P9-CQW-335

a call to die

david nasser

foreword by chris tomlin

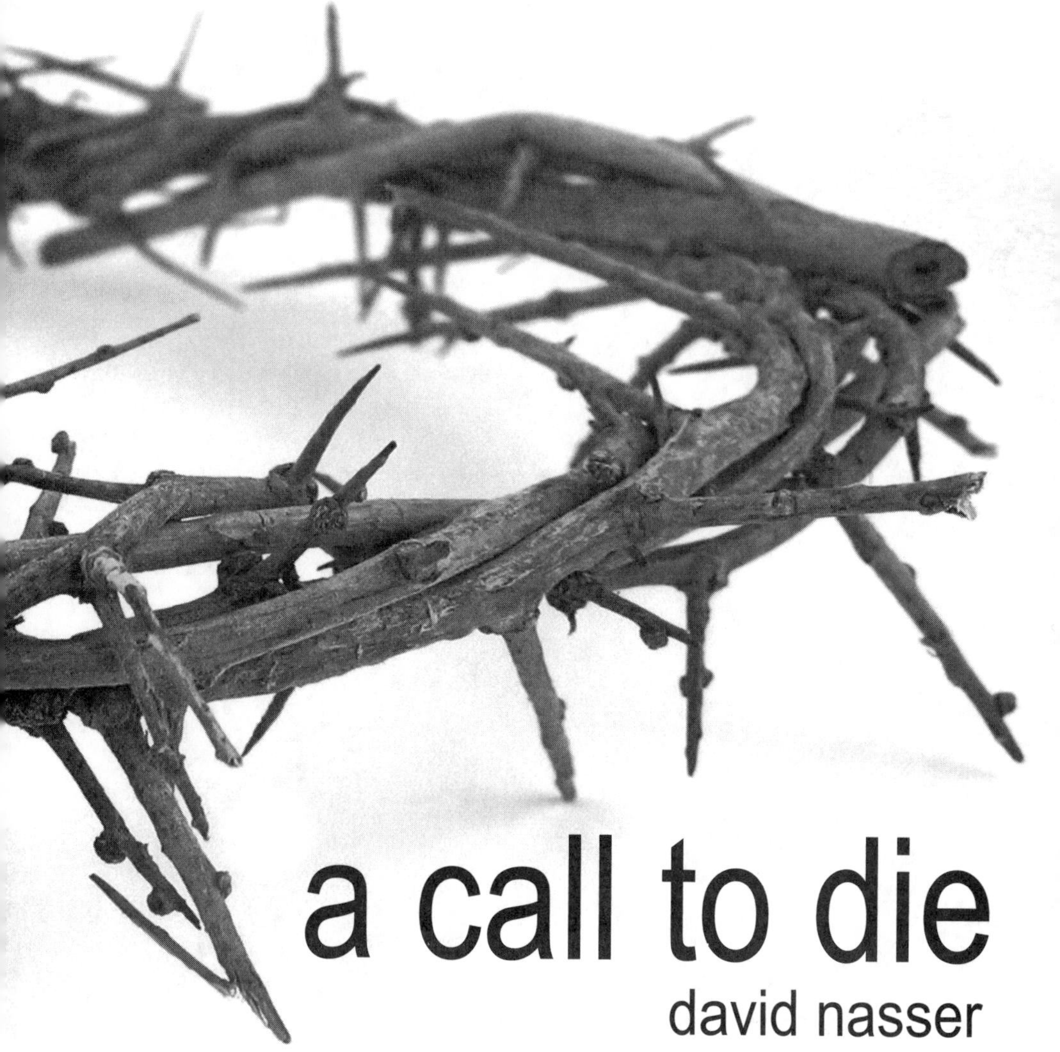

a call to die

david nasser

foreword by chris tomlin

a 40 day journey of fasting from the world & feasting on God

Redemptive art PUBLISHING

Published by Redemptive Art Publishing
Printed by Rose Printing

Printed in the United States of America

ISBN: 978-0-9792479-0-3

Designed by LeAnn Gentry
Previously published by Baxter Press, Friendswood, Texas.

I WANT TO THANK...

My Lord and Savior, Jesus Christ. May all of this bring glory and honor to Your Name.

My beautiful bride, Jennifer. You overwhelm me still.

My Nasser-Davis-Morgan family, especially my football teammates, Benjamin and Emmanuel and Rudy. I love you all more than words can express.

My pastor Buddy Gray and the rest of our Hunter Street Baptist Church family.

The devoted staff at DNO. Dana Davis, LeAnn Gentry, and Cathy Barnes. Everyone at Creative Trust and Word Distribution.

The Powells, the Himayas, the Engles, the Morgans, the Ngs, Chris Tomlin, our wonderful Board of Directors: Bob Thompson, Bill Greer, Phil Newberry, Bill Sonnes and also, Steve Richardson. Your friendship, support, wisdom, and prayers mean more to me than you can ever know.

Word Made Flesh, Scotty Paschel and the ICTA, Youth Specialties, Teen Mania, the many local churches that have partnered with us in ministry over the years; Randy Hall and our Student Life family; the Billy Graham Evangelistic Association, Premiere Productions, X-treme Conferences, the Scott Dawson Evangelistic Association, and Third Day. Thank you for the privilege of doing ministry with you.

My mentors in the ministry: Buddy Gray, Rick Stanley, Jay Strack, Dale Bynum, Ralph Bell, and Franklin Graham. Thank you for the godly example that you continue to be to me and many others.Everyone who specifically helped on this project:

- Jennifer, who took the photos,
- LeAnn, who did the cover graphics and layout,
- Jeanne Newberry, Vernard Gant, and Nastaran Morgan for their hours of proof reading wisdom,
- All of you who faithfully prayed for God to speak his words through us, and
- Pat Springle who helped in writing and editing this book.
- Joe Denny and Rose Printing.

Thank you all for putting your time and talents into this book so God can use it to change lives.

FOREWORD

by Chris Tomlin

This book has quite an interesting title. The simple yet powerfully gripping title is not some clever, controversial phrase David Nasser dreamed up to sell books. It is a simple invitation to all who would claim to follow the greatest revolutionary to walk this planet. It is an invitation from Jesus, the Son of God, to anyone who wants to find true life. But before I expound on that, I have to confess that there is a bit of irony in David asking me to pen a foreword for a book called *A Call To Die*. On a personal note, the irony I feel stems from the first time I met David. Let me explain.

I consider David one of my closest friends and he is truly one of my favorite people on earth. We have had the opportunity to see a lot of life, do a lot of life, and live a lot of life together, over the past several years. But on an evening in Memphis, Tennessee in the year 2000, our first encounter was almost our last. It was a night that almost ended in death! Through mutual friends, I had heard so much about David and was looking forward to meeting him. I was playing a concert on one side of town and he was speaking on another side. We had coordinated together and agreed to meet for dinner afterwards. At the end of dinner, David offered to give me a ride to my hotel since I didn't have a car and he had rented one. When we arrived at the hotel, David pulled up outside the main entrance to drop me off. It was a cold night so we sat there for a few minutes with the car heater on, talking and exchanging cell phone numbers. Then, with the car still running, David and I got out of the car to go and unload my stuff from the trunk. That's when it happened! That was the moment that we began to be carjacked. At first it was one guy. One determined criminal forcing his way into the drivers seat of the rental car and trying to drive away. What the thief wasn't planning on however was that David was not so quick to let him go without a fight. It was then that I saw a side of David that I will never forget. Rather than running for cover, David went after the guy to stop him. Before I knew what was happening, the thief was in the drivers seat of the car and David was halfway leaning into the car, trying to pull the criminal out. David was going all Chuck Norris on the guy! It was one of those, "Jesus loves you, but you're not stealing from me" moments. As if that wasn't shocking enough, from behind the bushes, two other guys appeared to help their failing buddy. One pulled a gun and pointed it at my face. I was frozen. I remember standing there, holding my guitar, frozen in time, and thinking this could be it. Talk about a "a call to die." I knew that I had to warn David that there was more than just one attacker, so I yelled, "David, he's got a gun." Stunned, David pulled his head out of the car and saw the two others. The man with the gun moved the weapon from my direction and began to point it at David's chest. What seemed at first to be a somewhat manageable drunk trying to steal a car had turned into an organized gang who was prepared to do whatever it took to steal this car. This was serious stuff. David started backing up, and the two new helpers jumped in the now officially stolen car and peeled away. We stood there speechless, thankful that by the grace of God, we were still alive. (The three guys were later apprehended after robbing several convenient stores and shooting someone. They even totaled the rental car before getting caught.)

Since that near death experience, David and I have been asked numerous times to tell the now famous story about the night that we first met. People laugh as David's take is always told with hints of how he saved my life, and my version is always about how I saved his. It's great that we can laugh about it now. However, it's important to note that whenever I've heard David tell the story, he has never forgotten to verbally admit that his instincts almost got the better of him that night. David has always been the first to confess that there is a thin line between fearlessness, and being dumb enough to die for a rental car; the fine line between not being passive and learning what battles to fight. Lesson learned. That night marked us forever. There is nothing like being car-jacked and very close to being shot to quickly bind you as brothers. So naturally, you see why I find it comically ironic that I am writing the foreword to David's book, *A Call to Die.* As a side note; David has a mean headlock and combination jab.

The experience as a whole taught me two things about my friend that has proven to be true time after time. He is not afraid to stand up and fight for what is right, and he is also not afraid to wear his humanity and shortcomings on his sleeve as well. I've heard it in his sermons, seen it in our friendship, and read it in this book.

The forty devotions of this book read as testimony to this fact. Page after page, you see the mixture of David's passionate and non-passive approach to the truth, mixed in with illustrations about his own depravity and need for a savior. The urgency that shouts from these pages never comes from an author who pretends to have it all figured out, but rather from someone who is in desperate need of grace as he answers the call. The call to daily die at the foot of the cross.

Nothing about the cross of Christ is passive, and to answer its call, we must be honest about our depravity and need for a savior. I pray that God uses this book to help you search within and see the cross for what it truly is. Yes, it was terrible, gruesome, and full of pain and darkness. It was a place for a criminal not an innocent man full of love. But for us now, the cross of our Lord Jesus is wonderful. It's a place of hope, life and ultimate love. It's where the worst of our humanity killed the Son of God, and in return He gave us life and a way to know our Father.

Years ago, I added a simple refrain to one of the great songs of our faith, "When I Survey the Wondrous Cross." You may know the song now by the title, "The Wonderful Cross." In this refrain, we sing...

O the wonderful cross
O the wonderful cross
Bids me come and die
And find that I may truly live

I believe this refrain is the heart of the book you have in your hands. We did not need a pat on the back or a slap on the wrist. We did not need a hand out for our poverty or even someone to post bond for us for our bad behavior. We were not bad people that God would have to make good. No, each of us were dead people that God would have to make alive. And praise His name! He did that through Jesus' work on the cross. You may be hearing this for the first time in life or maybe you could tell it back to me as if you were Billy Graham, but either way, it's as true today as ever. You and I can come to God through the sacrifice of His son.

And now that God, through Jesus, has made us alive how do we live out this life day to day? Well it seems to come full circle in Jesus' own words. In the book of Matthew 16:24-25, we find this passage.

"Then Jesus said to His disciples, 'If anyone wishes to come after Me, he must deny himself, and take up his cross and follow Me. For whoever wishes to save his life will lose it; but whoever loses his life for My sake will find it.'"

Here is the invitation. What would it look like if the greatest desire in our hearts was not just for ourselves? That you and I would give our lives away for the sake of the name and fame of God, and for His people. This course is a daily one. And I know you will find this book a great help to you along the way.

Sincerely,
Chris Tomlin

PROLOGUE

Not all babies are cute. To a mother holding her first born for the first time, the infant might look like an angelic vision, but to the unbiased eye, a cone shaped head, puffed up eyes, and curled up nose might resemble an alien more than the perfect "Gerber" baby. But who can blame a mother for being biased? Still, the mother has to wonder. *Does my child look as beautiful to others as it does to me?* Sure, the mother might see the obvious blemishes, but to her the beauty goes way beyond cosmetics. Her prayer is that others will look at her baby as she does. Beautiful for all the right reasons.

I will always remember the very moment that I held the first copy of *A Call to Die* in my hands. It felt as though I was a pregnant woman who was finally able to hold her newborn child in her arms, seconds after delivery. Sure, I had felt its birth pains and even seen with my own eyes the rough transcripts (sonograms for the sake of illustration), but finally it was here. The delivery came from the UPS man and not a doctor. It was in a church lobby and not a hospital, but it still felt like a birthday moment. We even had a birth certificate, complete with time of delivery and the official weight! I know because the UPS man asked me to sign for it. It was only a few small boxes containing 72 books in all, delivered at exactly 1:45 p.m. I tore the box open and pulled out the very first copy. As I held those 300 plus pages in my hands, tears filled my eyes. It was beautiful.

I didn't know if anyone else might agree, but to me it didn't matter. To me, and all who helped make this book a reality, the creation of it was an act of obedience and worship. The beauty was in the intent of writing a book for the glory of God, not based on how it would be received. I knew that this book was in no way perfect, with all its blemishes and shortcomings, but I loved this book. Why? Because it was written for my King. Many who had seen the transcripts had advised me that the book was going to fail and disappoint. Not so much because of the content, but the way it was presented. I was warned that unless drastic measures were taken it might tank. They had told me that the title was too strong, the chapters too long, and the call too severe. But to me, it didn't matter. This was what God had given us and the beauty was in the obedience. Maybe no one else would think this book was any good, but to me on that Friday afternoon in January, it was beautiful.

Only a few boxes were delivered to the conference that afternoon because many had told me that a church generation that cannot be motivated to read a one-page-a-day devotional, was sure to reject this intense devotional book. *A Call to Die* dared to challenge the reader to not only read five to six pages a day, but to then take the time to journal, meditate, memorize scripture, and last but not least, fast for 40 days. This was certainly nothing new, but in a world full of instant gratification and an "I want it now" mentality, it felt like an alien baby. I was told that my predominantly younger audience would probably not want this book. This is why I had only a few boxes delivered to the event which had more than 2,500 attendees. To me the book was beautiful, but I didn't know if anybody else would think so...

Oh you of little faith...

By the first night, we had sold out. And within two months we had sold over 4,000 books. It was not available through the web at that time. As a self-published item, we had no distribution to bookstores, and so every book was sold at events and conferences at which I was the speaker. If you're thinking, *So what? Good sales don't necessarily mean that this book resonated with people.* You're right. I wondered the same at first. The only thing that extraordinary book sales proved at first was that people were willing to buy a book based on a radical theme, or perhaps even their connection with the author who just spoke to them from a stage. Maybe even an impulse buy based out of pity. Kind of like complementing a mother about her baby being beautiful, although you know it's not really true. Was the book connecting with people once they took it home?

Soon after the book became more easily available, the emails, phone calls, and letters starting pouring in. They came from ministers, teenagers, parents, pastor search committees, and even death row inmates who were reading the book and taking the 40 day journey. Most messages were encouraging and affirming. People were kind enough to let us know what particular daily devotional was their favorite. I have to admit a few of the notes were also surprising.

One unexpected letter in particular was from a 60 year old woman who wrote to say that the day 37 devotional about honoring your parents really gripped her heart. At first I thought that this was a letter from a parent writing about her children's lack of honor towards her. But no, this was from a 60 year old child who had dishonored her 79 year old mother. She confessed that she had dishonored her elderly mother who had been living in a nursing home for years. She had unintentionally began to view her mother as a senile old dependant rather than a parent. "Since I was the one who took care of my mother by paying the bills for her nursing home, I saw myself as her authority. Most of our conversations were filled with me telling her what to do and how I wanted her to do it." In her own words, her tone of voice toward her mother, her attitude, her lack of respect, all of it was now under much needed conviction. She felt the call to die to her pride by repenting and asking for her mother's forgiveness. My surprise wasn't in the conviction, but in the age of the one being convicted. In those days, the audience that I primarily ministered to was a much younger crowd. So naturally I had written two particular chapters for what seemed to be the more youthful audience. To me, a chapter devoted to the call of honoring parents seemed to be an unlikely chapter for a 60 year old lady to really resonate with. But the truth is that there is no age of exemption on any of God's great commands.

The other chapter that seemed more geared toward younger readers was the chapter written on sexual purity. But again, how encouraging it has been to hear from so many of how God has used that chapter to convict about a sin that knows no boundary of age. I mean, how old do you have to be before sexual temptation is no longer an issue? The truth of God's Word applies to all, from the senior in high school to the senior citizen.

One common denominator in most of the feedback I've received from this book is that the 40 devotionals serve the purpose of an appetizer for a greater meal. After reading the devotionals, you are asked to study deeper the Word of God, to pray, meditate, journal, and fast. It has been through these disciplines that the Holy Spirit has intensified the message of truth and grace. As we hoped, the book has served as a gateway into something really magnificent: The devoted life.

It's now been seven years since the delivery day when I laid my hands on the first copy of *A Call to Die*. With more than 140,000 copies of this book in print so far, it has been affirming to see that by the grace of God, our act of obedience has been embraced by so many. It is humbling to think that God has undeservingly blessed this flawed and imperfect book to do such extraordinary things for His kingdom. Now, as it has become available in bookstores everywhere for the first time, I pray that God will continue to use it as an arrow to point you toward the only perfect book–His Word, the Bible. To me, that would be the most beautiful thing of all.

INTRODUCTION

"WHEN CHRIST CALLS A MAN, HE BIDS HIM COME AND DIE." — DIETRICH BONHOEFFER

A call to die? Not just strong words from a theologian and martyr, but our very call from Christ himself. Although statistics tell us that one out of one people die, we avoid the topic at all costs. We don't want to think about it. It's too morbid.

This forty-day journal, however, is not about physical death. On the contrary, in it we explore the meaning of spiritually dying to our desires so Christ can live in us. Romans 6:11 says, "Count yourselves dead to sin but alive to God in Christ Jesus." Paul says in Galatians 2:20, "I have been crucified with Christ and I no longer live, but Christ lives in me." If these two verses sound like paradoxes, they are. The Bible is full of paradoxes like this:

- We must become less so he can become greater.
- We must become a slave to righteousness so we can be set free.
- God's strength is made perfect in our weakness.

When we make the effort to look past the seeming contradiction of these words, we begin to understand the kind of life God wants us to live: a life emptied of ourselves and filled with him.

In this book we will examine some of the hard teachings of Christ, as well as God's disciplines for us as believers. *A Call to Die* is designed to help us find the consistency to explore God's word daily and find out what he is specifically calling us to do. For forty days we will memorize scripture and marinate our minds with God's word, we will write down what God is saying to us, and we will spend time reflecting on who God is and how he wants to transform our lives. Through this journey, God will use his Holy Spirit and his word to reveal to us what it means to die to ourselves so Christ can live through us. For every one of us, this journey will be different. The question is: Will you make the effort to find your tailor-made call to die?

The call to die is open to all of us who believe, but few of us will follow when we know the real cost of discipline. It's much easier to be a nice Christian than a radical one. It's much more fun to be entertained by Jesus and the church than to struggle and strain in the pursuit of purity and the presence of God. No, the call to die is not for everybody—only for those who are serious about experiencing the greatest adventure life has to offer. If you choose to answer that call, you will be in for some very hard moments, but take heart: It's well worth it in the end. "He who began a good work in you will carry it on to completion until the day of Christ Jesus" (Philippians 1:6).

If you choose to take this step and use this book for the next forty days, I guarantee that God will change your life. You will sense God's presence like never before; you will have a clearer direction for your future; you will feel the love of God more deeply; and you will see God use you in ways you never thought possible. In fact, I'm so sure of all this that I'll guarantee it.

You might be thinking, "David, how can you be so arrogant to guarantee that God will do these things?" Good question. You see, my confidence is not based on the pages of this book and my ideas. My trust is based on God's promise to the prophet Isaiah:

> "As the rain and the snow come down from heaven,
> and do not return to it without watering the earth
> and making it bud and flourish,
> so that it yields seed for the sower and bread for the eater,
> so is my word that goes out from my mouth:
> It will not return to me empty,
> but will accomplish what I desire
> and achieve the purpose for which I sent it"
> (Isaiah 55:10-11).

God's word has the power to change lives. If you marinate yourself in the truth of the Scriptures, I'm confident that God will do some amazing things in you and through you. Count on it.

The Commitment (How to use this book)

This book is not one to pick up in your spare time and read when you feel like killing a few minutes. It requires a rock-hard commitment of heart, time, and energy. Before you begin, look carefully at this list of requirements:

1. Spend One Hour

At least an hour each day for forty days. There is nothing "magical" about forty days, however, many times scripture makes reference to forty-day time periods. Jesus began his ministry by spending forty days in the wilderness fasting and praying.

2. Read

Read the text, think about the principles, and write your thoughts in the spaces provided. Writing sharpens your mind and opens your heart.

3. Memorize

Memorize the passage for the week.

4. Pray

Pray each day to apply the principles and truths.

5. Commit to Fast

As a statement to yourself and to God of your commitment to anything and everything to answer his call to follow him, make a decision to fast from something for these forty days. Fasting is denying yourself of something so you can focus more completely on God. Most often, people talk about fasting from food, but I'm not necessarily suggesting that here. We're talking about a forty-day diet, fasting from certain everyday things that occupy your time, so that it clears you to feast on God. Here are some ideas:

- You may decide to stop listening to secular music for these forty days so you can spend that time in prayer.
- You may decide to stop going to movies for this time so your mind isn't polluted with sex and violence.
- You may decide no television, internet, or video games. Then you can occupy that time with prayer and scripture reading.
- You may decide to give up lunch each day so you can spend that time memorizing scripture.
- You may decide to get off the phone after 8 o'clock so you have time to work on this book.

I'm certainly not going to tell you what your fast should be. Pray about it. God will be glad to show you! If you're still confused, pray again. I know that sometimes when God reveals something I should fast from, I have a tendency to compromise. Don't bargain with God. Fast from the thing that is most distracting to your spiritual life, and replace it with prayer, study, and worship.

A Word of Warning

Whenever people talk about a "radical commitment to Christ," they run the risk of misunderstanding what that means. In their desire to take radical action in their lives, some people set up a rigid set of do's and don'ts as a way of controlling their behavior. That seems right. It feels strong. It looks like real commitment. This causes us to become, in the words of the late evangelist and author David Busby, a "performaholic."

Don't do it! Don't become a Pharisee who lives by rules instead of relationship. God's call to us is first and foremost to love him with all our hearts and souls and minds. He will give us wisdom about changing our behavior, but don't let a rigid set of rules take over your life. In the next forty days, don't focus on changing your behavior, but more importantly, focus on letting Jesus change your identity.

Are you willing to make a commitment to fast, pray, memorize, and obey for forty days? The question shouldn't be, "Can I afford to do this?" but "Can I afford *not* to do this?" Take some time to talk to the Lord to tell him what you want to do. If you want to pursue him by using this book for forty days, pray for his strength and direction. If you feel strongly about taking this journey, a good place to start would be signing the following covenant with God.

INTRODUCTION

COVENANT

Lord Jesus, I am responding to the call to die to my selfish desires because I want to really live. I know I cannot do this on my own. I want to know you, love you, and serve you with all my heart. I make this commitment to spend at least an hour each day for the next forty days to read, pray, think, memorize, and respond to your direction. As a symbol of my commitment to you, for the next forty days I will fast from:

____

so that I may have greater focus and have the time to hear from you more clearly.

____

Signature   Date

I want to pray for you as you begin this journey.

> Jesus, you love us more than we can know, and you don't ask us to do anything you haven't already done before us. You were radically committed to the
>
> Father. You arranged your life so you could do what he wanted all day every day—even when it cost you your life. Give my friend the courage to die to selfish desires each day, to live for you and your purposes. Lord, I expect there to be some tough times, but I know you're with my friend. Keep him strong. Remind him that you're with him even when he may not feel your presence. In your strong name, amen.

You can pray this prayer or express your heart in your own way:

> Jesus, let the light of your presence shine on areas of my life that need to die, and let the fire of your Spirit burn those things away each day. Let my life be so consumed with your love and strength that I become a lighthouse for others, but Lord, only you can accomplish that in me. Have your way, Lord Jesus. Have your way. Amen.

Note:

Many of the passages of scripture we will use in this book are from the Gospel of Matthew. We could skip around and find lots of meaningful passages, but I wanted us to focus primarily on one book so you will become familiar and comfortable with it. During the course of these forty days, I encourage you to read Matthew's account of the life of Jesus several times. That will help you understand the context for the passages we explore in *A Call to Die*. All scripture references are taken from the New International Version of the Bible.

DAY 1

TAKE UP YOUR CROSS

"THEN JESUS SAID TO HIS DISCIPLES, 'IF ANYONE WOULD COME AFTER ME, HE MUST DENY HIMSELF AND TAKE UP HIS CROSS AND FOLLOW ME.'"
– MATTHEW 16:24

Jesus' words were unmistakable—and brutal—to his disciples. They knew what crosses were. No, they weren't silver charms worn on necklaces. They weren't the designs in tattoo parlors. The cross was an instrument of execution, one of the most violent and horrible ever invented by evil men. I can imagine the disciples gasping when Jesus uttered those words in Matthew 16:24. If we fully comprehend them, we will gasp, too.

But before we get to the cross, let's understand some things. Jesus begins this statement with a tiny but important word: *if.* He doesn't take it for granted that you and I will be willing to follow him along his path of radical obedience to the Father. Jesus is no bully. He doesn't try to get us to pack our bags for a guilt trip. No, he simply offers that path with all its hardships and joys, and says, "If you want the greatest adventure life has to offer, here's what the ticket will cost you." Quite frankly, the vast majority of Christians look at the brochure and say, "No thanks. The price is too high. I'll settle for something else." Only a few are willing to say, "Yes, Jesus. I want to go wherever you go." Fewer still stay on board for the whole journey. Jesus makes the offer, and he leads each of us in deciding what we want to do. The question isn't, "Do you do what you want to do?" but "Do you do what he wants you to do?" In this lies the opportunity to die.

He makes the price very clear. There are three parts. First, "deny yourself." Jesus is talking here about our innate selfishness:

- our selfish ambitions to rise above other people
- our selfish behaviors to get what we want when we want it
- our selfish attitudes of caring only for our own interests
- our selfish desires to put our needs first above anyone else

What does it mean to "deny" our selfish interests? Think of your selfishness as a hungry wolf that consumes anything and everything it can eat. To deny it means: don't feed it. Identify the sources of food for your selfishness, and stray away from those things!

- Deny reading books or magazines that stimulate those thoughts.
- Deny daydreaming about having more things or controlling people.
- Deny watching movies or television shows that feed those impulses.
- Deny listening to music that makes selfishness seem normal.
- Deny hanging out with people who drag you down and offer you selfish meat.
- Deny talking about people or things or yourself in ways that put people down.

- Deny gossiping, criticizing, cursing, lying, stealing, acting selfishly in any way, shape, or form.

"So, if I deny myself those things," you may ask, "what's left? Those things are my whole life!" For some of us, starving our selfishness will be a shock to our systems! That's all we've ever known! But after the shock wears off, we find there's plenty of good stuff to fill the hole in our time and affections.

Denying yourself means saying "No!" to selfishness. The next part of Jesus' statement is saying "Yes!" to him: "Take up your cross." Imagine being one of Jesus' disciples and hearing those words. As you walked down the roads near towns, you occasionally passed dying men hanging on crosses. They were murderers and traitors. The cross was the most extreme form of punishment in the Roman Empire, reserved only for the worst criminals. Jesus was saying "take up your cross"? It must have seemed insane to them! I'm sure they were confused.

A few months later, the disciples understood what Jesus meant. At that time, the perfect Son of God, the sinless Messiah, willingly "endured the cross, scorning its shame" (Hebrews 12:2) in obedience to the Father. He prayed so hard that blood vessels in his forehead burst from the strain. Drops of blood fell on the ground where he agonized with his Father about dying such a horrible death. But his commitment to obey the Father was greater than his desire for comfort and approval. So he went to the cross.

That's what it means for you and me, too: to obey God no matter what he asks us to do and no matter how much we don't want to do it. On a daily basis, we are to say "Yes!" to God by:

- Valuing what God says is important, and blowing off the things that aren't.
- Being loyal to the Father at all costs because he is worthy of our love.
- Obeying him wherever, whenever, and however he leads.

• Finding our ultimate reward in knowing our God is honored in our obedience.

OK, but what does "taking up our crosses" really look like? I believe we encounter this decision on two distinct levels. On one level, each of us faces a few dozen major decisions in our lives which are forks in the road: our choice of friends; which college to attend; what career to pursue; who to marry; how far to go in a significant relationship; what habits we will develop in high school, college, and in early years of adulthood; how to relate to someone who has hurt us deeply; whether we will fill our minds with trash or with healthy stuff; and other, much bigger decisions.

But on a different level, we make hundreds of choices each day and thousands each week that either say "Yes" or "No" to God. We may not realize that's what we are doing, but it is. We have choices: to set the alarm to get up a few minutes early to pray and read the Bible, or to get a little more sleep; to go to bed a few minutes early so we aren't wasted early in the morning when we know we should get up and spend time with God; to rob someone's reputation by gossiping about them or to keep quiet; to say something encouraging to someone instead of being sarcastic; to take time to listen to a boring person; to refuse to defend ourselves or talk about our success; to grab a sinful thought and replace it with truth from God's word; to overlook an unkind remark; or to give and serve when it would be easier to stay in our own selfish world.

In all this, Jesus is our example. He isn't asking us to do anything he hasn't already done to a far higher degree than we will ever do. Paul encouraged us to understand this in his letter to the Philippians. He wrote:

> "Your attitude should be the same as that of Christ Jesus: Who, being in very nature God, did not consider equality with God something to be grasped but made himself nothing, taking the very nature of a servant, being made in human likeness. And being found in appearance as a man, he humbled himself and became obedient to death—even death on a cross!" (Philippians 2:5-8).

So "taking up our crosses" means to value God above all else, to serve instead of demand our rights, and to be humble instead of proud—to the point of death.

The passionate motive that drove Jesus to the cross was us. Why us? Because our salvation ultimately brings glory to the Father.

> "Therefore God exalted him to the highest place and gave him the name that is above every name, that at the name of Jesus every knee should bow, in heaven and on earth and under the earth, and every tongue confess that Jesus Christ is Lord, to the glory of God the Father" (Philippians 2:9-11).

Jesus says in John 8:50: "I am not seeking glory for myself; but there is one who seeks it, and he is the judge." So there you have it—Jesus' motive for death. He went to the cross so that we would be saved and thus glorify the Father. Likewise, our motive for daily dying to ourselves should be to glorify God.

If we choose to deny ourselves and take up our crosses as Christ did in obedience to God, we too will bring glory to God and experience the presence of God in our lives. We will see his hand at work in us and through us. Broken hearts will be mended. People who have lost their way will find direction and meaning. Prodigals will return home. He will heal the hurts in our lives and give us hope and purpose. We will sense the love and power of God in a way we never thought possible. The Scriptures are full of these promises. We can't miss them!

Another benefit of denying ourselves and taking up our crosses is that we then are involved in the third part of Jesus' invitation: "follow me." As God strengthens us, we make those daily choices to say "No" to selfishness and say "Yes" to God, we walk side by side with Jesus Christ. When we read the Scriptures, we hear his voice. When we walk through our day, we sense his presence. When we obey him, we see his hand at work changing lives. My friend, *this* is the abundant life!

The benefits of a life of obedience are not just here and now. There will come a day that all of us will stand before Jesus to give an account of his or her life, and believers will be richly rewarded for everything we have done to honor Christ. I'm looking forward to that day!

The rewards are great, but so is the cost. It costs us everything. Like the hymn says, "I surrender *all*," not "I surrender 10%." No one will tell you that it's an easy road. Jesus himself faced hardship on the cross. He wept. He sweat. He asked his friends to pray. The result of his obedience was that God is exalted above all and Christ became the way for you and I to be forgiven. Man, I'm glad he didn't bail! You and I will face excruciating moments, too, when it seems God is asking too much and nobody is there for us. Those are the most painful, and the most important, times in our journey. We will feel alone, but we aren't. God is with us, and he has not forsaken us, especially in those times of need. Our obedience is worth it.

What is Jesus' call in this passage of scripture? It is a call to die, a call to let your selfishness starve to death because you don't feed it. If it won't starve, we have to grab our selfishness by the throat and strangle it. Once again, remember that we're talking spiritual, not physical issues. Because Satan is not gentle in dealing with us, we cannot be gentle in dealing with sin. In the place of this sin, we put Jesus squarely in the middle of our lives and choose to honor him all day, every day. Keep in mind that none of this can be accomplished apart from daily accepting the strength God gives us through his word and the Holy Spirit (Philippians 4:13).

Years ago, a young, uneducated man in Chicago named Dwight Moody heard a preacher challenge his audience: "The world has yet to see what God will do through one man whose heart is completely his." Moody responded instantly, "Lord, I want to be that man!" Over the course of the next few decades, God used Moody to lead thousands of people to Christ, to begin a Bible college, and to launch a missions movement that eventually sent over 30,000 young men and women to parts of the globe that had never heard of Jesus or had even seen a foreigner. Moody was committed to his heart being the sole and complete property of Jesus Christ. God poured out his Spirit on him.

How would you respond to that preacher's question today? Do you want to be that man or that woman?

—Be still. Listen to what God is saying to you.

1. What are some examples of selfish ambitions, behaviors, attitudes, and desires? Time to myself to relax & watch TV, impatience w/ my kids

2. Which of these have been part of your life in the past few days? Be specific and transparent. I've done ok the past few days b/c I've been busy @ work/home, kids busy, but I regularly am selfish about "me time."

3. What are the patterns of your selfishness? (Identify the three most selfish things you do on a regular basis?) - I Do not answer the phone. (Jake my time) - I do not answer the door. - Watch TV when I should be playing, reading, or being productive.

What is the attraction of these things? Rest, relaxation

What do they seem they will get for you? Peace, tranquility

What do they actually get for you? Feelings of isolation & alone.

4. How can you "starve" each of these things?

5. Write a paragraph on what it means to "take up your cross."

6. Describe the benefits of denying yourself and taking up your cross to follow Jesus.

7. Is the reward worth the price to you? Why or why not?

8. Read Matthew 16:24-27. Think about each verse, then use each verse as a guide as you pray and ask God to hide his word in your heart that you might not sin against him (Psalm 119).

Memorize John 3:16.

Let me say a few things to you about memorizing scripture. I hear people whine, "I can't memorize verses from the Bible. It's too hard!" That's ridiculous. These same people know every song on their favorite CD, and I know a couple of guys who can recite the entire dialogue from *The Three Amigos* word for word! The first thing I want you to realize is: yes, you can memorize verses from the Bible. Here are some things to help you:

1. Read it five or six times.

2. Memorize it in segments, a phrase at a time.

- After the first one, go to the second one.
- Then say both together to be sure you don't forget the first part. Keep going until you have the whole thing.
- Write it each segment as you get it clearly in your mind.
- Then write each verse when you have the verse learned. Writing strongly reinforces memory work. In fact, some people write the segments and the verses several times at the beginning of the process, too.

3. Memorize It Exactly

Memorize it exactly as it is written, even the punctuation. Yes, even the punctuation. If you get it down exactly, you will be far more likely to remember it accurately—and use it in your thoughts and prayers.

4. Write It

Write it on a card and put it in your pocket. Look at it several times a day to reinforce it in your mind.

5. Practice

Practice with a partner.

6. Meditate

Meditate often on the verses. Use them as guides for your prayers. Let the word of God sink deep into your heart so it changes your attitudes and actions.

7. Be Diligent

Memorizing scripture takes discipline, but it's well worth the effort. The verses you memorize will be with you the rest of your life. God can bring it to your mind whenever you need to be reminded of his truth and grace—like a refreshing glass of cold water on a hot summer day.

A CALL TO DIE

JOURNAL

Lord, today you are calling me to die to selfish desires by:

asking Jesus what He would want me to do with my time, talents.

You are calling me to obey in these areas:

- Time
- Energy
- Patience c̄ my Children

You are calling me to intimacy with you by:

- Talking c̄ you more
- Reading/Praying w/ you more

DAY 2

HARD WORDS

"ON HEARING IT, MANY OF HIS DISCIPLES SAID, 'THIS IS A HARD TEACHING. WHO CAN ACCEPT IT?' FROM THIS TIME MANY OF HIS DISCIPLES TURNED BACK AND NO LONGER FOLLOWED HIM." – JOHN 6:60, 66

During the middle period of his ministry, Jesus was popular—as popular as a top athlete or a rock star today. Thousands of people came to see him, hear him, and watch him. He didn't disappoint them. They saw him heal the sick and raise the dead. "Man!" they probably said to each other as they smiled and elbowed each other, "This guy is incredible! What's next?" At one point, fifteen to twenty thousand people (five thousand men and their families) stood on a hillside to see Jesus. They stayed a long time. Too long, in fact. They had nothing to eat. They couldn't make it to the local drive-thru, so Jesus took a boy's lunch and miraculously fed them all—with plenty left over. The crowd couldn't get enough of him.

But popularity was never Jesus' goal. He wanted to make disciples, not points. So at the height of his fame, he made sure no one misunderstood. He told them in no uncertain terms that he was God himself. He said, "I AM the bread of life." Sounds pretty simple, huh? But to the people of Jesus' day, his "I AM" statement sounded very much like the time when God revealed himself to Moses and called himself "I AM that I AM." Jesus was claiming to be that same God—with the implication that he should be worshipped, too.

"Wait a minute. I like the healing and raising and eating, but I don't know about this Deity thing..." They wanted Jesus to back down, to say, "Well, I sure don't want to offend anybody, so let me re-phrase that statement." Instead, Jesus cranked it up a notch. He told them bluntly, "I tell you the truth, unless you eat the flesh of the Son of Man and drink his blood, you have no life in you."

Eat his flesh? Drink his blood? That was too much for them, so the crowd melted away and the thousands of people went back to their homes. After watching them all walk away, Jesus stood there with only the Twelve next to him. Jesus gave them the same choice. He asked them, "You do not want to leave, too, do you?"

What do you think that moment was like for these guys. Wow, what a crossroads moment! This was the point at which they had to decide who Jesus was to them. Their man had been in the front car at the motorcade. The cheerleaders were doing cartwheels around him, and the mayor had given him the key to the city. (Maybe even a Nike sponsorship, who knows?) Things had been going great! Then he claimed to be worthy of worship and obedience, and all the people—that's *all* the people in the crowd—left. I can imagine the Twelve disciples shifting their feet and looking at the ground. Kind of embarrassing for all of them. Then Peter shrugged and said simply, "Lord, to whom shall we go? You have the words of eternal life. We believe and know that you are the Holy One of God." So the Twelve stayed with Jesus.

Jesus didn't come to entertain us. Jesus' ultimate goal in coming was to bring glory to the Father. Yes, in that lies the good news of our salvation through his death and resurrection, and the opportunity to be worshippers of him. However, there's a huge difference. It's not the *fun* news, but the *good* news. If we expect only to be entertained, we will leave him at the first request for sacrifice and obedience. The people in the crowd did. Many of us do, too. But hard words are just as much a part of being a disciple of Christ as all those promises we love to hear. In fact, if you don't hear any hard words from God, it's a good sign that you aren't his child at all. Solomon wrote about it; so did the writer to the Hebrews:

> "My son, do not make light of the Lord's discipline, and do not lose heart when he rebukes you, because the Lord disciplines those he loves, and he punishes everyone he accepts as a son" (Proverbs 3:11-12, Hebrews 12:5-6).

Only a loveless father refuses to correct his son or daughter, and our Heavenly Father is not that way at all. He loves us so much that his heart breaks when we get off the path he has charted for us, and he lovingly taps us on the shoulder and says, "Hey, it's me. Listen. You're messing up. Don't go that way. Come with me." At that point, we have a choice to respond or ignore him.

What are the hard words he speaks to us? These words usually identify something we value and that we insist on putting at the center of our lives where only Christ should be. It could be a cherished dream, a position we want to hold, money, possessions, or a person. When God needs to speak words of rebuke, he makes himself crystal clear.

A rich young man came to Jesus. He was, by all outward appearances, a very committed believer. The disciples probably looked at him and thought, "Hey, here's a guy who is on the same page with Jesus."

The man asked a good question: "Teacher, what good thing must I do to get eternal life?"

Jesus repeated some of the Ten Commandments (which the young man already knew very well), "Do not murder, do not commit adultery, do not steal, do not give false testimony, honor your father and mother, and love your neighbor as yourself."

The young man responded, "All these I have kept. What do I still lack?"

At that moment, Jesus saw an open door. He undoubtedly had seen it earlier in the conversation (after all, he's God!), but he waited until the man asked for more. Jesus saw deep into this man's heart. His money was most important to him, and Jesus pointed that out: "Go, sell your possessions and give them to the poor, and you will have treasure in heaven. Then come, follow me."

Matthew tells us: "When the young man heard this, he went away sad, because he had great wealth" (Matthew 19:16-22).

I've heard some speakers say that this passage shows that Jesus wants us to sell all we have and give the money to the poor, but I don't believe that's the point. The real point is that if we genuinely want to follow Christ, we need to be ready for him to point out those things that come between us and him, the thing or the person we cherish more than him. He knows that thing, that dream, or that person will be a wet blanket over our spiritual lives unless and until we move it to its right place. Sure, we can go to all the meetings and sing all the songs, but until it is removed, it will clog up the lines and short out the connection between us and God.

God's Spirit will shine his light on your particular idol when it's time. In some cases, God will say hard words to you about a secret sin you harbor: pornography, going too far physically in a relationship, lying, or harboring a grudge. But in many cases, the idols are not hidden at all; they are your greatest strengths and your most valued possessions:

- He may show you that you love your boyfriend, girlfriend, or yourself more than him.
- He may expose your bad attitudes.
- He may show you that academics, sports, or your daydreams are taking too much time and attention.

- He may show you that you care too much about popularity and acceptance.
- He may reveal the bitterness that resides in your heart.
- He may show you that your looks, clothes, car, music or some other possession is in his place in your heart.
- He may show you that your selfish ambition or jealousy is stealing your heart away from God.
- He may show you that you want to avoid making decisions, that you wiggle out from under authority, and that freedom has become your God.

We can't program when, how, and where the spotlight of the Spirit will shine on the hidden part of our hearts. God will do it when he's ready, not when we think we're ready. Do you think the rich young man expected Jesus to point out his attachment to money? Not a chance! He fully expected Jesus to be impressed with his commitment to God and to praise him for being such a good guy. But Jesus had a different agenda. Similarly, you may be proud of your commitment to Jesus and shocked when he points out an idol in your heart.

God may shine his light on you when you are working on today's material in this book, or he may do it when you are riding down the road some day next month. The point is, be receptive. When he speaks, be still. Listen. It's not necessarily audible. It's even louder. It is straight to the heart. God doesn't need your ears to get your attention. Obey. Will it be hard? You bet! You can count on it. But he speaks those hard words because he loves you so much, and he honors your commitment to follow him with all your heart. Think of him as a coach. He wouldn't be a good one if he didn't point out how you could be the best you can be, would he? You've chosen to be on the team, and it would be foolish not to listen to the best coach in the world.

Only this coach is your Father and Savior and Friend. He is kind at heart.

Has Jesus said some hard words to you already? How did you respond? If you didn't respond very well, you may need to remember that he didn't come to entertain us. He came to be our Lord. He's not an actor or a comedian; he's our Savior. If you and I have responded to him by saying, "Jesus, I will follow you," then he has the responsibility to show us those things that stand in our way.

Our "entertain me" culture has made us spiritually soft and emotionally mushy. We expect things to happen simply by pushing a button or clicking a mouse. Repenting of spiritual idolatry is hard, brutal work, and this culture has not prepared us for it. Still, it is essential if we intend to walk with God. When God shows you that something besides him is occupying the center of your life, don't expect it to just melt away. It won't. Don't expect it to step down graciously. It won't. Don't expect it to come out without a fight. It won't.

Don't be shocked when the Holy Spirit taps you on the shoulder, points to something in your life, and says, "My friend, you love this more than you love me. I will help you tear it from your heart and put me there." You will find a dozen reasons to leave it right where it is. Your heart will plead for more time or another chance. Be ruthless. Be brutal. Don't start to bargain. Grab the dragon by the throat and slay it with the Sword of Truth (the Bible). Don't listen to it plead or scream. Be done with it. The devil does not go easy on us. If you try to get rid of the sin gradually, it will find a way to hang on and you will be defeated. The quicker method is harsh, but it is the only effective way to deal with sin. Ask God to help you not get hung up on making excuses for your sin.

When this day happens, remember these things:

- Fix your eyes on Jesus.
- This may be a difficult day, but it will lead to new experience of the presence and power of God.
- Focus on passages of scripture to encourage and direct you as you respond to the Lord's light.
- Pray and ask God himself to help you with his Holy Spirit.

- Tell a godly friend or your youth pastor to get some insight, encouragement, and accountability.
- Stay in the fight. These things don't die once and for all. They try to crawl back into your heart again and again.

Have you heard hard words from the Lord? If not, you're in trouble. If you have, it proves you are God's loved child.

—Be still. Listen to what God is saying to you.

1. As you read these pages, did God shine his light on anything or anyone that is occupying his place in your heart? Explain:

   - Bad attitude @ work
   - Expecting a 12 yr. old to be cooperative & mature

   Has he shined his light on the deepest part of your heart before? If so, what happened? He has helped me, but it has taken a tremendous will to stay positive & focused on Him.

2. What are your strengths? How can these become idols? ?

   - Compassion/Empathy
   - Kindness

   I suppose if I focused on them.

3. What are some evidences of our "entertain me" culture?

Events that entertain more well-attended than Revival mtgs. Facebook, Internet/TV in general.

How do you think this culture has influenced you and your ability to make hard decisions?

Not sure??

4. Do you agree or disagree with this statement: Hard words are a sign of God's love for me. Explain your answer:

Agree - He loves me so much He wants to change me to be more like Him.

5. Read John 6:25-69. Think about each paragraph, then use each paragraph as a guide as you pray.

Memorize: Go over John 3:16 again.

DAY 2

JOURNAL

Lord, today you are calling me to die to selfish desires by:

- Spending more time c̄ Him

You are calling me to obey in these areas:

- Time
- Attitude toward difficulties

You are calling me to intimacy with you by:

- Focusing on what He wants for my heart/life.

DAY 3

RUINED

"'WOE TO ME!' I CRIED. 'I AM RUINED! FOR I AM A MAN OF UNCLEAN LIPS, AND I LIVE AMONG A PEOPLE OF UNCLEAN LIPS, AND MY EYES HAVE SEEN THE KING, THE LORD ALMIGHTY.'"
– ISAIAH 6:5

We are incredibly self-absorbed people. We think about ourselves all day every day: "Do I look good today?" "I wonder how I can get him to like me better?" "How can I get what I want when I want it?" "When am I going to get the promotion I deserve?" Self-absorption leads to two extremes: cockiness and shame. If we think we are doing well, we feel superior to other people, but if we perceive we aren't measuring up, we feel like failures. Pride and shame are both products of being self-absorbed.

In the Christian world, we sometimes unconsciously reinforce this self-absorption by focusing on "my growth," "my progress," and "my development." We talk about wanting to "be like Jesus," and some of us focus all our attention on comparing how we're doing today to how we were doing last week or last month. A friend of mine told me that this teaching almost drove him nuts. Instead of loving Jesus, he spent all his time comparing himself and worrying that he wasn't growing fast enough.

The prophet Isaiah was minding his own business one day when God broke through and revealed himself in a vision. Isaiah described the experience:

> "I saw the Lord seated on a throne, high and exalted, and the train of his robe filled the temple. Above him were seraphs, each with six wings: With two wings they covered their faces, with two they covered their feet, and with two they were flying. They were calling to one another:
>
> "Holy, holy, holy is the Lord Almighty;
> the whole earth is full of his glory.
> At the sound of their voices the doorposts and thresholds shook
> and the temple was filled with smoke.
>
> "'Woe to me!' I cried. 'I am ruined! For I am a man of unclean lips, and I live among a people of unclean lips, and my eyes have seen the King, the Lord Almighty'" (Isaiah 6:1-5).

If and when we get the slightest clue what God is really like, we quickly realize that we fall short—way short. The seraphs in this passage are angels with six wings. They used two of them to cover their eyes because God is so holy they had to protect themselves from his blinding light. These seraphs repeated this attribute of God three times: "Holy, holy, holy is the Lord Almighty." I think they wanted to make a point. His majesty and holiness swamp our petty selfishness, and our pride is shattered. We are broken, helpless, and hopeless—unless God himself touches us. I'm afraid that we have dumbed

Jesus down to our level these days. We treat him like a buddy we meet at the mall, or we call the Father "the man upstairs." Yes, Jesus calls us his friends, but be sure of this: Jesus stoops from the blinding majesty of his heavenly throne in order to stand next to us and call us friends. He didn't come from the next street over. He created the entire Universe!

Isaiah's response to the holiness of God is, "Woe is me!" This is the seventh time in his writing that the prophet proclaims "woe" on somebody. All the other times are God's judgment on others' sins. Now it is because his own sin is exposed in the light of the presence of God. At that moment, Isaiah recognized his true condition. He was ruined.

And in that sense, God wants to ruin our already dead lives in order to resurrect in us *real* life. Remember, the gospel of Jesus Christ is not the "Fun News." It is the "Good News," but we can't realize how good it is until we become aware—painfully aware—how bad we are. That realization always brings us face to face with change. All our self-centered plans and goals will be ruined. Relationships, how we spend time and money, laziness and discipline, how we love, and who we love and obey... everything will be turned upside down. Our lives will then be driven by conviction, not just convenience. God doesn't design this experience to crush you, but to cleanse you and fill you with himself. Out with the old life, in with the new, true life.

No one can make us have this kind of vision of God. God himself must reveal himself to us. We can prepare our hearts and put ourselves in a position to be receptive to God's voice, but ultimately, the Lord himself must break through our calloused hearts to show us what he is like. In my experience, this happens most often when I am aware of my need—my need of seeing the bigger picture. That's what happened to Isaiah, too. Notice that this vision of God occurred "in the year that King Uzziah died." The death of a king caused tremendous turmoil in a country. No one knew who would try to seize power through a coup or who would be kicked out or executed by the new king. The new man might continue the old policies and practices, or he may change everything. The whole culture could change overnight—and it often did just that.

In that unstable time, I believe Isaiah felt insecure. He was more open to God, and the Lord used that opening to speak to his heart. When you and I feel insecure, we are more open to God speaking to our hearts. Stability often produces passivity: the same old same old. But upheaval—a move, graduation, a job change, a broken relationship, sickness, a deep disappointment—breaks our hearts, reveals our needs, and somehow opens us to listen.

God revealed himself to Isaiah. As he got a glimpse of a holy, holy, holy God, Isaiah got a glimpse of his own depravity (unholy, unholy, unholy...). The prophet said, "I'm ruined! I'm not what I should be!" He had nowhere to run, nowhere to hide, no way to fix his problem. So God touched him:

> "Then one of the seraphs flew to me with a live coal in his hand, which he had taken with tongs from the altar. With it he touched my mouth and said, 'See, this has touched your lips; your guilt is taken away and your sin atoned for'" (Isaiah 6:6-7).

Remember, Isaiah had identified his sin as "unclean lips." Did that mean he cursed or gossiped all the time? Perhaps, but his sinful words were symptoms of a deeper problem. I believe he knew, as Jesus reflected centuries later, that "out of the abundance of the heart the mouth speaks." Our words reveal our hearts. Griping, gossiping, self-pity, and bitterness reveal a sin-filled heart. Encouragement, thankfulness, and love reveal a heart that accepts the fact that it's forgiven. Isaiah knew his unclean lips were the outward expression of the sin in his heart.

When a wound is infected, a doctor may stop the infection by cauterizing the wound. He takes a red hot tool and sears it, burning away the rotten flesh and leaving only what can heal. It is a drastic method, but it is effective. The seraph used that same healing touch on Isaiah. He picked up a burning coal and touched Isaiah's rancid lips. The flame seared the sin and burned away the guilt.

Some of us have a very wrong view of guilt and forgiveness. We think we d enough long enough to feel forgiven, but that's not forgiveness;)thers of us think that forgiveness is a simple, legal, emotionless ne forgiveness involves genuine sorrow. Paul wrote about this in his second letter to the believers in Corinth. He described the difference between "godly sorrow" and "worldly sorrow":

> "Even if I caused you sorrow by my letter, I do not regret it... I am happy, not because you were made sorry, but because your sorrow led you to repentance. For you became sorrowful as God intended and so were not harmed in any way by us. Godly sorrow brings repentance that leads to salvation and leaves no regret, but worldly sorrow brings death" (2 Corinthians 7:8-10).

Denial (saying, "Oh, it wasn't all that bad.") isn't godly sorrow. Self-hatred (saying, "I'm such a jerk! I can never be forgiven for that! I'm hopeless!") isn't either. Godly sorrow is the willingness to say, "Yes, Lord. You're right. That is sin, and I'm guilty." But it also involves allowing God to do spiritual surgery to cauterize the infected wound and forgive us. Just because we don't know how to forgive others or ourselves *doesn't* mean God doesn't know how. The sorrow God intends for us brings the refreshment of feeling forgiven, the determination not to sin again, and a focus on God, not on ourselves. Worldly sorrow brings "death," that morbid self-hatred that we are so bad we can never be forgiven, so we are helpless and hopeless. One results in joy and life; the other results in bitterness and depression.

Let me give you a word of warning. Sensitive, conscientious people run the risk of going overboard about finding and rooting out their sin. They desperately want to please God, and they think they can help him by looking for sin in their lives. They analyze every conversation and every action looking for sinful motives and wrong behavior. If this goes on long enough, they begin to find sin where there is none, and the focus of their lives becomes morbid self-absorption. Their noble desire to root out sin becomes a spiritual death trap of beating themselves up for any and all perceived wrongs. If you are a conscientious person (and you wouldn't be involved in this call to die if you weren't very serious about pleasing God), be careful not to try to do God's job for him. Relax. You can be very certain that the Holy Spirit will point out sin when he wants to. At that point, allow him to burn it away with the fire of his holiness and forgiveness, and give thanks for his grace and mercy. Then move on. I've seen the zeal of too many men and women lead them to destruction instead of joy. Don't let that happen to you.

And what is the response of someone whose deepest, darkest sins are exposed in the light of God's holiness and forgiven by the fire of his love? Isaiah tells us his experience:

> "Then I heard the voice of the Lord saying,
> 'Whom shall I send? And who will go for us?'
> And I said, 'Here am I. Send me!'
> He said, 'Go and tell this people...'" (Isaiah 6:8-9).

God's questions were not only for Isaiah. His call is for everybody who will listen and respond. The prophet heard and instantly responded, so God sent him to tell everybody who would listen about the greatness and healing power of God. Isaiah was eager to respond because all of his excuses had been burned away by that hot coal. When our sins are exposed in the light of God's presence, we feel ruined; but when we experience forgiveness in the depths of our souls, we become fresh, clean, and new. We are eager to please God in any way we can. When he calls, we hear and go.

Something else strange happens in us when we go from ruined to forgiven: we develop an unquenchable thirst for God. "Well," you may ask, "doesn't this experience of forgiveness deeply satisfy us?" Yes, it satisfies more than anything else in the world, but paradoxically, it leaves us longing for more; more of the goodness of God, more of his kindness and his power, more of his healing touch and the direction he gives. King David had a very close, intimate relationship with God, yet he wrote:

> "O God, you are my God, earnestly I seek you;

my soul thirsts for you, my body longs for you,
in a dry and weary land where there is no water" (Psalm 63:1).

Have you had an experience like Isaiah had? Have you realized how wonderful Jesus is, and in that realization come face to face with your own sinfulness? If you have, I hope you didn't respond in prideful denial or in self-hating shame. I hope you recognized the fact that you are ruined, and allowed the burning coal of God to cauterize your sin and heal your heart.

If you haven't had this experience, don't try to manufacture it. That won't work! God must do it in his way and in his time. Your role is to prepare yourself by feeding your mind and heart on the truth of the Scriptures and getting as close to God as you can. He'll do the rest. Count on it. The apostle Paul promised, "He who began a good work in you will carry it on to completion until the day of Christ Jesus" (Philippians 1:6).

Not long ago, one of my best friends, Michael John, was driving his SUV along the road one night and hit a deer. He called me on his cell phone a few minutes after it happened. That deer was stunned, but wasn't hurt. Neither was Michael John's SUV. Because there was no damage to his vehicle, the collision had no effect on Michael John's driving habits. A few weeks later, I was in a friend's car one night, and a deer ran out in front of us. We tried to miss it, but that deer went right over the car and landed behind us. It was shaken up, but it limped off into the woods. The car had some minimal damage. The encounter left us a little shaken, so it really affected how we drove for the next few weeks. A couple of months after that, a friend told me about a guy and his wife who were driving along on a pretty day with their windows down. They saw a deer stumbling down a hillside next to the road in front of them. They weren't too alarmed. They saw deer all the time, but this time the deer couldn't stop his slide. It got to the bottom of the steep hill right as their car drove past, and the deer somehow dove headfirst into the open window of the car! It was jumping and jiving in the woman's lap! The situation was starting to get dangerous! When it was all said and done, there was major damage to the car, and the experience forever changed the driving habits of that couple!

All three of these stories involved a collision with a deer, each with very different results. In the same way, each of us will have an encounter with God. For some of us, an encounter with God produces no change in who we are and how we live. For others, God might collide with us, and it changes us temporarily. However, for some of us, a head-on collision with the living, holy God will ruin us—alter us forever.

Which will be true of your collision with God?

—Be still. Listen to what God is saying to you.

1. What does it mean to have "a vision of God"?

To understand who and what He really is on a personal level.

2. Have you ever felt "ruined" like Isaiah did? If you have, describe that experience. If not, do you want that kind of experience? Why or why not?

Yes - I felt ashamed & unworthy of God's attention, love, & grace.

3. What does it mean to have God cauterize your rancid sins? What does it look like? ...feel like?

To have His pure and cleansing touch on my life so that my sins are forgiven & that ~~He~~ will help me to not sin again.

4. What are some results of being ruined and then healed? What were the results in Isaiah's life? What are the results in your life?

Isaiah wanted to tell everyone about Jesus love c̄ healing. A constant awareness of His presence c̄ a desire to please Him daily.

5. What are some differences (in the process and the results) between trying to root sin out of your life yourself and letting God do it?

Waiting on God takes time c̄ patience since He will do it in His perfect timing in my life. (Will not work if I try s̄ God.)

6. Read Isaiah 6:1-8. Think about each verse, then use each verse as a guide as you pray.

Memorize: Write John 3:16 and put your name where it says, "For God so loved..."

DAY 3

JOURNAL

Lord, today you are calling me to die to selfish desires by:

Putting others' needs before my own desires.

You are calling me to obey in these areas:

- Time management
- Patience in dealing with/ instructing my children
- Pleasing Him esp. @ work.

You are calling me to intimacy with you by:

Reading / praying more of day.

DAY 4

REWARDS

"THOSE WHO HONOR ME I WILL HONOR."
– 1 SAMUEL 2:30

The messages in these pages have been pretty brutal so far, haven't they? The call to die requires a will of steel to persevere and make those hard, thankless choices to honor God instead of serving selfish desires. (Remember Philippians 4:13.) But is it a thankless task? Is there encouragement to keep going? You bet there is!

One of the most important principles in the Bible is the law of sowing and reaping. We see this principle working over and over again. Paul stated it in his letter to the Galatian Christians:

> "Do not be deceived: God cannot be mocked. A man reaps what he sows. The one who sows to please his sinful nature, from that nature will reap destruction; the one who sows to please the Spirit, from the Spirit will reap eternal life. Let us not become weary

in doing good, for at the proper time we will reap a harvest if we do not give up" (Galatians 6:7-9).

The "law of the harvest" means that we reap *what* we sow, we reap *more than* we sow, and we reap *after* we sow. When a farmer scatters wheat seed, he doesn't expect to see corn growing there the next day, does he? No, he expects to harvest wheat, but he knows it will come several months later. He will be very disappointed if he doesn't reap fifty or a hundred times the amount of wheat he sowed into the soil in the Spring. The same principle is true for you and me, and it operates on both ends of the spectrum of sin and goodness.

If we spend our time and attention in the pursuit of success, we may achieve wealth and power, but we also continually compare our success with other people. We all know people who are obsessed with their rank on the pecking order of success, whether in school or business. They can't even enjoy the money or prestige this brings because they are afraid of slipping behind somebody—anybody—else.

In our day, many people yearn for perfection in some area of life. Some strain for that perfection in academics; some try for it in business or in their appearance. Many people work out incessantly and read all kinds of magazines to get the latest tips on how to have the perfect body. Where does it get them? They may have firm abs or trim thighs or great pecs, but they are also preoccupied with themselves all day every day. A small world.

Many people desire approval more than anything on earth. To get a smile and a nod, they do anything to please people. They change how they dress, what they like, how they talk, and what they do—just to fit the mold they think will impress that other person. What do these people reap? Worry. They are constantly anxious to know if they have done just the right thing. A person's rolled eyes or smirk destroys the approval addict's life.

And some people have only one simple goal in life: to be #1. They are driven to be on top, to dominate, to control their lives and the lives of those around them. They may use blatant methods of demanding and yelling, or they may be much more subtle in manipulating others to get what they want. Either way, people around them feel used and resentful, and the driven person's real need to be loved and to love in return is crushed in the vice of power.

All of these are attempts to be the center of attention. They may spring from insecurity or pride, but the result is the same: heartache. The desire for power and attention always reaps a painful, destructive harvest. The Lord said to a man who wanted power: "Should you then seek great things for yourself? Seek them not" (Jeremiah 45:5). That is God's message for you and me, too.

On the other hand, we can easily see the law of the harvest at work on the positive side, too. When we sow love and encouragement, we receive kind words back, if from no one else, from Christ. When we give freely to others with no strings attached, we get welcome surprises in return. When we speak truth, people are honest with us. To be sure, this is not a hard and fast rule. Just as weeds grow among the wheat the farmer sows, we aren't immune to some weeds of hurt others put in our lives when we sow love and kindness. But look at the overall pattern, and you'll see the law of the harvest working incredibly well. One conclusion we reach is that it is just plain silly not to sow truth, respect, and kindness. After all, that's what we want from others, isn't it? For sure, it's what God wants from and for us.

If we experience the love and forgiveness of God, our hearts are transformed. The Spirit changes our hearts so that we want more than anything else for God to be honored. As we grow in his love, we won't care as much if anyone even notices us. If our goal is to be happy, thousands of obstacles will get in our way, but if our goal is to honor God, we can accomplish that goal no matter what circumstances we encounter. The young German, Dietrich Bonhoeffer, was committed to honoring Christ, so he took an unpopular stand against Hitler and his Nazi regime. Bonhoeffer was imprisoned for speaking out boldly against Nazi oppression. Alone, facing a future of prison, loneliness, and death, Bonhoeffer never regretted his stance for Christ. He wrote: "I am sure of God's hand and guidance...You must never doubt that I am thankful and glad to go the way which I am being led. My past life is abundantly full of God's mercy, and, above all sin, stands the forgiving love of the Crucified."[1]

The desire for success, pleasure, and approval had been removed from Bonhoeffer's heart. He lived only with Christ's pleasures as his pleasure. Over and over again, he was dragged into court. The Nazi judge demanded that he recant. Again and again, he calmly explained that as a Christian, he was an enemy of Nazi Socialism, so they threw him back in his cell. Late in the war, some friends plotted to free Bonhoeffer, but he quickly realized that his escape would endanger the lives of his family and friends, so he refused. On the day he was executed, Bonhoeffer went to the gallows with his head up and his heart full. His faith and dignity impressed his fellow prisoners, and even the guards.

So what were Dietrich Bonhoeffer's rewards for a life of faithfulness, obedience, integrity, and eventually a martyr's death? His ultimate reward was the glory that he brought God, not only in his life, but also in his death. It *honored* the King. He felt the presence of God as only those can who live for Christ in the midst of great adversity. He possessed the "peace that passes all understanding." We can be assured that he is now experiencing incredible rewards as he sees his Lord face to face. Paul wrote about believers' future rewards:

> "For no one can lay any foundation other than the one already laid, which is Jesus Christ. If any man builds on this foundation using gold, silver, costly stones, wood, hay or straw, his work will

1 Dietrich bonhoeffer, Cost of Discipleship, (The MacMillan Company, New York: 1963) p. 17.

> be shown for what it is, because the Day will bring it to light. It will be revealed with fire, and the fire will test the quality of each man's work. If what he has built survives, he will receive his reward. If it is burned up, he will suffer loss; he himself will be saved, but only as one escaping through the flames" (1 Corinthians 3:11-15).

This is not the judgment regarding heaven and hell. Believers don't go through that. Judgment for believers is called The Judgment Seat of Christ. On that day, I will stand before Jesus and my entire life since I trusted Christ will be put on a "big video screen": every kind word I've spoken, and every time I've gossiped or been sarcastic; every time I've gone out of my way to help someone, and every time I've selfishly turned away; every time I've believed God to work in a difficult situation, and every time I've given up on him. On that day, all the things I've done that displease God will be burned up like "wood, hay, and straw." Swoooosh. Gone.

But for everything I've done to honor God, he will smile and say, "Well done, David. Enter into the joy of your Master!" I will receive a reward to enjoy for all eternity.

Please don't misunderstand. We're are not rewarded only for standing strong for Christ as we face execution. We are rewarded for even the smallest thing we do to honor God. Jesus made this point when he told people:

> "Anyone who receives a prophet because he is a prophet will receive a prophet's reward, and anyone who receives a righteous man because he is a righteous man will receive a righteous man's reward. And if anyone gives even a cup of cold water to one of these little ones because he is my disciple, I tell you the truth, he will certainly not lose his reward" (Matthew 10:41-42).

A kind word...a helping hand...a note of encouragement...a cup of water. If these are given because of our love for God, even the smallest act will receive an eternal reward. We may not be called to stand before a Nazi judge to defend our faith, but we have opportunities all day every day to extend love to the undeserving and unlovable, as Christ does to us.

I love the movie *Chariots of Fire*, the story of a Scottish athlete, Eric Liddell, who ran in the 1924 Olympics in Paris. Liddell was a Christian with strong convictions about keeping the Sabbath day for God. In the film, when he learns his first heat is scheduled for Sunday, he refuses to run. The British Olympic Committee and even the Prince of Wales encourage him to abandon his convictions just this once, but his decision is firm. Liddell, the greatest runner in the world in the 100 meters, takes himself out of the race. The news of Liddell's decision to put God ahead of his country is the sensation—and the controversy—of the games, but the story doesn't end there. Another British athlete who already has a medal offers Liddell his place in the 200 meter race on Monday. Liddell gratefully accepts.

On that day, as Liddell carefully digs out his starting spot, an American runner hands him a piece of paper. Liddell reads: "In the Good Book it says, 'He who honors me I will honor.' " The starting gun sounds, and Liddell runs with that piece of paper in his hand. He wins the race, and all of England and Scotland thrill in his victory! Eric Liddell becomes a national hero. However, even if Eric had lost the race, he had won the opportunity to bring glory to God through his actions.

Liddell was faced with honoring his God or pleasing his King. He chose his God. As the American already knew, God would honor him for that decision.

He will honor you, too. *Sometimes* we enjoy the harvest of rewards for walking with God soon after we sow good attitudes and actions. In other cases, the reward will come in the next life. But we can be sure of this, God notices, and he doesn't forget.

We will reap what we sow, more than we sow, and after we sow.

—Be still. Listen to what God is saying to you.

DAY 4

1. How have you seen the law of the harvest in people's spiritual lives (both positively and negatively)?

Those who give much & freely are honored by God. Those who are greedy & think only of themselves are lonely, sad, & depressed.

2. What are some things you are sowing "to please the sinful nature" these days?

Listening to negativity & gossip @ work.

What are you reaping?

discontent & loneliness @ work.

3. What are some things you are sowing "to please the Spirit"?

Giving of my time, energy, effort to my children, husb, church, friends.

What are you reaping?

Blessings of closer relationships & trusts

4. Does the thought of a "video" of your life at the Judgment Seat of Christ make you feel excited or anxious? Explain:

Both. I want my video to be of me choosing to honor / glorify God.

5. Do the rewards for following Christ seem fair? Why or why not?

Maybe not, here on Earth. I like comfort, & pleasure (vacay, meals out, new clothes / shoes for my fam). But He may choose to honor me after death in Heaven.

6. How will understanding that God will reward your faithfulness shape your decisions?

It gives me tremendous peace & joy that my Godly choices are noticed & pleasing to Him.

7. Read Galatians 6:7-9. Think about each verse, then use each verse as a guide as you pray.

Memorize: Say John 3:16 to a friend and describe what this verse means to you.

DAY 4

JOURNAL

Lord, today you are calling me to die to selfish desires by:

You are calling me to obey in these areas:

ditto

You are calling me to intimacy with you by:

ditto

DAY 5

EXCUSES, EXCUSES

"THEN A TEACHER OF THE LAW CAME TO HIM AND SAID, 'TEACHER, I WILL FOLLOW YOU WHEREVER YOU GO.' JESUS REPLIED, 'FOXES HAVE HOLES AND BIRDS OF THE AIR HAVE NESTS, BUT THE SON OF MAN HAS NO PLACE TO LAY HIS HEAD.' ANOTHER DISCIPLE SAID TO HIM, 'LORD, FIRST LET ME GO AND BURY MY FATHER.' BUT JESUS TOLD HIM, 'FOLLOW ME, AND LET THE DEAD BURY THEIR OWN DEAD.'"
– MATTHEW 8:19-22

Our struggle with excuses is the test of our commitment to Christ. Make no mistake: in a thousand choices to obey, we are faced with several thousand excuses to turn away. All of them seem "reasonable."

Look at the statement the lawyer made to Jesus: "I will follow you wherever you go." Wasn't that what Jesus was looking for? Wasn't that what he wanted every person to say? But look how the lawyer addressed Jesus. He called him "Teacher," not "Lord." This lawyer lived in comfort and wealth. He enjoyed Jesus' teaching, and he wanted to hear more, but all he wanted was intellectual stimulation. Jesus saw this man's heart, and he spoke to the cost of genuine commitment. If we are serious about following Christ, we give up our demands for comfort and we follow him to reach both the rich and the wealthy, the robed and the lepers. Our modern day example of this commitment was Mother Theresa of Calcutta, India. Her calling was to the sick and dying of one of the poorest cities in the world, yet her compassion for the poorest of the poor gave her a platform to speak of the love of God to presidents and kings. Foxes and birds may have homes, but the disciple of Christ doesn't demand or expect comfort. He follows his Lord anywhere and everywhere he leads.

The second man also stated his commitment to follow Jesus, but he had a very reasonable request. He wanted to fulfill a responsibility to his family to go and bury his father. Some Bible teachers tell us that this man's father may not have been dead yet, and this man's responsibility was to take care of his father through old age. Whether the man's father was already dead or heading in that direction, Jesus replied that our first responsibility as a disciple is to him, even more than to our families.

You and I face thousands of choices: some are large; some are relatively insignificant. For some we need to pray about and ask specific directions; some are clear and we just need to obey; while in others, God's word gives us general principles to follow. Should I watch this movie with skin and violence? Should I read my Bible? Should I reach out to the anti-social new guy at school or the office? Should I be respectful to my parents? Should I carve out time to pray? Should I be kind to a person new to our church? Should I follow God's leading to give to a missionary? Should I grab my tongue when I feel like cursing? Should I spend time on the sofa with my boyfriend or girlfriend late at night with nobody else around? Should I gossip about a mistake someone made? Should I date that person because he or she looks so hot? We face a zillion more choices just like these, big and small.

When those choices come, we often don't think through them very clearly. We just do what we've always done before—unless the Holy Spirit breaks in and says, "Hey! You've got a choice here. Be wise. I'll show you." Even then, we can think of lots of excuses to do the reasonable thing instead of the obedient thing. Here are a few:

- I'm only going to do it just this once.
- Nobody's looking.
- It's not going to hurt anybody.
- Everybody's doing it.
- Well, we're not living in Biblical times.
- If I do what God wants, people will misunderstand. They'll think I'm a religious fanatic or something.
- Doesn't God want me to fit in with my old friends?
- It's just too hard to do what God wants.
- I don't have time.
- Well, it's not exactly like that situation in the Bible when God specifically said, "No."
- I don't really know what God wants me to do. Until he makes it clear, I'm going to keep doing what I've been doing.

I think many of us hide behind the excuses of convenience and confusion. We don't do what God wants because it requires a little more effort and courage (OK, sometimes *a lot* more effort and courage!) than drifting along like we usually do. In this pampered culture, we don't want to do anything that requires more from us than we want to give. We hide behind imagined confusion. How many times have you heard people say (maybe even the person who looks at you in the mirror), "I'd do what God wants if I only knew what that was." Sometimes that is genuine and valid, but most of the time, we know good and well what God wants. We just don't want to do it. We try to shift the responsibility back on God as if to say, "Hey, God, you aren't clear enough. When you decide to show me clearly, then I'll obey. I know this is what the Bible says, but..." Do we seek God's will with all our hearts, or do we hear the truth from scripture after scripture and a dozen people and still say we are "confused?"

Don't feel alone in this problem of using excuses. I struggle with them, too. Several years ago, I went to Blockbuster to rent some videos. The problem was that I went at seven o'clock on Friday night. I walked over to the "New Release" wall. Nothing was left. The shelves were empty. I was bummed, but at that moment, one of the employees in a blue shirt came from behind the counter with a huge stack of returned videos to put back on the shelves. Everybody in the store saw him, and it was like we were magnetically drawn to him. He headed for the "A" section and put a couple of videos back up. I grabbed one. I didn't really care what it was. I just knew that I had to grab whatever I could get my hands on.

As soon as I looked at the title, I knew I had a decision to make. It was not the kind of video a committed Christian would watch. There are certain things that break the heart of God, and it's that cut and dry. Watching this kind of movie was one of those things. But immediately, I thought of a zillion excuses to shut up the voice inside me (the Holy Spirit) and rent that video. Wasn't I a strong enough Christian to overlook the bad parts and enjoy the good ones? Strong Christians don't let those things bother them, right? Wasn't watching it going to help me relate to other people more effectively?

I picked up a couple more videos and walked to the counter to pay for them. I gave the guy my credit card, signed for the videos, and he put them on the counter past the magnetic theft device. At that instant, I can imagine God leaning over and saying to his top angels, "Hey, Michael. Hey Gabriel. Watch this. Nasser's gonna get busted!"

When I walked past the magnetic thing and reached out to grab my videos, a student walked up to me. "Hey, David! Nasser! What's up?"

I said, "Hey, bud!" (which is ministerial for: "And you are...?")

"You don't remember me, do you?" he grinned. "You spoke at a camp last summer, and God changed my life. I've been going to a Bible study and growing in my faith. It's been fantastic! Some guys from the Bible study are coming over tonight to watch movies at my place. I know there's not much left at this time on Friday night..."

I could see the wheels turning. This guy had a brainstorm. "Hey, David, why don't you come over and we'll watch whatever you've rented! What did you get?"

I wanted to say, "Oh, *The Ten Commandments* and *Ben Hur*. You know, the same old, same old."

His eyes darted over to the stack of videos on the counter. There weren't any others up there, and he had seen my hand reaching for them a few seconds earlier. There was no way out of this one. He saw the title of that video I knew broke the heart of God, and this guy's smile vanished.

A blanket of conviction came down and enveloped me.

After an incredibly awkward moment, I turned to the blue shirted employee who didn't have a clue what was going on in this conversation, and said quietly, "I don't want these videos."

"Do you want your money back?"

"No. Just take them."

There was nothing more to say. I turned and walked past the stunned student and got in my car and drove home. When I got there, I went into my room, closed the door, and turned off the lights. I felt much more comfortable in the dark that night. I thought, *What have I become? Is the only way for God to speak to me for him to physically put somebody in front of me and tell me, "Hey, David! You are messing up! You are feasting at the wrong banqueting table! This is poison!"*

When I was standing in the aisle with that video in my hand, I was well aware that God is omnipresent. He was watching me. I hadn't forgotten that. But I thought, *So what? God is a God of grace. He doesn't expect me to be perfect. I'm only human. It won't be a regular thing.*

Don't misunderstand. This is not about setting up rules about not watching videos or about becoming a legalistic Pharisee. This is about becoming like the one who suffered and died to rescue you and me from hell. If we have the slightest clue about being bought by the blood of Jesus, we won't see how much we can get away with. We'll see how much we can honor him. True, there is not a sin that you or I could muster up that would make God say, "I don't love you anymore." But that doesn't mean we have the right to take his grace for granted.

Some people think that overcoming excuses and living out a genuine commitment to Jesus will make them really tough, and that toughness is a mark of real spirituality. I once heard a guy say, "If people don't hate me, then I must not be walking with God!" A radical commitment to Christ doesn't make you obnoxious. It makes you different. If it doesn't make you different, then it's not the real thing. Every time we say "No" to one of our excuses and "Yes" to Jesus, we know we must be closer to his heart, sensing his love. What kind of impact did Jesus have on people? Even the hardest sinners knew one thing about him: he loved them. Only the self-righteous religious leaders drew harsh words from Jesus, and that's because they were leading people away from God. To the prostitutes and other sinners, Jesus was the kindest, most loving person they had ever known. As we know him better, we will be kinder, more loving, more compassionate ...different, in a good way.

Recognize the excuses you use to say "No" or "Wait" or "But" to Jesus, and repent. Ask Christ to help you turn from those excuses and say "Yes" to him. It'll change your life—in a good way.

—Be still. Listen to what God is saying to you.

1. What are the most common excuses you hear people say for not doing what Jesus wants them to do?

?

2. What are your most common excuses?

I don't have time (but I am working on that w/ Jesus' help).

3. Think of three of your past choices (about your speech, your relationships, your time, etc.) What were some excuses you struggled with? What was the outcome?

4. Have you used convenience or confusion as excuses?

   Explain:

Convenience. yes

I want to do more for Jesus, but I get overwhelmed w/ all there is to do.

5. Write a paragraph on this topic: When I choose to disobey, I break God's heart.

When I choose to disobey, I break God's heart. I want God to be pleased w/ my choices, but I also want to know/feel like He's noticed my decisions for Him. I want to do His will always.

6. Agree or disagree: Obedience is loyalty to a person, not just following a rule.

Obedience is doing what God wants me to do, not just

Explain your response:

loyalty to a particular person, also of course He wouldn't want me gossiping about anyone

7. Read Matthew 8:19-22. Think about each verse, then use each verse as a guide as you pray.

Memorize Isaiah 26:8.

A CALL TO DIE

JOURNAL

Lord, today you are calling me to die to selfish desires by:

You are calling me to obey in these areas:

You are calling me to intimacy with you by:

DAY 6

GOD'S WORK

"THEREFORE, MY DEAR FRIENDS, AS YOU HAVE ALWAYS OBEYED—NOT ONLY IN MY PRESENCE, BUT NOW MUCH MORE IN MY ABSENCE—CONTINUE TO WORK OUT YOUR SALVATION WITH FEAR AND TREMBLING, FOR IT IS GOD WHO WORKS IN YOU TO WILL AND TO ACT ACCORDING TO HIS GOOD PURPOSE." – PHILIPPIANS 2:12-13

I value zeal for God. I value it a lot. That's what much of this book is about. But when young Christians (whether they are 16 or 76) become zealous for God, some of them make a big mistake. They want more than anything in the world for their lives to change, and they want to control their actions. To put the clamps on sinful behavior, they come up with rules to live by. Rigid rules.

Now, let's be honest. In the early stages of our commitment to be disciples of Christ, rules have a lot of validity. We need some guidelines to know what's acceptable and what's not. Otherwise, we might keep doing the same wicked things we used to do. When I first became a believer, I had a problem using foul language. Even as a brand new Christian, I knew cursing was dishonoring to God, so I asked all my new friends to punch me in the arm every time they heard me curse. Believe me, it didn't take long for me to change my language! Obviously, as I grew in my faith, I no longer needed this radical (and very painful!) rule applied in my life. My habit had changed.

In his letters to the churches, Paul often gave them lists of behaviors that dishonor God and those that honor him. He wanted there to be no misunderstanding, so he wrote it out in black and white. For example, to the Galatians he wrote: "The acts of the sinful nature are obvious: sexual immorality, impurity and debauchery; idolatry and witchcraft; hatred, discord, jealousy, fits of rage, selfish ambition, dissensions, factions and envy; drunkenness, orgies, and the like. I warn you, as I did before, that those who live like this will not inherit the kingdom of God. 'But,' Paul continued, 'the fruit of the Spirit is love, joy, peace, patience, kindness, goodness, faithfulness, gentleness and self-control. Against such things there is no law'" (Galatians 5:19-23).

Rules have their place, but if that's all there is to our Christianity, we become hardened, shallow, prideful, and judgmental. We become tangled up in all our rules. One of the most zealous young men of this century, Jim Elliot, recognized this problem in himself. He wanted more than anything in the world to please Jesus Christ. In his passion for purity, he set rules for himself: Don't waste time; don't date because dating robs you of your focus on Christ; don't spend time with people who aren't zealous for God; and so on and so on. These rigid rules seemed to fit his radical commitment, but in college, he realized that he was living by a "code of don'ts." Suddenly, the rules that seemed so right appeared to be sterile and empty. He realized his heart was full of pride because he had succeeded in following those rules, and his heart was also full of judgment for those who didn't. Jim Elliot repented of his strict "code of don'ts" and replaced it with more of the living, loving Lord.

Throughout Paul's letters, he reminded believers to experience the life-changing presence of God's Spirit. To the Galatians, he wrote, "So I say, live by the Spirit, and you will not gratify the desires of the sinful nature." The Holy Spirit works that miracle deep inside us, not just on the surface. He is at work in you right now. The Holy Spirit does many things in and through us. He:

- convicts us of sin so we can repent.
- comforts us when we are hurting.
- helps us understand the truth so we can walk in his light.
- strengthens us.
- gives us spiritual gifts.
- empowers us to minister to others.
- causes the love and life of Jesus to flow from our hearts and into the lives of others.

What does it look like for the Holy Spirit to be at work in us? Here's a MAP to guide you. The Spirit's work is a *mystery*, our walk then becomes an *adventure*, and seeing him at work deepens our *passion* for Jesus. Let's look at these:

Mystery—In his book, *Celebration of Discipline*, Richard Foster compares our walk with God to a wheat farmer. In order to bring in a harvest, a farmer must do certain things: plow the field, plant the seed, fertilize the seedlings, pull out the weeds, and kill the bugs. These are all essential parts of farming, but there's one thing the farmer can't do: make the wheat grow. In the same way, you and I have responsibility to do certain things to prepare ourselves: pray, read the scriptures, memorize verses, spend time with people who influence us to be holy, worship, and so on. But only the Holy Spirit himself can make the life of Christ flow in our hearts and change our desires. It is a great mystery of the faith that God would even want to hang out with sinners like you and me (well, me, anyway), but he does. Not only that, he wants to use us to reach other people with his wonderful truth and love.

Adventure—One thing about God is sure: He will always amaze us with how he'll use us. We have to keep our eyes open because he will blow our minds with where he will lead us. Sure, he lets us get into patterns that give us some stability, but as soon as we are established, he leads us in new directions to new experiences of enjoying him and letting him use us. You and I both know of countless stories of people who were willing (and sometimes only barely willing) to say "Yes" to the tap of God's Spirit on their shoulders, and God used them to bring light to dark hearts, and lives were changed forever.

Passion—I'm always amazed that God is willing to use somebody like me. His faithfulness to me makes me love him even more. The psalmist said, "I love the Lord, for he heard my voice; he heard my cry for mercy. Because he turned his ear to me, I will call on him as long as I live" (Psalm 116:1-2). The more we experience God's mercy, the more we love him. The more we see his power at work in us and through us, the more we are loyal to him. Passion takes root in gratitude. Take time to think about what God has done for you. Let the Holy Spirit remind you of how God's great grace has rescued you. No, many things may not have gone the way you hoped. But even in those disappointments, God is still God. He may have been directing you in a better direction. He may have been protecting you from harm you didn't see. He may have been testing you to strengthen you. He may have been stripping away some attitudes that hinder your relationship with him. He may have been preparing you for a deeper walk with him. Recognize that God is at work, and give thanks.

As we experience the mystery, adventure, and passion of walking closely with Jesus, following the rules won't be as much of a struggle because we won't want anything to hinder our walks. We'll be more patient with those who are at a different place than us. Instead of walking away in pride, we'll walk toward them in love. I'm convinced that many of the problems in churches occur because of this pride. One group is committed to following Christ, and they demand that others follow the rigid rules they set as a standard of godliness. That standard could be almost anything: church attendance, time devoted to ministry, giving, serving, or particular behaviors to avoid. Paul addressed this issue very clearly. He wrote:

> "Who are you to judge someone else's servant? To his own master he stands or falls. And he will stand, for the Lord is able to make him stand. One man considers one day more sacred than another; another man considers every day alike. Each one should be fully convinced in his own mind. Let us therefore make every effort to do what leads to peace and to mutual edification" (Romans 14:4-5, 19).

Think of how judgmental Jesus could have been! He could have blasted every person on the face of the earth for not being as committed to the Father as he was—and he would have been right. But just being right wasn't his purpose. He came to demonstrate the Father's love, to seek and to save the lost. To accomplish those purposes, he overlooks a lot of junk in people's lives—yours and mine.

The good news for you and me is that God is at work in us. The Spirit of God is convicting, encouraging, strengthening, and comforting us. You don't need to wonder if it's happening. It is! Our task is to notice the Spirit's work, to be sensitive to his voice, and to follow his leading.

I hope that these pages have stimulated your zeal for God and for doing good. I hope God has showed you behaviors and attitudes that are displeasing to him, and you have repented. But don't let your zeal for God be stuffed into rigid rules. Experience the presence of Christ. Let the Holy Spirit work his wonders in your heart. Obey out of gratitude. Let the love of God flow in you and through you to every person you meet.

—Be still. Listen to what God is saying to you.

1. Is it easier to follow rules or follow Christ? Explain your answer:

If we follow Christ, we want to do what He wants ∴ that makes it easier to do the right thing –

2. What are some rules zealous young Christians impose on themselves and others?

Be at the Church when the doors are open.
Do not go to movies
Alcohol is evil.

3. What are some positive results of having a "code of don'ts"?

discipline

What are some negative results?

Bondage

4. How have you seen the Holy Spirit at work in your life in the past week?

5. Were there times in the past week that you sensed God's Spirit speaking to you or nudging you and you failed to respond? If so, describe those times:

6. Are you a good farmer who does his part so the mystery of growth can occur? Why or why not?

   What practices need some work so the harvest will be more plentiful?

7. Write a prayer to God about how you want your relationship with him to be a mystery, and adventure, and full of passion. Thank him for his sacrifice for us.

8. Read Philippians 2:12-18. Think about each verse, then use each verse as a guide as you pray.

   Memorize: Write Isaiah 26:8 three times to reinforce it in your mind.

A CALL TO DIE

JOURNAL

Lord, today you are calling me to die to selfish desires by:

You are calling me to obey in these areas:

You are calling me to intimacy with you by:

DAY 6

Holy Bible

DAY 7

KNOW THE WORD

"FOR THE WORD OF GOD IS LIVING AND ACTIVE. SHARPER THAN ANY DOUBLE-EDGED SWORD, IT PENETRATES EVEN TO DIVIDING SOUL AND SPIRIT, JOINTS AND MARROW; IT JUDGES THE THOUGHTS AND ATTITUDES OF THE HEART. NOTHING IN ALL CREATION IS HIDDEN FROM GOD'S SIGHT. EVERYTHING IS UNCOVERED AND LAID BARE BEFORE THE EYES OF HIM TO WHOM WE MUST GIVE ACCOUNT."
– HEBREWS 4:12-13

Can you walk with God and not know God's word? That's a good question. Many people believe that God will somehow give them his treasure of wisdom and insight by osmosis. It doesn't happen like that. We have to mine for it, and the mine shaft goes through the pages of the Scriptures.

We Christians, including many who have been believers for several years, are clueless about the truth in the Bible. We can't find Psalms or Matthew, and we think Ruth and Timothy are in a new sit-com. We can't even quote a Bible verse for each year we've been believers. We know the theme songs of television shows and movies and a zillion songs on the radio, but we are biblically illiterate.

The Bible is the blueprint of life. The writer to the Hebrews said that the Scriptures are "living and active," not dead and buried like some of us think they are. God's truth may have been written centuries ago, but it is more up to date than any book on engineering, law, or medicine because it reveals timeless insight about man's heart and God's character. These don't change. The writer also stated that the word of God is sharp enough to cut through bones and marrow. Not long ago, doctors at the Livermore Institute invented a pipet, a water laser so sharp it can slice human hair lengthwise over 3000 times! God's word is even sharper, it cuts deeply and accurately into the most remote corner of our hearts, and then it heals and changes us.

If your house leaked in a huge thunderstorm and dripped on your computer, your posters, your clothes, and your bed, you'd notice! You'd probably do something about it—quick! Many of us have spiritual and moral leaks, but we don't have a sense of urgency to plug those leaks and protect our spiritual treasure. What is that treasure? The life-changing truth of God's word used by the Spirit of God to transform lives.

Do you need to know what is in the heart of God? Do you need wisdom when you are confused? Do you need peace when anxiety threatens to turn your world upside down? Do you need encouragement because you have failed or been betrayed? Of course, you do. We all do. How do we get the faith to believe God in good times and bad? It comes mostly through his word.

When your roof leaks, you call a repairman to come and take a look at it. He examines it carefully and gives you an estimate of what it will take to fix it. The question then becomes: Is the repair worth the cost? Becoming a student of God's word costs us some time, energy, and discipline. But it will result in a wealth of insight, direction, and understanding. Here are some ways to absorb God's truth.[2]

Hear the Word—In the field of education, experts tell us that about 10% of what we hear stays with us. At school or at work, we absorb and apply only a tenth of what we hear. The rest is flushed from our brains, and it's gone. That percentage is true in spiritual life, too: We absorb only about 10% of the sermons, seminars, and talks we hear. Paul wrote about how trust is generated: "Faith comes from hearing the message, and the message is heard through the word of Christ" (Romans 10:17). Hearing is important, but it is only a first step.

Read the Word—We absorb 25% of what we read. The physical and mental effort expended in reading pays greater dividends than simply hearing. In Deuteronomy 17:19, Moses said, "He is to read [the scriptures] all the days of his life so that he may learn to revere the Lord his God and follow carefully all the words of this law and these decrees." Reading reinforces truth so we can understand and obey God. The pages of the Bible are the source of God's wisdom about relationships; career; parents; dealing with tragedy, pain, and death; purpose; values; lifestyle; and all the principles you and I need to live successfully. Many Christians complain that they don't know what God's will is. You can know his will if you read his book.

Study the Word—Hearing and reading are effective, but not as effective as studying. That discipline allows us to take in and apply 50% of the truth. Solomon, the wisest man the world has ever known, wrote about the benefits of searching for the truth:

> "And if you call out for insight and cry aloud for understanding, and if you look for it as for silver and search for it as for

2 These principles are taken from a Christian Life and Witness class that I taught for the Billy Graham Evangelistic Association.

hidden treasure, then you will understand the fear of the Lord and find the knowledge of God.

"For the Lord gives wisdom, and from his mouth come knowledge and understanding. He holds victory in store for the upright, he is a shield to those whose walk is blameless" (Proverbs 2:3-7).

Years ago when I was a geeky preteen, I was a big fan of Michael Jackson. You may not realize it now, but there was a time in the music industry when Michael Jackson was somewhat cool. I remember being so excited when his "Thriller" album was released. I cut grass and cleaned pools to get enough money to get my own Michael Jackson jacket and "Thriller" cassette from Wal-Mart. When I finally had enough money, my dad drove me down there in his Buick Regal diesel (the ultimate "That's-OK-I'll-just-walk-to-school mobile"), and I bought the jacket and the cassette. As soon as I got in the car, I ripped the cover off the tape and devoured the lyrics. I studied the lyrics in the car all the way home. By the time we got home, I had memorized most of them. Even today when I see old clips of Michael Jackson and his "Thriller" music video, I can sing every song word for word. Why? Because I studied the lyrics. Why did I study them so much? Because I was passionate about Michael Jackson's music. Likewise, we will be motivated to study God's word when we become passionate about knowing God.

Memorize the Word—Studying God's word will have a huge impact on your life, but memorizing the Scriptures is even more effective in changing your life, because 80% of what we memorize stays with us. In Psalm 119:9, David wrote, "How can a young man keep his way pure? By living according to your word." A couple of verses later, he describes how the word penetrated his heart: "I have hidden your word in my heart that I might not sin against you." Memorizing God's truth makes it easily accessible for the Holy Spirit to use it any time, any place.

A few years before I met my wife Jennifer, I was speaking at a revival in Dothan, Alabama. After I spoke one night, I was hungry, so I walked into a restaurant connected to a hotel. The cute young hostess said, "Come this way. I'll show you to a table."

I said, "Thanks, but I'll just get it to go."

She brought the menu to me in the lobby, and I ordered a salad. A few minutes later, she brought dinner to me and handed me the dish with silverware and a linen napkin. She thought I was staying in the hotel connected to the restaurant, and she expected someone cleaning the room to bring the silverware back to the restaurant after I was finished. I told her, "I'm not staying at this hotel. I need a plastic knife and fork, please."

She then looked at me, smiled, and said, "I'll come over to your hotel when I get off at two in the morning, and I'll get it from you then."

I'd like to tell you that I wasn't interested in her coming to my lonely hotel room to see me. I'd like to tell you that all she was really interested in was the silverware. But neither of those statements were true.

At that moment, in God's perfect timing, the Holy Spirit reminded me of Hebrews 12:14: "Without holiness no man will see the Lord." I looked back at her and said, "Thanks, but no thanks. I'll just go now." God used the word I had stored in my memory to give me clear direction in that situation.

Meditate on the Word—An even more life-changing way to interact with truth is to meditate on it. In fact, I want you to cross out the word "meditate" and replace it with the word "marinate." God wants his word not just to be a "spice" that accents our life, but a daily marinating process that literally soaks into the core of who we are, forever changing our very identity.

One night when Jennifer and I were first married and she was still learning how to cook, she made me a special meal. Problem was, she didn't know how "special" she was really making it. She knew I loved the taste of Dale's Steak Sauce®, which is basically battery acid and worcestershire sauce, so she marinated some chicken in it—for two-and-a-half days! When I took that chicken out of the dish to grill it, I didn't know what it was, but it was no longer like the patterns of chicken. No matter what we did to that chicken (soaking it in Clorox®, putting it in the dryer—just kidding), it was not going back to the way it used to be. While that may be bad for chicken, it is great for Christians. We need to be so marinated in God's word that we are able to follow Paul's direction: "Do not conform any longer to the pattern of this world, but be transformed by the renewing of your mind" (Romans 12:2). Soaking yourself in God's word is 100% effective.

The truth found in the pages of the Bible are worth more than silver and gold. They hold the keys to success and fulfillment, but these treasures aren't available for free. They require tenacity and effort. Is that effort worth it to you?

—Be still. Listen to what God is saying to you.

1. Can a person walk with God and not know God's word? Why or why not? No — If you aren't familiar w/ God's word you can't walk w/ God & do His will

2. Where do you hear God's truth spoken?

   In the Bible, @ our Church, my husb. & Children, my friends

3. Describe your practice of reading the Scriptures? (What books do you read? Is there a pattern? Do you focus on some more than others? When do you read? How long each day?)

4. What does it mean to study God's word? What are some good study habits? Spending time regularly going over truth.

5. Has memorizing the verses in this book made an impact on your life? Explain: Yes. it is something to lean on when I need strength & to make sense of non-sensical things

6. What does it mean to meditate on God's word?

Read, Study, think on, listen to God's direction

What are some practices that make meditation meaningful to you?

7. How do the Holy Spirit and the Holy Book work together in a person's life to transform, encourage, and direct?

8. Read Hebrews 4:12-13. Think about each verse, then use each verse as a guide as you pray.

Memorize: Go over Isaiah 26:8 again. How can you apply this verse today?

A CALL TO DIE

JOURNAL

Lord, today you are calling me to die to selfish desires by:

You are calling me to obey in these areas:

You are calling me to intimacy with you by:

DAY 8

LIES, NOTHING BUT LIES

"THE ONE WHO RECEIVED THE SEED THAT FELL AMONG THE THORNS IS THE MAN WHO HEARS THE WORD, BUT THE WORRIES OF THIS LIFE AND THE DECEITFULNESS OF WEALTH CHOKE IT, MAKING IT UNFRUITFUL. BUT THE ONE WHO RECEIVED THE SEED THAT FELL ON GOOD SOIL IS THE MAN WHO HEARS THE WORD AND UNDERSTANDS IT. HE PRODUCES A CROP, YIELDING A HUNDRED, SIXTY OR THIRTY TIMES WHAT WAS SOWN." – MATTHEW 13:22-23

Only a few pages into the Bible we find Satan. What does he look like? He is beautiful. What is his purpose? To destroy people. In Genesis, it tells us that God had given Adam and Eve everything they could possibly want in a million years. Eden was heaven on earth. Out of all the wonderful things God gave this couple, he required one thing: Don't eat of a certain tree. He made his point crystal clear. But as my friend, evangelist and author Rick Stanley, always says, "The problem wasn't the apple on the tree, but the 'pair' on the ground."

Satan came to Eve and asked a simple question, "Did God really say, 'You must not eat from any tree in the garden?' " At first, Eve responded accurately, "No, God didn't say that. He said there is only one tree we can't eat from." But then she overstated God's requirement: "And we can't touch it or we'll die."

God never said that. Satan saw his opening and exclaimed, "You will not surely die. In fact, if you eat it, you'll really live!" Then Satan compounded his deception. He told her, "If you eat from that tree, you'll know both good and evil. You'll be just like God!"

Satan's plot was to plant a question in Eve's mind about God's intentions and character. If he could get just one of the people to doubt God, he had a chance of destroying the whole human race. Eve took the bait. She ate the fruit. Sin, misery, and destruction then entered human history.

Satan's purpose is the same today. For you. For me. He wants to destroy us. He uses lies of every stripe to get us to doubt God's intentions and character. We are at war. Let's see what we're up against:

Temptation—Matthew records Jesus' parable about the seed of God's word falling on four types of spiritual soil: the packed roadway, rocks, soil full of thorns, and good soil. Many believers fall in that third category. We respond to the gospel and grow for a while, but "the worries of this life and the deceitfulness of riches choke" our spiritual throats. What is he talking about? That's not too hard to figure out. What do most people spend their time thinking, dreaming, and talking about? Possessions, popularity, sex, prestige, and power. What do riches promise but fail to deliver? Happiness, comfort, and fulfillment.

Satan has a strong ally today in his attempts to tempt you and me to pursue those things instead of Christ: advertising. Think of all the magazine ads, television commercials, radio ads, and billboards you encounter every day. Every one of them claims its product or service will do something you must have. But it is the implicit, hidden promise that is so deceptively tempting. Toothpaste promises not just to clean your teeth but to get you the date of your dreams. A credit card promises not only to help you buy something conveniently but to give you ultimate peace and contentment. Beer promises not just to taste good, but to make you popular (and good looking, too! How does *that* work?). We are so submerged in the sea of advertising that we don't even notice the subtle, implicit messages. They are lies. You and I believe them far too often.

Accusation—When we give in to temptation and fall, Satan kicks us while we're down. He is called "the accuser of the brethren." At that moment, his beautiful mask of temptation is stripped off and he snarls, "See! You're a failure! How can you call yourself a Christian? God couldn't love anybody who is such a screw up like you!"

Have you ever heard those voices? Have you ever beat yourself up for doing something stupid? Satan wants us to focus on how awful we are instead of on God's wonderful forgiveness and strength. The more you grovel in the mud of self-contempt, the better Satan likes it. The more you focus on self, the less you focus on God.

John tells us what to do when we hear those voices of accusation: "My dear children, I write this to you so that you will not sin. But if anybody does sin, we have one who speaks to the Father in our defense—Jesus Christ, the Righteous One" (1 John 2:1). Picture a court room with you on trial for committing a sin. The Father is the judge. Satan is the prosecutor, and Jesus is your defense lawyer. Satan delivers a blistering attack—with lots of evidence against you. You are guilty. No question about it. Then Jesus gets up to speak. He says, "Yes, Judge, my client is guilty, but his penalty has already been paid. By me. In blood." The Father smiles and nods, "Paid in full. Case dismissed." That's a picture of what happens every time you sin and are accused by Satan.

Listen to your defender who paid your penalty. Love him for it. Thank him for it. Honor him in your lifestyle of worship.

Confusion—Satan wants to distort our view of God, to make us believe that God doesn't care or can't help. He uses bad teaching of the Scriptures, cults, some biology professors, and well-meaning friends to get us off track. Today, millions of people check out their horoscopes every day, but they fail to read God's word. Most high school and college students are taught that our existence is the product of matter and chance over billions of years instead of God's sovereign design. Some of these sources of "truth" look very appealing, even to some Christians. Paul reminded us that "Satan himself masquerades as an angel of light" (2 Corinthians 11:14).

Obstacles—If he can't tempt us to sin, if he can't get us to hate ourselves when we win, and if he can't confuse us, Satan will put obstacles in our way to try to prevent us from knowing and serving God. Chapter 10 of the book of Daniel records an amazing celestial struggle. Daniel prayed that God would give him wisdom. Nothing happened. Daniel kept praying for a week. Nothing. After three weeks, an angel appeared to him and told him that God had heard his prayer and sent an angel the day he began praying, but Satan sent a demon to stop the angel from coming to his aid. For three weeks, the angel and the demon fought it out in the heavens until finally, the angel won the battle and appeared to Daniel to guide him. Does something so dramatic happen to you and me today? Only if we are as serious about upholding the honor of God as Daniel was. I believe that Satan doesn't give as much merit to many of us because we aren't a threat to his purposes. But if we grow strong, he will oppose us.

Does that scare you? Does it make you not want to get too close to Jesus because you don't want to have to fight? You're in a fight whether you want to be or not. You and I experience temptations and accusations all day every day. Often, we are exposed to distortions of truth. If we are serious about taking the love of God to our friends and the world, Satan will put obstacles in our path.

Whose voice utters all these temptations and accusations? In the vast majority of cases, Satan uses our own voices to slam us. If he used a voice like the gravelly demonic voice in *The Exorcist*, we would realize it's him. But since he uses our own voices, our own words, our own inflections, we are much more easily duped. Don't accept every thought just because it happens in your head. Yank it out. Take it captive (see 2 Corinthians 10:4-5), and analyze it to see if it is of God or not. Check it out with the truth of God's word. (See how important it is to know God's word!)

Satan is a liar and a thief. He doesn't play fair. His goal is to keep people from God any way he can. If they become Christians, he wants to keep them off balance and focused on things that will make them empty and ineffective for Christ. The vast majority of our struggles with Satan take place in the realm of truth. He uses temptation, deception, and accusation to get us off base. We need to be strong in the word of God so we can fight effectively. Paul encouraged us in this fight:

> "Finally, be strong in the Lord and in his mighty power. Put on the full armor of God so that you can take your stand against the devil's schemes. For our struggle is not against flesh and blood, but against the rulers, against the authorities, against the powers of this dark world and against the spiritual forces of evil in the heavenly realms. Therefore put on the full armor of God, so that when the day of evil comes, you may be able to stand your ground, and after you have done everything, to stand" (Ephesians 6:10-13).

Since you began this study a week or so ago, have you had any odd, uncomfortable thoughts? Has it crossed your mind, "This is a joke. What's this business about me following Christ and honoring him—after what I've done, where I've been, and what I've seen?" Or maybe you've thought, "Yeah, I'm doing this 'dying for Jesus' thing really well. I hope people notice how much I'm growing. I'll be an example to those people who don't get it as quickly as I do." Satan wants to get each of us off track. For some, he uses hopelessness; for others, pride. He doesn't care which works on you...just so something works.

Don't take your eyes off Jesus. He is the beginning and the end, the top and the bottom of our faith. He supplies strength and power. But as you focus on him, realize there is another who wants desperately to make you stumble. Satan is deceptive, but Jesus is far more powerful, loving, and wise. Keep your eyes on him. Don't be surprised if the fire gets hotter. That's a sign that you are on the right path! But don't get burned, either.

—Be still. Listen to what God is saying to you.

1. Make a list of five commercials and ads. What do they promise the product or service will do? What is the implicit promise of how it will give you peace, success, popularity, or power?

2. What are some examples of . . .

   temptations?

   accusations?

   confusion?

   obstacles?

3. Which do you struggle with most? Explain:

4. Describe Jesus' role as your defense attorney. How does that make you feel?

5. Read 2 Corinthians 10:4-5. What does it mean to take our thoughts captive to Christ?

6. Are you more susceptible to hopelessness or pride in Satan getting you off track? Explain:

7. Read Matthew 13:1-9, 18-23. Think about each verse, then use each verse as a guide as you pray.

   Memorize: Repeat John 3:16 and Isaiah 26:8 several times until you can say them without looking.

A CALL TO DIE

JOURNAL

Lord, today you are calling me to die to selfish desires by:

You are calling me to obey in these areas:

You are calling me to intimacy with you by:

DAY 8

DAY 9

WHAT'S YOUR TREASURE?

"THE KINGDOM OF HEAVEN IS LIKE TREASURE HIDDEN IN A FIELD. WHEN A MAN FOUND IT, HE HID IT AGAIN, AND THEN IN HIS JOY WENT AND SOLD ALL HE HAD AND BOUGHT THAT FIELD. AGAIN, THE KINGDOM OF HEAVEN IS LIKE A MERCHANT LOOKING FOR FINE PEARLS. WHEN HE FOUND ONE OF GREAT VALUE, HE WENT AWAY AND SOLD EVERYTHING HE HAD AND BOUGHT IT." – MATTHEW 13:44-46

On July 20th, 1985, Mel Fisher leaned over the side of his salvage boat off the Florida Keys. As he had done thousands of times before, he watched the bubbles from the scuba tanks and waited for some good news. For seventeen years, Fisher had looked for the wreck of the Nuestra Senora de Atocha, a Spanish galleon that sank in a hurricane in 1622. For years, divers found many other wrecks, but none would compare to the Atocha. Ancient documents in the General Archive of the Indies in Seville, Spain, said that this ship carried enormous quantities of gold, silver, and jewels from Havana to Spain. The man who found it would be rich beyond his wildest imagination.

Everybody in Key West knew Fisher had looked for the Atocha day after day and year after year, and many of them laughed at his inept efforts. Then, on July 20th, 1975, Fisher's son Dirk found a bronze cannon from the Atocha. Surely riches were just around the corner. But instead of riches, Fisher found only heartache when Dirk, his wife, and another diver were killed a week later when their boat capsized.

Fisher buried them, and he kept up the search.

In the next few years, Fisher found a few coins, a few gold platters, and a few emeralds...just enough to keep investors interested. But they failed to find the main compartment of treasure.

On that afternoon in 1985, Fisher tried a new salvage technique. He rigged up his engines to blow water through a tube to hose off the sea floor. It stirred up an immense quantity of sand in the water. After it settled, he sent his divers down for a look. Fisher stood at the side watching. Always watching.

After only a few minutes, a diver surfaced, ripped off his mask and yelled, "It's here! We've found the main pile!"

Imagine being that diver as he swam down through the settling sand and suddenly gazed on a stack of gold and silver bars eight feet wide, five feet high, and twenty feet long! It contained over 7000 ounces of gold, 1000 silver bars, and 530,000 doubloons. Gold necklaces, platters, and candelabras littered the ocean bottom. The divers scooped up double-handfuls of huge emeralds. On that first day, the divers brought up so much treasure that the salvage boat almost sank! It took the 70-man crew two and a half years to recover it all. The haul was valued at $400 million.

Mel Fisher had quite a treasure, but he had given up practically everything to get it: his reputation, his comfort, the lives of his family. But the value of the treasure was worth more to him than anything in the world. Sadly, we know that Fisher's treasure was only earthly, and many would say he still came out short. But you can't deny his passion and commitment.

The double parables of Jesus in some ways teach the same lesson, only in the spiritual realm. These stories are similar, yet there is a difference. In both cases, the men valued what they found so much that they instantly gave up everything to acquire the treasure. Yet in the first story, the man stumbled across the treasure, and in the second, the man had been searching for it all his life. The treasure in the field may have been hidden there by a family to protect their possessions when an invading army came through. The man in that story wasn't looking for anything—except a shortcut home. Maybe a recent rain unearthed the box. He saw it out of the corner of his eye and stopped to investigate. When he saw the valuables inside, he quickly hid it again, ran home, and sold all he had so he could buy that land and own the treasure. The pearl merchant had seen thousands of fine pearls. He was an expert. But he had never seen one like this. He simply had to have it, but the price was high. He quickly calculated that he could have it only if he sold all he had to raise the capital. It was an easy decision for him because the value of the pearl far outweighed his own possessions.

In these stories, the treasure and the pearl are symbols of Christ. Some of us stumble across him. We are going our own way, minding our own business, and somehow, some way we realize, "Jesus is real. He can be my Savior!" Others of us have a tug in our hearts for years. We search for truth by going to every conceivable source of spiritual nourishment. We try astrology and angels; we read the Baghavad-Gita and Joseph Smith; we meditate on a hill and read Darwin. We watch Sally Jesse and Oprah. But none of these satisfy us. Maybe we have been turned off by arrogant Christians, so we discounted Christ. But now, we examine the Christian faith one more time—and we see Jesus.

Either way, whether by surprise (though it is never a surprise from God's sovereign point of view) or by careful, diligent search, we find Christ. He is so wonderful that our instantaneous response is to gladly forsake anything and everything to become intimate with him. Nothing else matters because, quite literally, nothing else matters.

Soon we realize that all the things that seemed so important a moment ago: the success, the money, the prestige, the possessions...all will pass like a vapor in the wind. They appear for only a moment in time, then they're gone without a trace. That insight changes our outlook. It rivets our affections on the one who is eternal, and we determine to live every moment of every day to honor him and advance his kingdom. After all, it's the only reasonable thing to do!

If Christ is our treasure, we have a completely different perspective on earthly things: we can enjoy them, and we can use them, but they never own us. If God gives us earthly riches, we are thankful. If not, we are content. These things simply are not important to us.

But for many of us, those things certainly are important to us. We love what Jesus does for us more than we love him. We look for promises that he will give us whatever we want, and we are angry when they don't come—or if they don't come fast enough. We demand his blessings instead of accepting them from his hand with gratitude. Please don't misunderstand me: I'm not saying that it is wrong to claim God's promises and enjoy his blessings. Answers to prayer are wonderful! But we need to be careful not to let those blessings crawl into the center of our hearts. They are evidences of his goodness and power, and they point us back—always back—to him.

We today are thrill-seekers. Extreme sports are the rave right now, and man, they are incredible! But I'm afraid too many Christians unknowingly expect Jesus to provide adrenalin-pumping experiences. To be sure, some of the things Jesus asks us to do are challenging to the extreme. We get a rush! But above all else, God values our faithfulness to obey him. Patient endurance is not all that exciting most of the time, and if we expect (and demand) spiritual thrills all the time, we will soon be disappointed and walk away.

How can we tell what we treasure? If we are serious about denying our selfish ambitions and taking up our crosses because we treasure Christ above all else, we can count on two things: encouragement and testing. God will lead us to passages of scripture and godly people to fan the flame in our hearts. Imagine how thrilled he is when you and I say, "God, I will do anything to follow you and honor you!" But he also tests that commitment. He brings failure and pain into our lives, not to discourage us but to refine our desires and burn away the stuff that gets in our way. When we say that he is our treasure, he tests us by either giving us those things that compete with him or he takes them away. You may receive an award or experience great success. At that moment, you have a choice of what to treasure. Or you may be rejected by someone you value or fail in an important goal. At that moment, you can choose whether to value the loss and sink into despair or to treasure Christ and say, "Lord, it hurts, but your love is far greater than my loss." Either way, in success or in failure, our true hearts are revealed and we can grow.

Jim Elliot was only a young man, but he realized that the things most people value are worthless. From an eternal point of view, all the money, awards, and comforts will burn up. They may seem important now, but they will vanish. Only what we do for Christ has lasting value. Elliot said, "He is no fool to give what he cannot keep to gain what he cannot lose."

If Christ is our treasure, no one can steal him, no one can damage him, no one can take our satisfaction away.

—Be still. Listen to what God is saying to you.

1. What are some ways you can tell what someone values? (Think about your family and friends. What are some neon signs in their lives of what is important to them?)

2. How did you feel the day you discovered Jesus?

Ashamed, grateful,.

3. Write a paragraph about this statement: If Christ is our treasure, it changes our outlook on success, pleasure, and approval.

Outward pleasures diminish in value. When we seek Christ, success, pleasure, & approval looks & feels different.

4. What does it mean to enjoy God's blessings without demanding them?

Being grateful when they come, but not having a negative attitude when they don't.

5. Has God encouraged you in your commitment to treasure him? If so, how?

6. Has God tested you in your commitment? If so, how?

7. State Jim Elliot's quote in your own words: "He is no fool to give what he cannot keep to gain what he cannot lose."

The person who understands that by giving something away in this life will gain peace, joy, lasting contentment from Jesus

8. Read Matthew 13:44-46. Think about each verse, then use each verse as a guide as you pray.

Memorize Galatians 2:20.

A CALL TO DIE

JOURNAL

Lord, today you are calling me to die to selfish desires by:

You are calling me to obey in these areas:

You are calling me to intimacy with you by:

DAY 10

RUBBISH... WHAT DOES THAT MEAN?

"BUT WHATEVER WAS TO MY PROFIT I NOW CONSIDER LOSS FOR THE SAKE OF CHRIST. WHAT IS MORE, I CONSIDER EVERYTHING A LOSS COMPARED TO THE SURPASSING GREATNESS OF KNOWING CHRIST JESUS MY LORD, FOR WHOSE SAKE I HAVE LOST ALL THINGS. I CONSIDER THEM RUBBISH, THAT I MAY GAIN CHRIST..." – PHILIPPIANS 3:7-8

The apostle Paul picks up the theme of what has value (similar to the parables about the treasure and the pearl in Matthew 13) and describes his perspective in his letter to the Philippians. Paul was the brightest young star in Judaism. If religion had been a sport, he would have been the top draft choice! When he walked in the door, people stopped and stared. They listened carefully to every word he said because they realized he was going somewhere fast, and they didn't want to be left behind. That kind of popularity and power is pretty intoxicating for a young man (or a young woman) to experience.

But something happened to Paul. He met Jesus.

In this letter, Paul reminds the believers where he came from: "If anyone else thinks he has reasons to put confidence in the flesh, I have more." Then he lists his impeccable credentials. "Circumcised on the eighth day, of the people of Israel, of the tribe of Benjamin, a Hebrew of Hebrews; in regard to the law, a Pharisee; as for zeal, persecuting the church; as for legalistic righteousness, faultless" (Philippians 3:4-6). If anybody had reason to trust in his family position, Paul did. If anybody had reason to boast in his success, he did. If anybody could point to radical commitments and a faultless lifestyle, Paul could. He had it all!

And it was all worth less than nothing.

Paul and others had thought all these things were "profit" to him because they gave him position and clout, but when he experienced "the surpassing greatness of knowing Christ Jesus my Lord," all those things paled into insignificance. But that's not quite accurate. Paul said that those things that had seemed so important before are now considered "rubbish." The Bible translators looked at the word Paul used in the original language and said, "Nah, we can't use that word. It's too vulgar. We'll use 'rubbish' instead." Unless you are British, you probably don't use the word "rubbish" much. Frankly, I feel uncomfortable using the literal translation in my book. But you do the math. You know what he's talking about. Let's just say "waste."

When you see a pile of dog waste (or "rubbish") on the sidewalk, you don't stop and admire it saying, "Oh, Helen, look at that! Isn't it lovely." (Well, some guys I know might...) No, you say, "Ugghh! Don't step in that!"

Paul was saying the prestige, possessions, and power he enjoyed were actually hindrances to him, and he was going to be careful not to step in them! Dietrich Bonhoeffer said of this realization: "The call of Jesus teaches us that our relation to the world has been built on an illusion."[3] The promise of the world is an illusion. We thought the promises and the substance were real, but

3 Bonhoeffer, *Cost of Discipleship*, p. 80.

they aren't. We thought those things would satisfy, but they can't. We thought they were treasures, but they are "rubbish." They are, indeed, waste, when we compare them to "the surpassing value of knowing Christ Jesus my Lord."

Notice in this passage how many times Paul uses the word *consider*:

- "Whatever was to my profit I now consider loss."
- "What is more, I consider everything a loss compared to the surpassing greatness of knowing Christ."
- "I consider them rubbish."

To *consider* something means we carefully reflect; we work at understanding; we pursue the hidden truth. Illusions don't die easily. Paul had to take time and effort to search the Scriptures and compare the real truth to what he had thought was truth. I get the idea it was a real struggle, like mining for gold through painstaking, gruelling labor. That's how wealth is accumulated: the wealth of gold and the wealth of spiritual riches.

Paul's considering also led him to reflect deeply on his sinfulness and God's great grace. He wanted to "be found in him, not having a righteousness of my own that comes from the law, but that which is through faith in Christ." Paul had tried the first way: doing everything in the attempt to measure up to God's standard. But his struggle to be good only revealed the sin in his heart. His righteousness was a gift from God, bought by Jesus, and gratefully accepted. Paul tells us in Ephesians 2:8-9 that it is by *grace* we're saved through faith—it's not by anything we could do. This realization sharpened his view that Jesus is the greatest treasure in the universe.

Paul's search for truth shattered the illusion in his life, and it led him to take action. Christ was not just his treasure in theory but in fact. Paul's consuming desire was to honor Christ and glorify him all day, every day through his obedience. God led him on the most exciting adventures any believer has ever experienced, to great joys and incredible hardships, to fantastic blessings and alarming threats. At every step, God made himself very real to Paul—just as he will for you and me if we value him as highly.

How did Paul relate to riches and honor after the illusion was blown to bits? His attitude was: "Riches? Who cares?" "Fame? So what?" "Awards or comfort? OK, no big deal." Later in his letter to the Philippians, Paul shared his secret:

> "I know what it is to be in need, and I know what it is to have plenty. I have learned the secret of being content in any and every situation, whether well fed or hungry, whether living in plenty or in want. I can do everything through him who gives me strength" (Philippians 4:12-13).

Paul's secret was to find joy, contentment, and pleasure not in outward things but in Christ alone—and Christ never changes.

When we "consider" the truth and that truth shatters our illusions, it sinks deep into our hearts and changes our lives. Suddenly, the things that seemed so important become nuisances and Jesus consumes us.

C. T. Studd was the Michael Jordan of his day in England. As a student at Cambridge University, he was the best athlete in the world, and everywhere he went people adored him. His family was rich and lived on a large estate, and he was the talk of the country. What could be better for a young athlete? If television and product endorsements had been around in the late 19th century, Studd would have had dozens of offers to put his face on cereal, phone service, shoes, and soft drinks.

But Studd considered Christ, and the direction of his life changed. He, along with many others in a great movement of God at that time, decided to give up his career and go overseas to spread the gospel. Six other young men at Cambridge believed God was leading them to China, a country that was almost as remote and forbidding in that day as the moon. Many people, including some of Studd's family members, were appalled at the decision of these seven young men to go to China. They thought it was a tragic waste of their intellect, ability, and potential. Still, these seven young men were determined to go.

As a further display of his commitment, Studd gave away his inheritance from his father's estate so that he would have no advantage—and no distractions—in his missionary work. He and his friends served in the China Inland Mission for many years. Later, even in ill health after returning to England, Studd answered a call to go to Africa because he saw a sign on a door saying "Cannibals Want Missionaries." Christ and his cause were more important to him than anything the world offered: prestige as the greatest athlete of his day, wealth, or comfort. It was all rubbish to C. T. Studd.

The task for you and me is to shatter the illusion that is so pervasive in our culture—and in our hearts. That illusion doesn't die the moment we trust Christ, but at least we are connected to the teacher. Our job is to go to school, to consider the facts of what has value and what does not. In that school we will find that very few people—and very few Christians—know fact from illusion. We will learn to sift through the talks and books and tapes we hear to look for the golden nuggets of God's perspective. Sadly, they are hard to find. Too much of our teaching and songs tell us we can have Jesus and comfort, Jesus and prestige, Jesus and power. They may even tell us the bold lie that Jesus' reason for coming was primarily to give us comfort, prestige, and power!

Learn to be a good listener. Don't react too quickly to what you hear. Think about it. Pray that God will give you insight. Talk to others who are seeking godly wisdom, too.

The results of considering and getting God's perspective is not violence or judgment against those who aren't clued in yet. It is thankfulness, contentment, firmness without hardness, and a zeal to tell everybody you know about the incredible treasure you've found.

—Be still. Listen to what God is saying to you.

1. What are your "credentials" of power, prestige, and popularity?

- grad. college / degree
- we know many people in this small community

2. What are some ways most people use these to get where they want to go?

3. In what ways can they be hindrances to a committed Christian?

We can lean on our own strength & understanding.

4. What are some evidences in your life that the world's values are an illusion?

Went to mission field in 1999 - left family, job, prestige behind.

5. Describe what it would mean for you to really "consider" what Paul had to say.

6. How would your life be different if you genuinely believed the things the world values are rubbish and knowing Christ is the most valuable thing in the world?

I believe that He is.

7. Read Philippians 3:1-14. Think about each verse, then use each verse as a guide as you pray.

Memorize: Write Galatians 2:20 three times.

A CALL TO DIE

JOURNAL

Lord, today you are calling me to die to selfish desires by:

You are calling me to obey in these areas:

You are calling me to intimacy with you by:

D A Y   1 1

BOUGHT AND PAID FOR

"DO YOU NOT KNOW THAT YOUR BODY IS A TEMPLE OF THE HOLY SPIRIT, WHO IS IN YOU, WHOM YOU HAVE RECEIVED FROM GOD? YOU ARE NOT YOUR OWN; YOU WERE BOUGHT AT A PRICE. THEREFORE HONOR GOD WITH YOUR BODY."
–1 CORINTHIANS 6:19-20

We talk about "my time" and "my things." We get upset when somebody interrupts "my rest" and violates "my rights." Our goal is to be self-actualized and self-fulfilled. But we are empty.

When we focus on meeting our own needs, we are slaves to ourselves and our sins. Paul talked about slavery in his letter to the Romans, and his perspective is just as relevant today as it was in the first century: "Don't you know that...you are slaves to the one whom you obey—whether you are slaves to sin, which leads to death, or to obedience, which leads to righteousness?"

(Romans 6:16).

What is the character of a slave? He is devoted to his master, and he obeys without question. Paul said that people who choose to disobey God are slaves to sin. We make people, possessions, or lust our master; and as slaves, we spend our time, resources, and energy to fulfill our master's wishes. Does this sound too harsh? Too dramatic? Watch people and see how devoted they are to whatever turns them on. What do they think about and talk about every spare minute? What activities do they organize their time around? What do they daydream about?

Look around today; it's all around us. We buy clothes and show them off; we shed more tears when our favorite show gets cancelled than when we see things that break the heart of God—and then there's music. Enough said. We jockey for position in the group to impress certain people. Who is our master then? Where your greatest passion lies, there lies your God. Some guys live for sports. The thrill of the game consumes their thoughts. Are sports wrong? Is it sin to pay football or baseball or basketball or anything else? That's not the question. The more important question is: What or who are you living for? If Christ is your Lord and he leads you to play sports, play with all your heart to honor him. But don't let anything—*anything*—occupy God's place in your heart. Having sin as your master leads to death. What does that look like?

The sins of lust, greed, envy, and jealousy gnaw at our hearts like a cancer. They cut off the life-giving flow of the Spirit in our minds, and we fail to exercise our muscles of faith so they wither. Spiritual vitality is drained away until ultimately, we don't respond to God's voice. Instead of forgiveness, we are crushed by guilt. Instead of thankfulness, we are bitter at God and at others who have hurt us. Instead of sensing God's presence, we feel alone and empty. Instead of seeing God use us to change lives, we realize we have become millstones that drag others down. That's spiritual death. That's the effect of letting sin be our master.

But Christ can be our master. Instead of letting lust, greed, and the thirst for approval dictate our lives, we can obey our loving Lord. When we are devoted to him, he gives us new eyes to see all that goes on around us. Instead of believing popularity and possessions will bring us happiness, the light comes on and we see the emptiness in the lives of those who pursue those things. But we don't hate or judge them for it. We realize, "I was right there, too. I was just as foolish and empty. Maybe Jesus will use me to be a light in that person's life."

When Jesus is our master, our minds are absorbed with pleasing him and advancing his kingdom. We will defend his honor at all costs, because we remember with gratitude the sacrifice he made. How do we get that perspective? Here are some truths to keep in mind:

1. You have been bought with a price.

A payment has been made. A purchase has been completed. No, I'm not talking about a new pair of jeans at the mall. I'm talking about Jesus purchasing you and me. Paul told the Corinthian believers, "You are not your own; you were bought at a price." The modern preoccupation with "my" this and "my" that has no place in the life of a person who has been redeemed (bought) by the blood of the Savior. The question for me each day should not be, "What do I want to do today?" It is "Jesus, I'm yours. What do you want to do with me today?" Contrary to popular perception, Jesus is not a good luck charm to help me do well at the things I've chosen to do. He is my Master, the one who rescued me from hell and gave me life. When I was the master of my own life (or at least, when I *thought* I was master of my own life), I was headed for eternal destruction. The ransom to get me out was high—exceptionally high. I could never pay it, but Jesus did. Today, I am not my own. I belong to him. That means that every moment of my time is his, everything I own is his, and every step I take is his.

Some of us have a misconception of authority. Maybe we've been hurt by parents or teachers. Maybe we got on the wrong side of the law and we despise anyone telling us what to do. Some of us have wonderful parents and can say, "I know what Jesus is like because my mom and dad are strong and loving, too," but others of us have to say, "The Heavenly Father is very different from my earthly father." Either way, we can have an accurate view of him through scripture.

In his letters, Paul often calls himself and us "bondservants." Moses gives us a beautiful description of a bondservant in Exodus 21. In those days, a Hebrew who owed too much to another would become an indentured servant, a slave, until he paid off his debt. On the day he was to be set free, the slave had a choice. If the master had been loving toward him, he could choose to remain as a bondslave, one who has chosen to remain because he wants to continue to enjoy his master's love and kindness. If that was his choice, his ear was pierced with a tool as a sign to all that being loved was more important to him than being free. It is the same with you and me. Christ has set us free, but if we feel his love and kindness, we can choose to be his faithful, loyal, committed bondservant.

2. Release your grip on sin.

Being a bondservant of Christ is not a once-and-for-all thing. We make choices to obey and honor him—or not—dozens of times a day. When God shows us areas of our lives that are too important to us, we need to say, "Yes, Lord. You are right. Help me rip these things from my heart." Jim Elliot prayed that God would give him the strength to let go of his sinful desires. He wrote:

> "Father, let me be weak that I might loose my clutch on everything temporal. My life, my reputation, my possessions, Lord, let me loose the tension of the grasping hand. Even, Father, would I lose the love of fondling. How often I have released a grasp only to retain what I prized by 'harmless' longing, the *fondling* touch. Rather, open my hand to receive the nail of Calvary, as Christ's was opened—that I, releasing all, might be released, unleashed from all that binds me now." [4]

4 Elizabeth Elliot, *Shadow of the Almighty*, (HapperSanFrandcisco, 1957), p. 59.

Jim Elliot realized that it was not wise to get as close to sin as he could without actually sinning. The battle, he knew, was in the desire even reach in the direction of sin. A better reach is for the "nail of Calvary"—the nail of dying to selfish desires, the nail of obedience.

3. Realize that all you have is a gift from God.

Does this mean that relationships, money, and things are evil and wrong? No, but we need to see all these as gifts from God, not as possessions to hoard. Paul wrote to the Corinthians: "What do you have that you did not receive? And if you did receive it, why do you boast as though you did not?" (1 Corinthians 4:7). If we see everything we have as a gift, we are much more thankful for what we have, and we are not as disappointed if we don't have as much as someone else. Our strengths, too, are gifts from the Lord. There's no reason to boast about them because we didn't manufacture them. On the other hand, there's no room for false modesty, either. When someone compliments us, instead of trying to look humble and saying, "It wasn't me. It was the Lord," we can say simply, "Thanks. I'm glad the Lord uses the gifts he gave me."

When we realize all our possessions are a gift from God, we are much more openhanded and generous with them. "God loves a cheerful giver," and it is a joy to use every possession and every minute to honor him and help people. It's much easier to give away something that I realize does not belong to me in the first place. A wise man of God, Mr. Dale Bynum, once told me something that I've never forgotten—"Hold things loosely."

When we realize we are not our own because we have been bought with a price, our perspective on joys and difficulties changes. A friend sent me a letter with these thoughts in them:

- When I feel alone, I can pray, "Lord, I belong to you, and I know I'm not alone in this situation."
- When I'm bored and my mind drifts into fantasies of a more thrilling life, I can pray, "I belong to you, Lord, and you have

the right to determine my circumstances. Teach me lessons of faithfulness today."

- When things are going great, I can pray, "I belong to you, Lord, and I realize that you are the source of all good things."
- When I feel hurt and anxious, I can pray, "I belong to you, Lord, and I know you are going to work this out for good in some way. I trust you."

One of the greatest—and rarest—perceptions for a follower of Jesus Christ is to be gripped with the truth that we are not our own any longer. We've been bought at a very high price. We belong to one who loves us and is as near to us as our breath. That makes all the difference.

—Be still. Listen to what God is saying to you.

1. Write a paragraph about what it means to be a slave of sin. (Consider: devotion, attitude, time, effect on relationships, effect on spiritual life, etc.) We devote a lot of time focused on something temporary, not eternal. It gets our focus off of Him.

2. How does realizing you have been bought change your perspective on God, on yourself, on your activities, and on your desires? I want to serve & please God in all I say / do.

3. Read Jim Elliot's prayer again. Paraphrase it here: Lord, help me to focus & think on the things of you, not to get sidetracked.

4. Does this prayer express your heart? Why or why not?

5. How does it affect you to realize that all you have is a gift from God?

6. Look over the "I belong to you, Lord" statements. Do any of them apply to you today? If so, which ones? How will that perspective help you?

7. Look at your schedule, goals, and secrets for the next 24 hours. How do they reflect you being a bondservant of Jesus Christ? How do they reflect you being a slave of sin?

What are you going to change?

8. Read 1 Corinthians 6:18-20. Think about each verse, then use each verse as a guide as you pray.

Memorize: Say Galatians 2:20 aloud. How can you apply this verse today?

A CALL TO DIE

JOURNAL

Lord, today you are calling me to die to selfish desires by:

You are calling me to obey in these areas:

You are calling me to intimacy with you by:

DAY 12

DEATH...AND YOUR GOOD CLOTHES

"PUT TO DEATH, THEREFORE, WHATEVER BELONGS TO YOUR EARTHLY NATURE...DO NOT LIE TO EACH OTHER, SINCE YOU HAVE TAKEN OFF YOUR OLD SELF WITH ITS PRACTICES AND HAVE PUT ON THE NEW SELF, WHICH IS BEING RENEWED IN KNOWLEDGE IN THE IMAGE OF ITS CREATOR." – COLOSSIANS 3:5, 9-10

When we become Christians, many wonderful things happen to us. We are forgiven, we have eternal life, we become God's children, and the Holy Spirit guides us. But we are still human. Very human. Even when we determine to live wholeheartedly for Christ, our sinful nature doesn't vanish. Some of us are confused about this. We think, "Shouldn't I struggle less with sin and selfishness as I get closer to God?" Well, yes and no. I believe we struggle with different sins as we grow in our faith. At first, the battle is over the outward sins like cursing, sexual immorality, gossip, violence, etc. After we walk with God and spend time with his people for a while, those don't seem as attractive as they used to. Now we struggle with other sins, more under-the-surface sins like pride, greed, the lust for power and popularity, etc. We can mask those by carrying a Bible and using Christian lingo, but some of us pridefully use our Christianity as a platform for success, pleasure, and approval.

Paul realized that sin continues to rear its ugly head until we die or are raptured, and he wrote in letter after letter how to help people deal effectively with their sin. He instructed us to be ruthless. Brutal. Show no mercy to sin. If we let sin have its way, it will take root and destroy us, so don't mess around. Kill it. Paul wrote to the Colossians, "Put to death, therefore, whatever belongs to your earthly nature." He wrote the believers in Rome: "For if you live according to the sinful nature, you will die; but if by the Spirit you put to death the misdeeds of the body, you will live" (Romans 8:13). At least Paul was consistent!

What was Paul talking about that needs to be brutally killed? He gives us lists in several different letters. To the Colossians, he wrote: "Sexual immorality, impurity, lust, evil desires and greed, which is idolatry; anger, rage, malice, slander, and filthy language." How bad are these sins? Paul tells us: "Because of these, the wrath of God is coming."

The sins of our earthly nature (that is, all our sinful attitudes and behaviors) deserve the righteous condemnation of God Almighty. They aren't cute. They aren't funny. They aren't attractive. They stink in God's nostrils... and if we understand their destruction in our lives and to others, they will stink in ours, too. If a rabid wolf came in your room right now, you wouldn't pet it. You wouldn't study it. You wouldn't talk sweetly to it. No, you'd kill it because it can't be redeemed. It can only be killed. That's the ruthlessness Paul wants us to have with our sin. All of it. From the visible pride and gossip to secret sins like lust and self-righteousness. The active sin of trying to take revenge on someone who has hurt us and the passive sin of failing to help someone in need. Showing off how much we've learned about God, or our failure to trust God when he has proven so faithful. All of it.

Be ruthless and brutal. Kill those sins. Dead. How do we kill them? The truth of the Scriptures is called "the sword of the Spirit." We let the truth of God sink deep into our hearts. We let that truth guide us, encourage us to make good decisions, and remind us of the consequences of our choices. Through the pages of the Bible, we understand what honors the Father and what breaks his heart. Then we realize our attitudes and actions are not in a vacuum; they are done in the very presence of the one who rescued us from hell. That realization gives us conviction to act—decisively and ruthlessly—on the truth. (See again the importance of knowing the word!)

But focusing on death is not all there is to it. Who does that? Undertakers! That's not the life Christ wants for us! Yes, we need to kill sin when it rears its head, but we need to focus our attention on enjoying God, which leads to doing what is right. To illustrate this daily decision, Paul talks about clothes. Yes, clothes. He says we have "taken off" our "old self with its practices"—that's the killing and death part—and now he instructs us to "put on the new self which is being renewed in knowledge in the image of its Creator." Follow the bread crumbs. He's being very practical and clear. When you recognize your shirt is dirty, you take it off and throw it in the basket (or in my case, on the floor) and you put on something clean. This simple process requires perception, a decision, and action. We perceive sinful behavior is harmful, and we choose to quit doing it. We don't stop there and think about it for three weeks. We replace it with a behavior that is good and godly. Like what? Paul gives us a clear list:

- Perceive that you are God's beloved child, and choose to be compassionate, kind, humble, gentle, and patient.
- When people are difficult, bear with them without griping. However, if a difficult person becomes abusive, seek Christian counsel immediately.

- When they hurt you, forgive them. How much? "Just as the Lord forgave you."

- When relationships get frayed by conflict, let your love stitch the relationship back together.
- When you are anxious, let Christ's peace rule in your heart.
- When you are confused, let God's word "dwell richly in you."
- When you walk, talk, sleep, eat, study, work, and relate to anybody and everybody, do it all to honor Jesus Christ who bought you.
- Finally, be sure, in good times and in bad, to give thanks to God for his goodness and faithfulness.

These are not emotions. They are choices. We need to determine to act in ways that clothe us in Christ's love, strength, and wisdom no matter how we feel—often *in spite of* how we feel; not emotion, but devotion. That's obedience to the Master. How do we know what needs to be discarded and what needs to be worn? The answer is found in another question: What breaks God's heart and what honors him? Study the gospels and see what made Jesus angry or sad, and what gave him delight. That will tell you what needs to be thrown out and what is worthy of putting on.

But these choices are not "grind it out" empty decisions. Over and over again, Paul reminds us that we have the example of Christ, his incredible love and forgiveness, and the strength provided by the Holy Spirit to keep us going. We have God's fantastic wealth of resources given to us by God himself. When we look in the closet to find something to put on, we find the royal clothes of the King of kings, the love, power, wisdom, and forgiveness he gives us to face any situation.

We have to recognize these clothes. Did you pick that up in Paul's words to the Colossians? He said the new self "is being renewed in knowledge in the image of its Creator." You and I have to gain the knowledge of God's clothes and character so we will know what to take from the closet. It doesn't just happen. In this passive, instant society where knowledge comes at the click of a mouse, many of us think knowledge should come into our brains by osmosis. Spiritual insight doesn't happen that way. (Remember Day 7?) Those who know the heart of God are those who have looked for it like an explorer. God wants to be known, but he wants to be known by those who are genuine seekers. He makes the gospel very clear and accessible, but he reserves the deepest secrets of his heart for those who respond to his call to follow him in true discipleship. Then..."he rewards those who earnestly seek him" (Hebrews 11:6).

You can't put on clothes that you can't find in your closet. They are there for you. Right now. You can find some very easily. Don't be too quickly satisfied with the first thing you find. Sure, it's wonderful to wear anything of God's character. But there's more. Always more.

As you experience the joys and trials of life, you will find many situations in which you say, "I need God to work here." "I need God to give me hope and wisdom." "I know I need to forgive but I can't do it on my own." That's the time to go to the closet and ask God to open your eyes to the treasures of his wardrobe. He never asks you to put on anything he hasn't worn himself. Even in his relationship with you. Do you need patience? He has been patient with you. Do you need wisdom? He is always perceptive in how he treats you and me, even when we don't see it. Do you need strength? He endured the cross for you and me. Do you need to forgive someone who has hurt you and doesn't even care? Jesus knows exactly what awful things you and I have done, what evil we have thought, what secrets we have kept, and he has forgiven them all. If we experience his forgiveness for our deepest sins, we will be much more likely to forgive others who hurt us. Christ will give us the strength.

Your schedule, your goals, your relationships are clothes. Some of them are dirty and need to be taken off and thrown away. This means, spiritually speaking, your freedom comes from walking away from these things. The clothes that are of God can be worn with confidence and thankfulness. After all, they are God's presents to us.

—Be still. Listen to what God is saying to you.

1. Describe what it means to put a sin "to death":

Walk away from it & don't think on it.

2. What are some of your sins you need to spiritually kill?

- impatience
-

Are these obvious or hidden to others? Does that make a difference in your commitment to be ruthless with them? Why or why not?

obvious to my family

3. What might happen to someone who focuses only on getting rid of their sin without shifting their attention to the love and strength of God?

4. What clothes have you found and put on from God's closet in the past week? What were the situations? How did putting on those characteristics help you?

- Empathy
- Kindness
- Compassion

5. How can you seek greater knowledge of God? Be specific.

   Spend more time reading His word, praying & listening to His voice.

   Do you long for that depth in your relationship with him? Why or why not?

   Yes - I want to be all He wants me to be.

6. Read Colossians 3:12-17. Make a list of things you can "put on" from this passage:

7. Read Colossians 3:1-11. Think about each verse, then use each verse as a guide as you pray.

   Memorize: Repeat John 3:16, Isaiah 26:8, and Galatians 2:20.

A CALL TO DIE

JOURNAL

Lord, today you are calling me to die to selfish desires by:

You are calling me to obey in these areas:

You are calling me to intimacy with you by:

DAY 12

GRACE: CHEAP OR COSTLY?

"FOR CHRIST'S LOVE COMPELS US, BECAUSE WE ARE CONVINCED THAT ONE DIED FOR ALL, AND THEREFORE ALL DIED. AND HE DIED FOR ALL, THAT THOSE WHO LIVE SHOULD NO LONGER LIVE FOR THEMSELVES BUT FOR HIM WHO DIED FOR THEM AND WAS RAISED AGAIN." – 2 CORINTHIANS 5:14-15

God's grace is an incredible thing. We sing about it. We hear sermons about it. We can never get enough of it. Yet too many of us misunderstand it.

Mercy can be defined as "not getting what we deserve." We are sinners who deserve God's righteous wrath, but in his mercy, he forgives us. We don't go to hell. Grace goes even farther: It means we "get what we don't deserve." Christ paid the debt we owed for our own sin. Not only did we *not* get what we deserve, Jesus got what we had coming to us. He then offers us what we *don't* deserve—forgiveness and salvation. We become sons and daughters of the King of the universe, we are co-heirs with Christ in all the riches of heaven, the Holy Spirit comes to live inside us, we are given God's "precious and magnificent promises," and on and on.

Paul tells us this grace is a free gift (Romans 6:23), ours simply for the taking. He also reminds us that there is no possible way to earn it by doing enough good things. Grace is too wonderful to be earned (Titus 3:3-7). Grace is like an unlimited credit card with Jesus paying the bill.

God's incredible grace is rich and free. Yet we often take it for granted. How wonderful that Christ pays for all our sins. However, as sinful people we often take advantage of this. We shouldn't say, "I'll just do what I want and 'charge it'—he's paid for it anyway." Have you ever done something really special for somebody, and that person really appreciated it? How did the giving and thankful response affect the relationship? It brought you closer together, didn't it? Have you done something wonderful—even sacrificial—for someone, but he shrugged and hardly even acknowledged your efforts? How did that reaction shape the relationship? Sadly, that's the way many of us treat the grace of God.

When we take God's grace for granted, we cheapen it. Cheap grace is the sterile doctrine of forgiveness divorced from Jesus himself. It is the teaching of Christian freedom that is neat and clean, separated from the blood and agony of the cross. Cheap grace is grace without obedience, right doctrine without passion, the shell without the substance. In this teaching of the free gift of grace, forgiveness is taken for granted so we don't need to face Jesus with our sin. We feel no deep sorrow over our moral failures, and the deep desire to be delivered from sin is missing. You see, it's already paid for, so it's no big deal!

Going along with this misperception of the grace of God is the idea that the Christian life should be effortless. "If God loves me so much and is so powerful," the thought goes, "then he won't ask me to do anything too hard, and he'll give me everything I need." When we feel God is asking us to make a hard choice, we get confused...and we quit the game. If we only signed on for a pleasure cruise, being a disciple of Jesus Christ will be a big disappointment!

The opposite of cheap grace is costly grace. Our forgiveness and eternal life cost the Father the life of his Son. It cost Jesus the anguish of Gethsemane and the agony of Calvary. The nails were not symbolic; they were made of iron. The whip and the crown of thorns were not theoretical. They cut his flesh and his blood flowed. His death was not just an example to us. It caused a tectonic earthquake in the history of the Universe and in the lives of every person who has ever lived. The grace of God is centered in, and cannot possibly be divorced from, a person. He is the treasure more worthy than anything we have. He is the one we worship and obey because he is worthy. He is the one whose love so overwhelmed the apostle John that it changed his identity. He called himself "the disciple whom Jesus loved." It changed his life.

Paul's statement about the love of Jesus in his second letter to the Corinthians is often quoted, but this statement is inextricably linked to the cost and our reasonable response: "For Christ's love compels us, because we are convinced that one died for all, and therefore all died. And he died for all, that those who live should no longer live for themselves but for him who died for them and was raised again" (2 Corinthians 5:14-15). I believe this means that grace is not the real thing unless it makes a real difference in our lives. We need, Paul said, to be "convinced" that the price Jesus paid rescued us from eternal damnation and gave us hope, life, and forgiveness. When we understand even a little of the price Jesus paid, it transforms us. We no longer live for ourselves but for him.

Paul described one of the effects of this transforming grace in his letter to Titus. He wrote: "For the grace of God that brings salvation has appeared to all men. It teaches us to say 'No' to ungodliness and worldly passions, and to live self-controlled, upright and godly lives in this present age" (Titus 2:11-12). The grace of God doesn't make it OK to sin because the price has already been paid. No, it transforms us. It exposes sin and produces in us a genuine sorrow for it. It creates in us a tremendous passion to do what is right in the sight of God.

When God's grace takes root, incredible things happen in us and through us. Jesus talked about this at a feast in Jerusalem. He said, "If anyone is thirsty, let him come to me and drink. Whoever believes in me, as the Scripture has said, streams of living water will flow from within him" (John 7:37-38). The problem today is that too many of us are satisfied, not thirsty. An anemic, distorted doctrine of cheap grace has prevented us from catching real passion for our Savior. That thirst comes from tasting a little of his great love and forgiveness, not just the teaching about it but experiencing it from the hand and heart of Jesus himself—and we want more!

Do you see the difference? Does it tug at your heart? We certainly don't want to go back to a doctrine of works-righteousness to prove that we are worthy of God's mercy. Not at all! That's not what we're talking about. But we need to be careful not to strip, in our minds, the person of Jesus from the doctrine of grace. It isn't a principle that saves us. It is Jesus. It isn't just teaching that compels us. It is the love of Christ. His grace is, indeed, free to us, but it cost him his life.

What does it look like for a person to be gripped with costly grace? We find many descriptions and examples in the Scriptures. In his first letter, John said a person who is transformed by God's grace loves God, obeys God, and loves others. We can make our own list, including:

- a thirst to know God better,
- carving out time to spend with God,
- feasting on God's word,
- gaining insight about God, life, self, and others,
- an edge, an intensity about the right things,
- identifying the right enemies,
- a heart of thankfulness,
- willingness to listen to God,
- glad obedience,

- enjoying the adventure of faith, taking risks in obedience,
- practical service to help people,
- our personality is Spirit-purged and Spirit-inspired,
- purer motives, and
- telling others people about God's great grace.

The response Jesus, Paul, and John talked about was a full-out, take-no-prisoners commitment to love, honor, and obey Jesus Christ. In our day, our "me first, me last, me all the time" mentality distorts and dilutes this kind of radical commitment. Many of us are willing to be disciples, but on our terms. We are willing to follow Christ, as long as he leads in a certain way or provides certain things for us to enjoy. We are willing to be radical, as long as we determine the outcome. Do you see anything a bit off base in this perspective? I'm sure you do. When we set conditions on Christ's Lordship in our lives, we are untrue to both him and to ourselves. Lordship means complete, full obedience. That is a frightening thing unless and until we realize Christ loves us more than we can possibly imagine and following him opens the door to the most exciting, fulfilling life we can imagine—but the road is sometimes hard and long. Oh, we want the exciting, fulfilling part. It's the hard and long deal we aren't willing to buy.

Full commitment to Christ is both a decision and a process. At each moment, we are asked to live completely for him and not for ourselves. We make that choice dozens of times each day. If we are serious about following him, God will take us deeper, ever deeper, into the depths of his heart. There we will have even more difficult decisions to make because the light will shine in the crevices of our hearts and we will find selfishness we never knew existed. Then, again as always, we need to focus on the costly grace bought for us by Jesus Christ. We cling to him and let him change our lives.

When you sing about God's grace and talk to your friends about it, remember the difference between cheap grace and costly grace. Remember that Jesus personally paid the price for you. Grace is not just a doctrine of freedom. It is an incredible price, and if we grasp it, grace changes our lives forever.

—Be still. Listen to what God is saying to you.

1. Describe the differences between cheap grace and costly grace. (Consider: response to sin, love for God, obedience, relationships with believers, desire for others to know Christ, etc.)

Taking for granted that God will always forgive my sin is cheap grace. Choosing the harder option, & sacrificing is often costly.

2. When, where, and how have you seen grace treated as an "unlimited credit card"? What were the results in people's lives—especially yours?

3. When, where, and how have you seen costly grace taught and lived? What were the results in people's lives—especially yours?

Difficult choices ~~were~~ led to the richest experiences of our lives.

4. Does cheap grace or costly grace make you spiritually "thirsty"? Explain: When I realize that I am being asked to do something difficult for Jesus, It draws me closer to Him (thirsty) and I need Him more

5. Which is honestly more attractive to you: cheap grace or costly grace? Explain:

Costley - I want to be all God wants me to be - esp. for my Husb. & girls / & friends.

6. Have you entered into discipleship "on your own terms"? How can you tell?

7. What will God need to do in your heart so that you value costly grace more?

8. Read 2 Corinthians 5:1-21. Think about each verse, then use each verse as a guide as you pray.

Memorize Psalm 56:3-4.

A CALL TO DIE

JOURNAL

Lord, today you are calling me to die to selfish desires by:

You are calling me to obey in these areas:

You are calling me to intimacy with you by:

DAY 14

TOO FULL TO EAT?

"BLESSED ARE THOSE WHO HUNGER AND THIRST FOR RIGHTEOUSNESS, FOR THEY WILL BE FILLED."
– MATTHEW 5:6

You and I are at the banquet table of God's presence and truth, but too often we are so full of junk that we're not hungry. In actuality, spiritually, we are starving to death. We have settled for garbage instead of feasting on the nourishment God richly provides.

Chris Heurtz is a young man who is the head of Word Made Flesh Ministries in India and all around Asia. This ministry provides shelters for homeless people, those with AIDS, and those inflicted with other diseases. Years ago when he was a college student, Chris went to Calcutta to work with Mother Teresa at the House of the Dying. Calcutta and Mexico City are the largest cities in the world, but Calcutta is the poorest. Most of the thirteen million people there are destitute. Air pollution is oppressive. Poverty and disease are the way of life—and death—for most people. Every morning city maintenance workers find bodies on the sidewalk and in the street of those who died during the night. At the House of the Dying, Chris' job was to look for dying people on the street and bring them in to give them a place to die with dignity. Their goal was not to cure these people. It was to give them a dignified place to die. Chris and his fellow workers lovingly cared for them, gave them a good meal, and shared the Gospel with them so they could die in peace.

In Calcutta, 70% of the homeless population have the lung disease of tuberculosis. When you walk down the street, you find thousands of old men and women coughing up their lungs. Day after day, hour after hour. Chris' ministry was to find those who had only hours or days to live and invite them, "Come with me. I'll give you a place to lie down." Upon arrival, their heads were shaved, and they were given a shower and a bowl of hot food. Chris then replaced their ragged, soiled clothes with clean ones. There, these men and women sat with other dying people who coughed their lungs out into a jar that was passed around. When it was full, the jar was thrown into the garbage with the soiled clothes and infested hair.

Lepers came in with their flesh rotting and their noses, fingers, and toes missing. Their clothes had the stink of rotted flesh. At the House of the Dying, Chris and the other ministers washed these lepers' skin and gave them clean clothes to wear. The job of one of the workers was to stick a syringe into their pus-filled sores and extract the poisonous disease. Each syringe was used for person after person and day after day until it was too dull to pierce skin. Then it was thrown into the garbage can.

Children infected with AIDS, usually girls about four or five years old, were brought to the House of the Dying. How did these little girls get AIDS? By a blood transfusion? No. The dominant faith in India is the Hindu religion. One sect of Hindus believes their men can get rid of a sexually transmitted disease by sleeping with a virgin—that means a four or five year-old child. Many children older than this are already prostitutes. Chris Heurtz brought these children from the streets, and he listened to their screams and weeping.

Chris once said, "We prayed the crying wouldn't stop, because their crying meant they were still alive." Lepers, children with AIDS, men and women with terminal tuberculosis—those were the ones Chris and his partners at the House of the Dying looked for each day. That's a far cry from our neat and clean existence, isn't it? At first, the disease and death would gross anybody out, but after a while, Chris saw hurting people in desperate need, not ugly people who interrupted his life.

Chris said, "One thing I begged not to do was taking out the garbage. The stench was almost unbearable. Can you imagine the disease, ragged clothing, and half-eaten food? I begged them not to ask me to do it. It haunted me forever after the first time I took out the garbage. As soon as we walked out the back door toward the dump, children came out of the alleys and ripped open the bags to get whatever was there. I yelled, 'Don't eat this garbage! It's full of disease and death!' But they were so hungry that they ate garbage because that was all they could find. They had no other choice. I wept as I saw them scramble through the spilled jars of disease, the clothing stained with rotten flesh, and used syringes, trying to get scraps of last night's dinner that a dying person didn't eat." Disturbing image, isn't it?! But in all honesty, how far are we from this spiritually? Can you see yourself feasting at the dumpster of this world?

Many of us are like those kids scrambling for garbage. We elbow each other at the mall, at the theatre, in the back seat, at home, at work, on the net, and at school in our hunger for food, but the food we lunge and fight for is rotten and diseased—and we eat it. We eat it every time we fill our minds and hearts with sexually suggestive movies or music, every time we make fun of somebody for whom Christ died, every time we value the praise of people more than the praise of God, every time we live to get revenge on someone who has hurt us, and every time we try to put things in God's place in our hearts. We are so full of this junk that we aren't hungry for the food that really satisfies and nourishes. Sure, we may listen to a message or a song about God, and that message has as much appeal as another bite of pizza when we are so full we're about to explode. Our souls are full of so much garbage that we don't even recognize our need for God's food.

It is a spiritual paradox that when we are thirsty for God and we drink, he satisfies us and yet leaves us thirsting for him even more. When we are hungry for God and eat his nourishing word, we are refreshingly satisfied and yet we are hungry for much more. Augustine said, "You have made us for yourself, O God, and our hearts are restless until they find their rest in you." This is the same perspective that the prophet Jeremiah spoke:

> "When your words came, I ate them; they were my
> joy and my heart's delight, for I bear your name,
> O Lord God Almighty" (Jeremiah 15:16).

Eating requires intention, selection, and effort. We don't eat by being in the same room with food. We don't take in the grace and truth of God by being in a sanctuary or at a retreat. We have to take initiative to eat because we recognize our need for the spiritual nourishment it can provide. We also need to be very selective when sifting through the options given to us by the world. Think of how many foods there are in the grocery store. You have lots of options! You have lots of options to eat spiritually, too—but remember, some of the foods you eat will poison you. It takes effort. Hear, read, study, memorize, and meditate on the word of God.

Jeremiah had one other insight about "eating God's word." He realized that it only made sense for him to eat it because he bore God's name. We are God's. We call ourselves "Christians." We call him Lord, Savior, Father, and Friend. In many places in the Scriptures, we read that God provides a banquet for his people. God's banquet doesn't have flat Coke and leftover Spaghetti-O's! It has the finest, richest, most delicious spiritual food we can ever eat! When we eat it, we are filled with the love, peace, joy, and strength God richly provides. Nothing even compares!

So why are we so content to keep running out in the alley to rip open the garbage bags of this world to eat that poison? It just doesn't make sense.

DAY 14

—Be still. Listen to what God is saying to you.

1. Describe what you think Chris felt like when he watched those children rip open the garbage to get scraps of food:

extremely sad & wishing that it could be different.

2. In your life, what are some things that promise to satisfy us but in reality poison you?

Replaying events/thoughts in my mind.

Have you experienced this poison in your own life? Explain:

3. List all the sources of poison (or at least not nourishing spiritual/emotional/relational food) around you:

4. Describe a time when God's truth and grace was a "joy and a delight to your heart":

    Still is.

5. Where, when, and how can you make better selections about what you feast on?

6. Read Jeremiah 15:16. Think about this verse, then use it as a guide as you pray.

    Memorize: Write Psalm 56:3-4 three times.

DAY 14

JOURNAL

Lord, today you are calling me to die to selfish desires by:

You are calling me to obey in these areas:

You are calling me to intimacy with you by:

DAY 15

THE RISK OF GRACE

"AND AS FOR US, WHY DO WE ENDANGER OURSELVES EVERY HOUR? I DIE EVERY DAY— I MEAN THAT, BROTHERS—JUST AS SURELY AS I GLORY OVER YOU IN CHRIST JESUS OUR LORD."
–1 CORINTHIANS 15:30-31

When you and I follow Christ, there is no telling where he will lead us! His love, mercy, and grace convinces us to go with him to the ends of the earth (usually beginning with a step across the street), and so the adventure begins.

We usually think of grace as comforting and encouraging, and certainly it is. But those who drink deeply of the grace of God obey him, and obeying a radical like Jesus Christ always involves risk. In college I did a little rock climbing. I don't know how smart it is to dangle from a rope hundreds of feet on the side of a cliff, but it sure was fun. Man, do I have stories to tell of close calls and narrow escapes! My wife, Jennifer, loves whitewater rafting. The rougher the water, the better she likes it. Waterfalls, hydraulics, dents, bangs, and spills...she loves to tell her stories of the one that almost got her! Adventure always involves risk: in rock climbing, whitewater rafting, and following Jesus.

Far too many of us are content with being comfortable in our faith. As long as Jesus doesn't ask too much of us, as long as we get enough good feelings, as long as it's fun to be a Christian, as long as nobody turns up their nose at us when they find out we believe, we hang in there. But that perspective is phony Christianity. It's not the real thing.

In the desert of Midian, Moses was content with being comfortable. He had tried to follow God forty years before, but in his zeal he sinned: He murdered an Egyptian. Instead of letting God take care of the injustice that he  saw, Moses took matters into his own hands. He played God. A modern day example would be the so-called Christian who murders an abortion doctor in the "name of Jesus." Moses was banished to the backside of nowhere where he tended sheep and got on with his comfortable life. Then one day, God got his attention. Moses saw a bush burning but not consumed by the fire. He was enough of an outdoorsman to know this was really strange! God was speaking to him! God gave Moses a new direction in his life, a new purpose, and a new identity. God turned Moses' life upside down. His comfortable existence quickly became an amazing adventure. When Moses walked down from the mountain, his face glowed because he had a glimpse of God. People were amazed at the sight. They asked Moses, "What in the world happened to you?"

He was never the same. When God encounters us, some of us aren't fazed a bit; some feel close to God for a while then fall away; and some are changed forever. God had promised to use Moses to set the enslaved children of Israel free. What a great job! So Moses set out with his brother Aaron to tell Pharaoh what God said.

What happened then? Did God make things work out as Moses assumed they would? Well, no, not exactly. The Pharaoh laughed in the face of this shepherd who demanded obedience from the most powerful king in the world, and the Pharaoh punished the people of Israel for Moses' silly demands. The Israelites' work load was made much harder, and they blamed Moses. (No kidding!)

Instead of leading the people out of Egypt in triumph, Moses was ridiculed by Pharaoh and his court and condemned by God's people. Is that the price of obedience? Moses struggled with God about his call. Did he misunderstand God's words? No. Was God backing out on the deal? No. Was God's plan as simple and neat as Moses had thought? No. The path of obedience and deliverance was through the valley of suffering: for Moses and for the children of Israel.

A woman named Corrie ten Boom knew something of suffering and obedience. She lost her entire family during World War II in a Nazi death camp. She and her family embraced the call of God to serve him and speak the truth no matter what the cost—even when it cost them their lives. Corrie noticed that Jesus obeyed the Father and experienced incredible suffering on the cross although he wanted to avoid it. Even though she also endured terrible suffering, her will to obey overcame her desire to escape pain.

You and I are only disciples if we follow the example of our Lord in all things, including suffering and the resurrection (your new life). So much for the entertainment brand of Christianity...

Is it worth it? That's the question you and I have to answer from time to time. Certainly, when we see God work in us and through us and lives are changed forever, it looks like a good deal! But think of Jesus in the Garden of Gethsemane. He was alone. His closest friends were asleep instead of supporting him, and soon they would run away. His Father was leading him to suffer the weight of the sins of the entire world. It didn't look all that attractive to him at that moment, but he obeyed anyway. Think of Moses after Pharaoh laughed at him and increased the work load of the Jews. Moses had planned on a triumph, but he faced a disaster. Moses could have quit right then, but he fell on his face before God to get wisdom and strength.

One of my favorite chapters in the Bible is Hebrews 11, God's "Hall of Fame." The first several verses tell of men and women who trusted God and obeyed him in the face of suffering, and God delivered them and worked miracles for them. The writer sums up by relating:

> "And what more shall I say? I do not have time to tell about Gideon, Barak, Samson, Jephthah, David, Samuel and the prophets, who through faith conquered kingdoms, administered justice, and gained what was promised; who shut the mouths of lions, quenched the fury of the flames, and escaped the edge of the sword; whose weakness was turned to strength; and who became powerful in battle and routed foreign armies. Women received back their dead, raised to life again" (Hebrews 11:32-35a).

These are great stories. Wonderful encouragement. But then the writer continues with a different list:

> "Others were tortured and refused to be released, so that they might gain a better resurrection. Some faced jeers and flogging, while still others were chained and put in prison. They were stoned; they were sawed in two; they were put to death by the sword. They went about in sheepskins and goatskins, destitute, persecuted and mistreated—" (Hebrews 11:35b-37).

Jeers? Flogging? Destitute? Sawed in two? Most of us didn't sign on for that course. The tests are just too hard. Why did these people hang in there in the face of such suffering without relief? Because they were convinced that "they would receive what was promised," not in this life, but in the one to come. They were sure that obedience would be rewarded—someday.

Moses endured rejection and failure because he was convinced God would fulfill his promises. Jesus endured the cross because he knew his obedience would result in our salvation, which ultimately brings glory to God. (If you haven't figured it out yet, this is what it's all about—bringing glory to God.) Those who suffered in Hebrews 11 endured because they knew that God would be glorified and that he would reward them for their faith. Not now. But someday.

If you and I are serious about following Christ, we can be assured of two things: suffering and God's strength to endure it in faith.

A couple of valid questions are: "Why does God allow suffering in our lives?" and "Why doesn't he rescue us out of it immediately?" Pain produces character in our lives like no amount of pleasure possibly can. Failure and rejection force us to seek God's face just as Moses did. When we go to him in desperation, our ears and our hearts are more open to him than ever before. In that face-to-face encounter, God can expose and purge away impurities in our behavior and our motivations. We see our selfishness as never before, and we also experience God's grace as never before. Failure and rejection have a way of stripping us of dependence on our own abilities. We realize we can't accomplish a thing apart from God's direction and power. As our motives are purified and our faith grows, we are better able to rest in and trust in God's hands. This will allow us to become more useful in his loving hands.

I sure wish these lessons could be given by injection, but they are learned only in the tough school of suffering. I'm not talking about self-inflicted suffering, or the suffering brought about by unwise thoughts, motives or actions. I'm talking about the specific trials that God allows us to go through to make us more like Christ. It doesn't happen just once. Resistance and repetition of exercise makes muscles grow. Suffering and repetition of trusting God in those painful times makes our faith grow in him.

God is much more interested in our faith in him growing than in our comfort and pleasure. Are we?

—Be still. Listen to what God is saying to you.

DAY 15

1. What are some kinds of suffering described in today's lesson?

Torture, jeers, flogging, Chained in prison.

2. What are some reasons we suffer for following Christ?

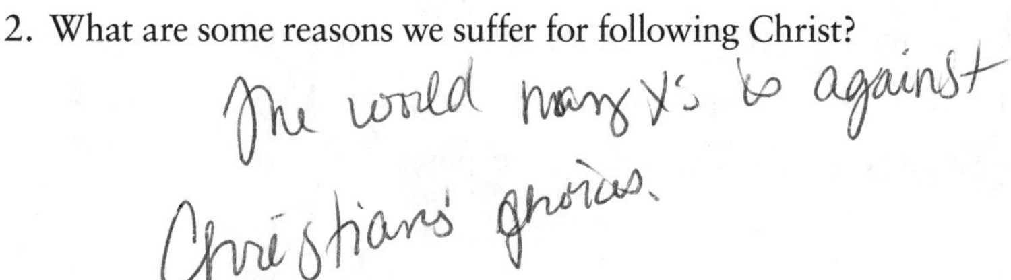

In what ways do we suffer when we don't follow Christ?

3. How do most Christians respond to suffering?

What are the results of these responses?

4. How has our entertainment-driven culture affected your view of suffering?

5. What are some ways you have suffered for your faith in the past several weeks or months? How did you respond each time? How would it have helped you if you had understood the purposes of suffering?

   How will your response be different next time?

6. What rewards does scripture say the Christians in Hebrews Chapter 11 received?

7. Read Hebrews 11. Think about each section or paragraph, then use them as guides as you pray.

   Memorize: Say Psalm 56:3-4 aloud. How can you apply this verse today?

DAY 15

JOURNAL

Lord, today you are calling me to die to selfish desires by:

You are calling me to obey in these areas:

You are calling me to intimacy with you by:

DAY 16

GOD'S CURRICULUM

"CONSIDER IT PURE JOY, MY BROTHERS, WHENEVER YOU FACE TRIALS OF MANY KINDS, BECAUSE YOU KNOW THAT THE TESTING OF YOUR FAITH DEVELOPS PERSEVERANCE. PERSEVERANCE MUST FINISH ITS WORK SO THAT YOU MAY BE MATURE AND COMPLETE, NOT LACKING ANYTHING." – JAMES 1:2-4

I don't know about you, but when I was in school, I didn't exactly think tests in Algebra or Biology (or Phys Ed for that matter) were "pure joy." I hated tests. Is James nuts? Did he lose it after writing only one verse? No, he had a much clearer perspective on the value of testing than I ever did when I was in school. He had God's perspective.

God's curriculum in the school of faith is much different from what most of us want. We look forward to recess; he wants to prepare us for a career in knowing and serving him. We long for easier days with no obstacles to overcome; he tests us to force us to learn crucial lessons. In his school, he knows exactly what we need, and he tailors the courses to fit each of us uniquely. Sure, we have recess and we have times to hang out with our friends in the fellowship hall of life. But we also have labs where we are forced to apply what we've learned, or realize we haven't learned our lessons yet.

In his school, God's curriculum for you and me includes:

- enough joy to encourage us.
- enough love to strengthen us.
- enough success to build our confidence.
- enough suffering to force us to depend on him.
- enough confusion to make us seek his face.

God's highest goal for you and me is not that we would enjoy school. His purpose is for us to enjoy him as he builds our faith. Not to bring success, but to build our faith. Not to make us happy, but to build our faith. Not to provide wonderful friends, but to build our faith. Not to make us comfortable, but to build our faith.

Get the picture? Most of us don't. We show how clueless we are when we whine and complain and quit when we don't get exactly what we want from God. Here's a news flash: God may have a different curriculum than we think he does.

In fact, he almost always has a different curriculum than we think he does. The prophet Isaiah recorded God's words of rebuke and assurance. He reminded the people that he is smarter than they are, and he assured them that his ways are always far better than anything they could imagine. Isaiah quoted God:

> "For my thoughts are not your thoughts, neither are your ways my ways," declares the Lord. As the heavens are higher than the earth, so are my ways higher than your ways and my thoughts than your thoughts" (Isaiah 55:8-9).

Difficulties, failure, rejection, and confusion are God's way of saying, "Hey, I'm over here! I've got something terrific to teach you. Pay attention."

God's usual method of instruction is to impart truth, followed with an affirmation like an answered prayer, and then test us to see if we really believe him. Just like school, the test comes after the classwork is done and the examples are finished. Then we find out what we know—and believe. Tests are not the same as temptations. A temptation has its source in the enemy of our souls, and its purpose is to cause us to fall. A test is given to us by God, and its purpose is to strengthen us. Actually, a single event can be both a test and a temptation, depending on how we respond.

People who have walked with God closely for a long time almost universally experience a particularly difficult type of test: darkness. Things are rocking along really well...God is rich and real and he is answering prayer... lives are changed and great things are happening. Then, nothing. A steel canopy is put over our heads and our prayers bounce off. It seems as though the spiritual phone lines are cut. We can't call out, and God doesn't call in. The modem won't connect. The light of God's presence, which we treasured so much the day before, has gone out. We feel the barrenness of being alone. Very alone.

I believe this "dark night of the soul" is one of the most severe tests for those who are serious about walking with God. God doesn't give this test to young Christians. The darkness that immature believers experience has a different source, usually their sins.

When we fail to respond to the light of God's Spirit exposing our sins, we put a layer of doubt and disobedience over the light. If we continue to refuse to respond, those layers become opaque, and the light is effectively dimmed. The solution for this darkness is confession, repentance, and obedience. God usually responds to the one who repents by showering his love and light in fresh, strong ways.

The darkness mature believers endure is different. Very different. Those who suffer this darkness search their souls for sin. They plead with God to show them any obstruction, but they hear only silence. Deafening silence. Isaiah gave hope, perspective and warning to these people:

> "Who among you fears the Lord
> and obeys the word of his servant?
> Let him who walks in the dark, who has no light,
> trust in the name of the Lord and rely on his God.
> But now, all you who light fires
> and provide yourselves with flaming torches,
> go, walk in the light of your fires
> and of the torches you have set ablaze.
> This is what you shall receive from my hand:
> You will lie down in torment" (Isaiah 50:10-11).

If you and I are committed to loving and serving Christ, sooner or later we will enter a time of darkness. If we search and find no sin that is blocking God's light, we need to take heart from the prophet Isaiah and trust in the unchanging character of God. If we try to light our own flames by generating emotion and looking for new spiritual experiences, we will only hurt ourselves and feel tormented. Darkness is a severe test, and God reserves it for those who are ready. You may not be at that point in your walk right now, but when the emptiness of darkness covers your spiritual life, remember these words.

Many times the tests God gives us are not only for us. God uses them to get the attention of those around us, too. When our family left Iran years ago, we used my mother's heart problems as an excuse to leave the country. A few years after that, it wasn't an excuse anymore. The doctors told her she needed to have two clogged arteries in her heart opened and two valves replaced, so our whole family took her to the hospital. They wheeled her into the operating room for an initial angiogram. I don't know if you've ever experienced the feeling of someone that you love looking at you from a hospital stretcher, saying, "If I don't see you in a few hours, I'll see you in heaven. This is not 'Goodbye.' " It was the summit of fear for me. My brother Benjamin didn't understand how serious the procedure might be, but the rest of us did. My Mom was a strong believer by this time, but my Dad still held to his Muslim background. My sister and I prayed with my Mom. Then the nurses wheeled her away. We sat in the waiting room and waited.

After a little while, a red light flashed above the door of the operating room where they'd taken my Mom. My sister had been allowed to stand just inside that door, and she ran out to tell us Mom had almost died. She had a rare allergic reaction to the dye they injected into her in order to do the angiogram. "That red light on the ceiling," my sister explained as she gasped for breath, "is a signal something is wrong. Really wrong. Pray that it won't flash on again during the rest of the operation."

We sat back down and waited nervously. In a few minutes, the red light began flashing like crazy again. We heard someone say, "Code Red in Room 324!" We knew Mom had another allergic reaction and was dying. My sister, Benjamin, and I ran to the door of the operating room and got on our knees. We prayed, "Oh, Jesus, don't let my Mom die! Please don't let her die!" After a few seconds, I felt a hand on my back, and I saw a hand extend past me to the door. It was the first time in my Dad's life that he kneeled and acknowledged Jesus. He prayed, "Jesus, don't let her die. Please, Jesus!"

A few minutes later, the door opened and the doctor told us that they had to resuscitate her to bring her back, but she was going to be OK. We were so happy God had granted our requests!

A week or so after the official open heart surgery, Mom was at home, and my sister and I related the story of praying in front of the operating room door. We told her about Dad calling out to Jesus for her. She was astonished and asked Dad, "Did you really pray to Jesus?"

He looked sheepish and mumbled, "Yes."

"Do you believe in Jesus now?"

"Yes."

My Dad then prayed to receive Christ as his Savior.

God had a curriculum for each of us that day of Mom's surgery. Each of us faced a test to see if we would trust him, to see if we would cry out to him when no one else could come through for us. We passed the test, and our faith was the catalyst for my Dad calling out to Jesus.

Sometimes we recognize the tests before they happen. Most of the time they are pop quizzes that catch us when we're not looking. The tests come in all shapes, sizes, and times, and God uses them to produce character and faith deep in our hearts. That's his curriculum. Don't play hookey from his school.

—Be still. Listen to what God is saying to you.

1. Describe some recent experiences in which God gave you:
   —enough joy to encourage you.

   —enough love to strengthen you.

   —enough success to build your confidence.

   —enough suffering to force you to depend on him.

   —enough confusion to make you seek his face.

2. What are some differences between God's curriculum and what we usually want his curriculum to be?

3. Have you experienced any times of a "dark night of the soul"? If so, describe that time:

   absolutely yes - in 1999-2003

4. Read Isaiah 55:9 again. Does this passage encourage you or discourage you? Explain:

5. Read Romans 5:3-5. What does Paul say about God's curriculum in our lives?

6. Read James 1:2-7. Think about each verse, then use it as a guide as you pray.

   Memorize: Go over the last three passages of scripture you have memorized (Isaiah 26:8; Galatians 2:20; and Psalm 56:3-4) until you can say them without looking.

DAY 16

JOURNAL

Lord, today you are calling me to die to selfish desires by:

You are calling me to obey in these areas:

You are calling me to intimacy with you by:

DAY 17

THE CRUCIBLE OF CHOICE

"GOING A LITTLE FARTHER, HE FELL WITH HIS FACE TO THE GROUND AND PRAYED, 'MY FATHER, IF IT IS POSSIBLE, MAY THIS CUP BE TAKEN FROM ME. YET NOT AS I WILL, BUT AS YOU WILL...' HE WENT AWAY A SECOND TIME AND PRAYED, 'MY FATHER, IF IT IS NOT POSSIBLE FOR THIS CUP TO BE TAKEN AWAY UNLESS I DRINK IT, MAY YOUR WILL BE DONE.'"
– MATTHEW 26:39, 42

Every step of Jesus' life had led to the hill outside Jerusalem where he was to die. He knew the prophesies. He knew the Messiah had to die for the sins of the world. He had told his disciples over and over again that he was going to be killed, and he rebuked them when they tried to talk him out of it. But now the time had come. His death wasn't just theory anymore. It was reality. He faced excruciating pain and agonizing death.

Over those last three years, Jesus had many pleasant times with his followers. They had talked with him about the Father, they had laughed and told stories, and they had seen Jesus heal the sick and raise the dead. Those were some good times—really good times. The disciples had also watched as the Pharisees and Sadducees accused Jesus of all kinds of heresy. These religious bigots confused people, but Jesus defended the truth with grace and strength. In a way, even those times were good, too.

But as the cross drew closer, the good times quickly evaporated. It was now Jesus' last night with the disciples. He told them all the things they needed to know, but they still didn't get it. He told them he was going to die a horrible death. He asked them to pray for him. They went to sleep. As Jesus fell on his face in prayer, he was utterly and absolutely alone. In a few hours he was going to take on his shoulders all the ugliness and pain of hatred, selfishness, murder, rape, envy, and every other sin of every single man, woman, and child who ever lived or ever would live. For a time, Jesus would be pushed away from perfect unity with his Father. He would pay for all our sins alone. The lies and taunts and spit of those lining the streets and those near the cross would compound his pain. The whip, the nails, and the thorns would sear his flesh, and awful thirst would make his tongue swell and cling to the roof of his mouth. He would be alone. He knew all this was coming, and in his flesh, Jesus wanted out.

As you and I walk with God, we feel the daily shaping of the word and the Spirit shaving off unwanted mess and conforming the contours of our attitudes and behavior to be more like Christ. That is a continuous process, day after day. But so often, we experience the collision of our will against God's. The reality of his call to obey breaks in and we simply don't want to do it. In our flesh...we want out. However, as Christ chose obedience in his spirit, we, too, may choose obedience through his grace.

Jesus first asked the Father to take the cup of sacrifice away from him, but he affirmed his willingness to drink it. Then, when he sensed the Father's confirmation, he accepted it as final. Between those two moments was a struggle in his soul so titanic in its intensity that the blood vessels in his forehead broke and blood dripped from his face. The collision of wills took Jesus to the brink. It takes us there, too.

The cup the Father wanted Jesus to drink was one of sacrifice: spiritual, emotional, and physical pain for a purpose. The prospect of all that pain made the heart of Jesus shudder. But in the crucible of the choice, Jesus followed the Father after all. You and I only rarely are faced with any choice that even vaguely compares, but this account is written for our instruction, as an example of how to respond when we are faced with a choice of this magnitude. What might it look like in our lives? I believe it invariably involves sacrifice. We want a certain person or a certain thing or a certain career, but God breaks in and says, "No, my child. I have chosen a different way for you. Follow me."

My little brother Benjamin (I say "little," but he outmuscles me by about twenty pounds), has Down's Syndrome. He's very, very special in many ways. Benjamin, much like other people with Down's, is *very* routine-oriented. Breaking a habit for him literally takes a miracle. One of his most deeply rooted habits was his love for country music. He was an Iranian redneck! He had the three-pound belt buckle; starched Wranglers; numerous cowboy hats; a full country stage complete with drum set, guitars, lighting, and sound equipment; and just about every country CD out there—you get the point. Needless to say, for his high school graduation gift, he asked me and Jennifer to get him tickets to see his favorite country music stars at an all day festival. $400 got him the best seats in the house. For days and days, all Benjamin could talk about was the festival. The problem was that the only person available to take him was Mom, who happens to be the Iranian version of Grace Kelly—sophisticated and reserved—not your typical country music fan. However, she loves Benjamin so much that she gladly volunteered.

The day after the concert, I called Benjamin to see if he had a good time and if Mom had survived. When he picked up the phone, Ben told me he could not talk now because he was saying goodbye. Before I could ask, "Goodbye to what?", Mom picked up the phone. Excitedly, she began to tell me what was going on. Apparently, after having been at the concert all day, on the drive home Ben looked at Mom and said, "God didn't like some of the stuff that happened at the festival today, did he?" As Mom and Ben reflected on the behaviors they had seen—the cursing, drinking, suggestive clothing, drugs, etc.—Ben came to the conclusion that it broke the heart of God. Some of it had even happened on stage. To Benjamin it was simple. What he saw broke the heart of God, so it broke the heart of Benjamin. He decided right then and there that he didn't need to have anything to do with country music.

That morning when I called the house, Ben was putting all his country CDs into a box and was going to get rid of them. As someone ingrained in the habit, this was a major sacrifice, probably one of the toughest of his life. To some, this might sound like legalism, but in the crucible of the choice, Ben followed the Father. He didn't see the point in offering anything to God that cost him nothing (2 Samuel 24:24).

That was over a year ago, and I have seen Benjamin in his struggles and victories in this particular situation. Through his fast from country music, Ben has discovered a new appetite for worshipping God through Christian music.

Now don't go off and misinterpret this. I'm not saying "no secular music, no movies, no secular books, no video games for the rest of your life." You don't have to sit around all day every day listening to sermons on tape. That's why at the beginning of this forty-day journey I asked you to seek, through the word and prayer, the boundaries God would have for you. I'm just saying, "Let's be gut-level honest here. If it doesn't cost you anything, it's not worth anything." Need more clarity? Do whatever you want. But if it pleases you, all the while contradicting the word of God, you are pleasing your own god—but you are your own god.

In Psalm 63, David declares, "Oh God, you are my God." He's not stuttering. David's saying the Lord of his life is the Lord of Lords. The question is not during the easy decision times of life, but in the crucible of choice: Who is your God?

—Be still. Listen to what God is saying to you.

1. Describe the emotions and thoughts Jesus may have had as he prayed in the Garden of Gethsemane:

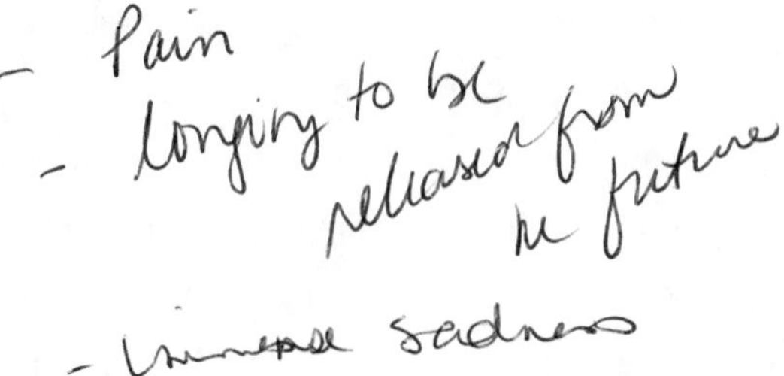

2. What does a "collision of wills" mean to you?

3. What are some things God has told you to do that you didn't want to do?

- music
- free time
- going out of my way

4. How did you respond in each case? What were the results?

- I want to obey.
- I feel encouraged. He is with me. He cares about the best for me.

5. When you are faced with critical choices to obey God, what are your most common excuses?

6. What are some things in your life God may be asking you to sacrifice to him?

7. Read Matthew 26:36-46. Think about each paragraph, then use it as a guide as you pray.

Memorize Psalm 115:1, 17-18.

A CALL TO DIE

JOURNAL

Lord, today you are calling me to die to selfish desires by:

You are calling me to obey in these areas:

You are calling me to intimacy with you by:

DAY 18

THE CROSS: ARE YOU BEYOND IT?

"FOR GOD SO LOVED THE WORLD THAT HE GAVE HIS ONE AND ONLY SON, THAT WHOEVER BELIEVES IN HIM SHALL NOT PERISH BUT HAVE ETERNAL LIFE."
– JOHN 3:16

Sometimes I hear people say, "We need to move beyond Jesus dying on the cross to 'deeper' things." Like what? What is "deeper" than the God of the Universe becoming a man and showing his incredible love by dying to rescue you and me from eternal damnation? The cross of Christ is not only the source of our salvation, it is our highest motivation, our clearest example of obedience, and it draws us to rich intimacy with one who loves us that much. I believe we never "get beyond" the cross. We only go deeper into our grasp of what it means in every relationship, every desire, every goal, and every decision.

Jesus is a king whose reign had one purpose: to demonstrate his love for us by sacrificing himself in our place. We deserve death; he took our place. But we often yawn at the gospel. We see Bible verses spray-painted on highway overpasses, and we drive by without a thought. We see "John 3:16" signs waved at sports events, and we wonder why somebody would be willing to look so silly in public. We wear silver crosses as jewelry, but we've forgotten about the real blood on the real wood of Jesus' cross. Not long ago, I even saw a guy selling crosses that you activate by twisting them so they glow in the dark. The cross seems to have become trivial and irrelevant.

A few years ago, our family went to Paris, and we went to the Louvre, the second largest museum in the world. My brother Benjamin went with us. The Louvre has some of the greatest pieces of art and artifacts of history in the world—and lots of them. It would take years to see it all! I was really excited about seeing da Vinci's *Mona Lisa*. We weaved our way through room after room of incredible paintings. Benjamin was right there with us, jammin' to music on his Walkman. By the time we got to the room where the *Mona Lisa* hangs, I turned around to say something to Ben. He was gone! Somehow we lost Ben in the labyrinth of rooms in the Louvre! I looked everywhere for him, but nobody spoke my language. I went to room after room, past thousands of people. I looked everywhere, then I remembered that a while back we had passed a huge painting of Jesus on the cross. I ran back to that painting. There was Benjamin. He had pulled up a chair in front of the painting of Jesus hanging on the cross, and he was weeping. Benjy didn't care about the *Mona Lisa* or the French Impressionists or Picasso. All that mattered to him was the cross of Jesus Christ.

A lot of us think, *I've done that. I became a Christian when I was five... or fifteen...or fifty five. I'm looking for more now.* If that's your attitude, you have no idea what the cross is about. We need to think about the cross of Jesus every day of our lives. We never get any deeper than the cross. Everything we say and do needs to be filtered through the sacrifice Christ made on the cross. At every crossroad in life, the question is not necessarily, "What would Jesus do?", but more accurately, "What has he already done on the cross?" and

"Will my decision honor the cross?" When you read Paul's letters, how often do you see the cross described as the foundation for the broad scope of what he writes about? All the time! It defines our identity as children of God; it explains how we can be disconnected from sin; it gives us hope that we have a future resurrection; it gives us the example of how much to obey the Father; it shows us how much we are forgiven and how much we can forgive those who hurt us; and it measures the depth of God's great love for us. (There's more, but that's enough to make the point.) Do we choose not to sin only because we don't want to get caught? Hopefully there's a higher, more compelling motivation: to please the one who laid down his life for us.

The great English pastor, Charles Spurgeon, said, "If you sin, sin boldly. Every time you sin, you are saying that sin is worth more to you than the cross of Jesus Christ." Spurgeon was certainly not advocating sin, but he recognized that those who are very aware of their sin can become very aware of God's great forgiveness. If we sin boldly, we will be slapped in the face with the absurdity of what we are choosing in light of what Christ did on the cross. Some of us need to be slapped in the face.

The movie, *Saving Private Ryan*, was a graphic display of World War II soldiers' courage in the face of death. These men obeyed orders to move forward under heavy fire. Friends were blown apart next to them, but they kept moving forward. Thousands of these brave men shed their blood for our freedom, yours and mine. Many people consider this movie, probably more than any other movie out there, a realistic portrayal of how much we owe these men for what they did for us as American citizens. Their sacrifice was great. Freedom and courage weren't theories to them. They were blood and guts and raw obedience when everything in them said, "Hide! Go back!" They went on. They paid a high price to preserve our freedom.

The sacrifice these soldiers made for our physical freedom made me think of the price Jesus paid for our spiritual freedom. Everything in him wanted to hide and run away because he knew exactly what he faced. Yet he went on. The whip tore chunks of skin and left his flesh exposed and bleeding. The nails ripped through real muscle and tendons and bone. It wasn't antiseptically clean. It was dirty, and it took hours, all to "demonstrate his love for us" beyond a shadow of a doubt. He paid a price, and we owe him everything.

One of the errors people have made about Jesus over the years is to say that his death on the cross is primarily a man's "wonderful example" to us. Well, yes, it is a wonderful example of his obedience, but he is not just a man. He is the pre-existent, immutable, holy God. He is the Creator, who chose to stoop to become a man to do what no one, not even the greatest example, could do for us: pay for our sins.

We get a better concept of Christ when we think of him as both Savior and Creator. All that we see, and all that exists far beyond what we can see, didn't "just happen." The vast scope and the incredible complexity of the Universe required a purposeful Creator.

The scope of creation is illustrated by a few facts:

- there are 2.5 million galaxies
- there are 25 sextillion stars
- the nearest galaxy is 750,000 light-years away
- our Sun is only 93 million miles
- the Sun is 3.5 million times bigger than the earth

The complexity is illustrated in creation's incredible precision:

- if our Sun were 10% closer to the Earth, we'd fry
- if it were 10% farther away, we'd freeze
- the Earth travels around the Sun at 70,000 mph, 19 miles a second. If it traveled more slowly or more quickly, the seasons wouldn't provide change for life as we know it to exist
- our air contains 22% oxygen, just the right amount for life to exist

The laws of teleology (there's a new word for you) tell us that intricacy in order demands a Creator. Nature tends toward randomness, not order, so when we find order, we can assume there has to be someone who created it. For example, if you find a watch in the woods, you can assume it didn't "just happen." It is the product of a watchmaker. In the same way, when we look at the incredible intricacy of the Universe, we can assume there is someone who created it. There is: God, made known to us through Jesus Christ.

From time to time, I find a few people who think it's cool to be an atheist. I look at them and say, "You know, the Bible actually states, 'There is no God.' "

Their eyes widen. I can see the wheels turning. They usually say, "Really? Well, sure, I, uh..."

I tell them, "Let me show you." I turn in my Bible to Psalm 14 and point to the first verse. It reads: "The fool says in his heart, 'There is no God.' "

At that instant, the light comes on. They know they've been had! Yes, God exists, and he went out of his way to be sure we know who he is and what he's like. His name is Jesus.

When Jesus met with Nicodemus and told him about God's love in John 3, he made it clear that he wasn't going to die only for the Jews. The Father also was giving his Son for a black man in Africa, a Chinese woman in a village outside Beijing, a white girl in St. Louis, and an Iranian kid who fled his country when it came apart at the seams. For you and for me.

"But," some people complain, "Christians are so arrogant. They say Jesus is the only way." No, it's not arrogant for God to humble himself to become a man and die a horrible death to pay for the sins of everyone who ever lived and then to say, "My forgiveness is yours if you want it." If there was another way, then God was cruel to have his Son die. If that's true, then he died for nothing. Muslims say Jesus was a prophet and a man of truth, but Jesus said "I am THE way," not just "a way" (John 14:6).

Don't take the cross of Jesus for granted. Don't trivialize it by wearing it as a token without feeling intense gratitude for what it means. Don't reduce Jesus' death to only an example to follow. It is more. Much more. Our entire lives and all of our eternity will be spent trying to grasp the power and the depth of what the cross of Jesus means. There is nothing deeper.

—Be still. Listen to what God is saying to you.

1. Read Luke 7:36-50. Describe the woman. What did she do? Why did she do it?

   Describe Simon the Pharisee. What was his response to the woman? Why?

   Paraphrase the parable Jesus told Simon:

   What does this passage say about gratitude and indifference?

   Which are you more like, the woman or Simon? Explain:

2. How can the cross shape:
   —your identity?

   —your motivations?

—your goals and desires?

—how you relate to other people, especially those who have hurt you?

Kindness to them, for Jesus' sake not for my own.

3. Is it healthy to dwell on the gore of the cross? Why or why not?

For me - no

4. Should a Christian wear cross jewelry or t-shirts? Why or why not?

I don't have a problem with it. I think it is an outward expression of faith s̄ saying a word.

5. Read John 3:1-21. Think about each paragraph, then use it as a guide as you pray.

Memorize: Write Psalm 115:1, 17-18 three times.

A CALL TO DIE

JOURNAL

Lord, today you are calling me to die to selfish desires by:

You are calling me to obey in these areas:

You are calling me to intimacy with you by:

DAY 19

"GOD-AND"

"BUT I AM AFRAID THAT JUST AS EVE WAS DECEIVED BY THE SERPENT'S CUNNING, YOUR MINDS MAY SOMEHOW BE LED ASTRAY FROM YOUR SINCERE AND PURE DEVOTION TO CHRIST." – 2 CORINTHIANS 11:3

When the serpent came to Eve in the Garden, he told her that she could have it all. God had given her clear instructions not to eat from a certain tree, but that, the serpent insisted, was a silly rule. She could have a rich relationship with God *and* the ability to do whatever she wanted. She was wrong, and it cost her.

We are incredibly self-centered people. We focus on *our* wants and *our* needs and *our* goals and *our* dreams and *our* time and *our* everything else. When we become Christians, this self-centeredness dies hard. Very hard. Unfortunately, some Christian churches and speakers reinforce this focus on self by promising that we can have God and whatever we want. It sounds like this:

- If you trust God, he'll pave the way to your success.
- If you walk with Jesus, he'll give you the circumstances you always wanted.
- If you only believe God, he'll bless you with financial wealth.
- If you trust Christ, you'll have perfect rest.

Has God promised those things? Well, yes and no. He has promised that if we are absolutely sold out to him, we will experience blessings beyond our wildest dreams. But if we love him with all our hearts, the greatest blessing will be knowing and loving him. We won't care that much about earthly blessings, will we?

The problem is not success, peace, wealth, and rest. Certainly, God gives those to some of us. The problem is when those blessings climb up to the center of our hearts and compete with Jesus for our affections. Those gifts are not wrong—unless they take God's rightful place in our lives. At that point, we begin using God to get what we want instead of worshipping him. We demand that God give us these things and we are bitterly disappointed when he doesn't. God isn't interested in being used to fulfill our selfish goals. He is interested in being our Lord and us putting him first.

How can we tell if we want these things too much? Here are four ways:

1. What do we pray about?

If our prayers are primarily centered on getting more of God's blessings, then we may be using God to get what we want. The prayers Paul wrote out in his letters are full of praise and thanksgiving. They are full of God, not man. When Paul prays, he asks for insight into the depths of God's love, for wisdom to know his will, and the strength to carry it out. Paul doesn't first bring a grocery list of wants to God for his personal gain. Requests are an important part of his prayers, but these requests are in the context of praise and even the petitions focus on doing the will of God, not pleasing ourselves.

2. How do we respond when someone has more than we do?

One of the best indicators of the condition of the human heart is comparison. When we see someone get a new car, new clothes, a new job, or an athletic scholarship, are we sincerely glad for them, or do we smile and pat them on the back but think, "She doesn't deserve that. I do!"? When our hearts are full of Christ, we have our treasure in abundance. We don't long for more stuff. If we get something new, that's great. If not, it's no big deal. Envy and jealousy will eat us alive. They are rooted in the lust to have more, and comparison is their fertile soil.

3. Do we get angry when God doesn't give us what we want?

If we have a "God-and" demand, we are sure we deserve whatever anyone else has—and a little bit more. When we don't get what we demand, we get mad. That anger may only simmer if we are good at masking it, but if we are immature or volatile, we may explode in our anger at God.

4. Do we feel sorry for ourselves when God doesn't come through the way we wanted?

Instead of thankfulness, our mouths spit out self-pity. "Why me? Why is it always me? Doesn't God care about me anymore?" Feelings of disappointment are normal when things don't go as we expected, but that can drive us to God to say, "Lord, what do you want to teach me from this?" That plea is a long way from, "Lord, I can't believe you let this happen to me!"

A "God and" perspective, trying to use God to get our wants met, quickly leads to a "God, but" reaction. When we are focused on our wants and our needs, we find lots of things get in the way, including obeying God. When he calls us to follow him, we reply, "Lord, but you don't understand. Serving you that way doesn't fit in with my hope of being successful and popular. I'll wait for you to ask me to do something else." But "something else" never comes. When we insist on God being on our terms, he refuses to play that game. We drift away in our anger and self-pity, blaming God or us.

the parable of the four soils, and do you remember of the seedlings in the soil that had thorns and weeds? of riches and the worries of the world. That's exactly ut here: when wealth, popularity, comfort, rest, and entertainment, compete with the growing seedling of God's word in your life. What do you do with weeds in the garden? You identify them (don't yank out the flowers!) and pull them out by the roots. That's what you do with spiritual weeds, too.

Believers who have walked with God for a while face another, more subtle "God and" problem. They sometimes confuse devotion to Christ with Christian disciplines of prayer, Bible study, serving, and giving. Those are meant to open our eyes and draw us close to Christ himself, not become a substitute for him. Prayer doesn't save us. Bible study is not our Lord. Serving and giving don't fill the deepest holes in our hearts. Christ does. These activities take on their direction and meaning if, and only if, they are focused on knowing and loving Jesus.

At one point, the religious leaders argued with Jesus about who he was and why he came. They were terrific students of the Scriptures, but they missed the real message there. Jesus told them, "You diligently study the Scriptures because you think that by them you possess eternal life. These are the Scriptures that testify about me, yet you refuse to come to me to have life" (John 5:39-40).

The message is clear: When you pray, don't just go through the motions and hope God is happy with the effort. Look for Jesus. Listen. When you study the Bible, look for Jesus in each thought and each verse, and talk to him about what you find. When you worship, sing to Jesus himself, not for those

around you. When you serve others, serve as if you were serving the Lord Jesus himself.

I think all of us have to wrestle with "God and" conflicts in our hearts from time to time. They are harder to identify than outright sin because our selfishness is mingled with Christian lingo and practices. We may look just fine on the outside while we are practicing idolatry on the inside. Simplicity and purity of devotion to Christ are developed when the light of God's Spirit shines on that conflict and says, "This is not the way, my child." At that moment, we have a choice. The decision is not just one of right and wrong; it is one of loyalty or disloyalty. When the prodigal son came home and confessed his sin to his father, he was welcomed warmly back into a rich, intimate, affectionate relationship. I can imagine that his love for his father and the simplicity of his loyalty to him grew exponentially that day.

When God shines his light on the hidden crevices of your soul and shows you that a blessing or a discipline is competing with your affection for Jesus, don't be shocked. Say, "Yes, Lord. I agree. I want to be completely loyal to you and you alone."

He will be honored by that loyalty to him.

—Be still. Listen to what God is saying to you.

1. What are some ways we use God to get what we want instead of loving and serving him?

2. Look at the evidences of "God and" in our lives. Do you see any of these in your life? Explain:
   —Self-focused prayers:

   —Comparison:

—Anger when we don't get what we expect God to give us:

—Self-pity:

3. What are some reasons we may let Bible study, prayer, serving, and giving compete with our loyalty to Christ? Why do we get confused about the role of these things?

4. Does it make a difference whether you see this idolatry as loyalty and disloyalty to Christ himself instead of merely right and wrong?

5. Describe what it means for you to have a "simple and pure devotion to Christ":

6. Read Luke 15:11-32. Think about each paragraph, then use it as a guide as you pray.

   Memorize: Say Psalm 115:1, 17-18 aloud. How can you apply this passage today?

DAY 19

JOURNAL

Lord, today you are calling me to die to selfish desires by:

You are calling me to obey in these areas:

You are calling me to intimacy with you by:

DAY 20

GROW UP

"WE HAVE MUCH TO SAY ABOUT THIS, BUT IT IS HARD TO EXPLAIN BECAUSE YOU ARE SLOW TO LEARN. IN FACT, THOUGH BY THIS TIME YOU OUGHT TO BE TEACHERS, YOU NEED SOMEONE TO TEACH YOU THE ELEMENTARY TRUTHS OF GOD'S WORD ALL OVER AGAIN. YOU NEED MILK, NOT SOLID FOOD!"
– HEBREWS 5:11-12

A month before Jennifer and I got married, my Dad generously offered to pay for our honeymoon—anywhere we wanted to go.

We went to London. Dad paid for the plane flights, the hotel, the food, and even the theater tickets. However, for snacks inside the theater, we were on our own. If you've ever been to the theater, you know how expensive snacks are. Jennifer and I were excited about seeing Victor Hugo's *Les Miserables*. It was phenomenal! Our next show was *The Phantom of the Opera*. We both dressed nicely because we made reservations at a swank restaurant after the show. Jennifer had on a beautiful pink linen dress. I wore my best suit. We bought some chocolate-covered almonds earlier that day to take into the theater with us to hold us over until dinner. When we got inside, Jennifer took out the bag of chocolates, put it on her lap, and began feeding them to me.

The theater was cold, so I gave Jennifer my jacket to put over her lap. Meanwhile, unknown to us, the chocolates in Jennifer's lap had spilled out, and because it was warm under the jacket, they melted all over the front of her dress. After a couple of hours, she got up at an intermission to go to the restroom. Pink linen and dark chocolate. Not a pretty sight! She and I were really bummed out (although we both had to admit, it looked pretty funny!).

We left the theater and walked toward Piccadilly Circus (which is not really a circus at all) to get a cab to go back to our room and change clothes. We could still salvage the evening if we hurried. As we walked, we stepped between two guys on the sidewalk who were in a heavy debate. I was walking toward that cab stand as fast as I could go, but Jennifer stopped to listen to them. One of them said, "The Holy Koran says this about God." Then he quoted a passage from the Koran.

The other guy was a Christian. He came back, "Yeah, but the Bible says, 'For God so loved the world...'" He explained the gospel as best he could. Jennifer stopped. When I looked back at her, I could tell she was going to be there for a while. I could see the wheels turning in her mind. When I walked back to her, she whispered, "God brought us to London and made me drip chocolate on my dress so we'd walk by this place to hear these two people talk about God. David, you used to be a Muslim and now you're a Christian! God put you here!"

She was right. What are the odds of this happening—a Christian evangelist who was converted from the Muslim faith walking past these guys? God had orchestrated a chocolate mess to get me here to talk to them. I asked if I could say something to them, and they both nodded. I told them my testimony about how I used to be a Muslim and how Jesus Christ paid for my sins. I explained how my life now had purpose and meaning.

Jennifer watched and beamed. She seemed so proud of me. I used all the verses I'd ever learned. As the conversation went on (forget about dinner, this was a God thing!), the Christian used all the passages of scripture he had memorized. Then the conversation took a strange turn. The Muslim had quoted lots of passages from the Koran, but now he was quoting the Bible—to prove it wrong. He knew more scripture than we knew put together. The other guy and I were out of bullets. This Muslim had a full clip. He asked with a smile, "Would you like me to quote the book of Romans for you?"

I don't know how the other Christian guy felt, but I felt ashamed. After a while, I'd had enough. I called for a cab. I had come to the harsh reality in front of my new bride that I was a spiritual illiterate. It was time for me to grow up in my biblical knowledge.

The writer to the Hebrews told his readers it was time for them to grow up. That wasn't a very pleasant message, but it was a necessary one. On that afternoon in London, I needed to hear it. Maybe you need to hear it, too. Imagine having a great Christian teacher sit down with you and look you in the eyes and say, "Friend, I'd like to teach you a lot more, but you just aren't ready for it. I want to give you meat, but you are a spiritual baby. Yes, I know you've been a Christian for a while, but you haven't grown. You're still a baby in the faith. Instead of always being fed, you should be giving out truth and grace to other people. In fact, you've forgotten what I taught you before. You need to hear the basics again to get it right."

How would you feel if a Bible teacher you respected said that to you? Yeah, I know how you feel. That's exactly how I felt that day in London. If you've been a Christian more than a year or so, you ought to be imparting God's word to others, not stuck dealing with childish things. If you've been a believer for a while, the issues you should be dealing with are things like: how to teach the Scriptures more effectively, how to serve better, how many people to take to camp or a retreat, and how to become more intimate with

Jesus. The issue is not if you study the Bible but what advanced Bible study methods are most effective for you.

One of the things that demonstrates how far we've come is how we respond to sin. Those who are stuck as infant Christians get as close to sin as they can, or they dive right in. God's holiness judges the sin of the world—and the sin in your life and my life. Yes, we're forgiven, but God still hates the sin in our lives. Do we hate it? If we do, it will break our hearts when we sin, and we'll be incredibly grateful when we experience his forgiveness. He loves us even when we are still infant Christians, but he doesn't want us to stay that way. Peter tells us there is a primary reason why people fail to grow spiritually. Peter lists characteristics of people who are growing spiritually, then he writes:

> "For if you possess these qualities in increasing
> measure, they will keep you from being ineffective and unpro-
> ductive in your knowledge of our Lord
> Jesus Christ. But if anyone does not have them, he is nearsighted
> and blind, and has forgotten that he has been cleansed from his
> past sins" (2 Peter 1:8-9).

Thankfulness for our forgiveness and glad obedience are the signs of someone who is growing in his faith.

When I was a bachelor, I wanted to buy a VCR. You know how all bachelors have to have the nice stereo equipment. We'll have a car that costs $300 with $5000 worth of stereo equipment in it. I went to the store. There were a lot of them, but I bought the best one, the "Billy Graham" of VCRs. Today, years later, it is sitting on my bookcase and still flashing "12:00" because I never bothered to find out how to program it. Not long ago, Jennifer and I moved. In all the papers we were packing, I found the instruction manual to that VCR. Finally, I decided to read it and find out the full potential it had.

Some of us have had life's instruction manual sitting around for years, but we haven't read it. You and I need to find our Bibles and read them. In those pages, we find out how to become men and women who desire to please the heart of God. When we feel his love and we want to honor him more than anything in the world, our desires change. Our lifestyle changes. I like movies. It's easy for me to say, "I know that movie has a lot of vulgarities and/or violence in it, but it's really funny." Have you ever said that? Sure, you have. My rationale is, "What difference does it make if I watch this movie? I'll just charge it to my unlimited grace credit card." But instead of taking advantage of God's grace, maybe I could take the adventure of holiness and obedience. Maybe I could value him above convenience and a moment of pleasure. Maybe I could rearrange my life to be sure that everything I do, every moment of my life, is glorifying to the one who bought me.

If you are involved in sports or drill team or anything else so much that you don't have time for God's word, you need to get out of what you're doing. Quit football? Maybe. Leave the drama club? Maybe. At least make sure you carve out plenty of time to feast on God's word. If you can't make God's truth a high priority, you need to reschedule your time.

—Be still. Listen to what God is saying to you.

1. What are the choices new Christians often face about their lifestyle?

2. What are some of the choices more mature Christians face?

3. Read 2 Peter 1:5-11. Does there seem to be a progression of characteristics in verses 5 through 7? If so, what is that progression about?

   Paraphrase verse 8:

   Paraphrase verse 9:

4. Are you growing, or are you stuck because you are blind or nearsighted? Explain:

5. In what way is a constant appreciation of Christ's forgiveness for our sins the gas that fuels our growth?

6. Read Hebrews 5:11-12. Think about each paragraph, then use it as a guide as you pray.

   Memorize: Go over the last three passages of scripture you have memorized (Galatians 2:20; Psalm 56:3-4; and Psalm 115:1, 17-18) until you can say them without looking.

DAY 20

JOURNAL

Lord, today you re calling me to die to selfish desires by:

You are calling me to obey in these areas:

You are calling me to intimacy with you by:

DAY 21

TRUE WORSHIP

"THEREFORE, I URGE YOU, BROTHERS, IN VIEW OF GOD'S MERCY, TO OFFER YOUR BODIES AS LIVING SACRIFICES, HOLY AND PLEASING TO GOD—THIS IS YOUR SPIRITUAL ACT OF WORSHIP." – ROMANS 12:1

Too often, the concept of worship is confusing to us. We think it is the hour on Sunday morning when older people put on suits and dresses to sing old songs. Or we think it is the sing-along before the message at camp or at youth group. We miss the point of true worship. I've heard people say, "I'm so committed to Jesus that I'm going to raise my hands when I sing!" My friends, raising our hands when we sing is not the highest form of worship.

When we are walking with Christ, our lives are acts of worship all day every day. Every single thing we do to honor God is worship. It is a lifestyle, not just a group of songs. God is looking for a generation of "walking worshipers," not just people who sing songs to him. When Jesus talked to the

Samaritan woman as she came to the well to get water, he told her, "Yet a time is coming and has now come when the true worshipers will worship the Father in spirit and truth, for they are the kind of worshipers the Father seeks" (John 4:23). I sure want to be the kind of worshiper the Father seeks, don't you? In spirit and truth, with a full heart and with integrity in our actions. Today, the words of praise we sing are too often disconnected from our hearts and our actions. "Walking worshipers" connect the dots; their words match their actions.

Recently I was on a television program, and the host asked me, "David, you are on the forefront of youth ministry today. What do you see as the next trend in worship?"

I answered, "*Authentic* worship, I hope."

He was a bit confused by my answer, so I decided to clarify what I meant. I explained that the new wave of contemporary worship songs is fantastic, if—and only if—the sentiment in those songs is translated into heart, hands, and feet. Authentic worship is what Paul talked about in Romans 12, and it is what Jesus meant in John 4. Worship is turning your mind's attention and your heart's affection to God. It is declaring, by word and deed, God's great goodness, power, and mercy.

Please don't misunderstand. I'm not saying that singing worship songs is wrong. But I believe we need to pay attention to what we are singing. When we sing, we can connect the dots by doing four things:

1. Let the song be a spotlight on your heart.

Worship songs bring us into the presence of God. Sometimes that experience is wonderfully comforting, but sometimes God chooses to shine his light on sin in our lives. Do you remember Isaiah's experience? He came to the throne of God and showed him his sin. Isaiah cried, "Woe is me! I'm a man of unclean lips." His honesty was a step toward forgiveness and healing.

When you sing praises to God, allow him to show you any sin you haven't dealt with yet, and thank him for his forgiveness.

2. Let the songs be the cry of your heart.

When you sing to Jesus, "You are my everything," you may realize that he doesn't have your whole heart. But use the song to tell him that you want him to be your everything. Make the song your prayer.

3. Let the song be a benchmark of integrity.

Think about the words and the message they express. If they don't communicate your heart, and if you don't want to use the song as a prayer for God to change you, be honest about it. Don't sing. I hope some of us will have the courage to close our mouths and sit down when a song doesn't match our heart's desire. When those around you are singing, "Lord, you are more precious than silver," be honest with God and with yourself about the condition of your heart. If you want your heart to change, sing passionately. If you'd rather value other things more than Jesus, don't sing. Worship in spirit and truth. Be authentic in your heart. God can handle your honesty, and being real with him may be a turning point in your walk of faith.

4. Let the song be translated into action.

When a song talks about crying out to God, take some time to be alone with God to pray. When a song encourages you to serve God by helping others, take steps to help someone you know. When a song describes the love Christians have for one another, choose to listen to someone you've tried to avoid, or offer a kind word to someone who isn't so cool.

If you've come back from a retreat or some other terrific spiritual experience, it's easy to drift back into the "same old same old" patterns of life. Don't let that happen. Let your life be consumed with "walking worship." Let the beauty and power of the songs you sing change how you treat people. Don't go back and show the church "how committed" you are by demanding that they change from their hymnals to new contemporary worship books. Don't demonstrate your "passion for Jesus" by standing up during one of the songs on Sunday morning and raising your hands—and demanding that others do it, too. Instead, find some elderly widow in the church and cut her grass for the summer, or rake her yard all winter. For no pay. Do it as an act of worship to God, and don't tell anybody in the world about it. If you call attention to yourself, you're doing it for your own glory, not God's.

Sometimes it is wrong to do the right thing. That happens when we do the right thing for the wrong reason. Serving God for selfish reasons (to get people to notice how spiritual we are) is sin, not worship. Don't do it! In one of his letters to Timothy, Paul described a list of sins. The last one in the list was people who are "lovers of pleasure rather than lovers of God—having a form of godliness but denying its power. Have nothing to do with them" (2 Timothy 3:4b-5). Don't let yourself be one of those who goes through the right motions for the wrong reasons. When you realize you have those wrong motives (and all of us do from time to time), take that opportunity to repent. Soak up the grace of God, and ask him to change your heart. If you want to tell people how much you are serving God, keep quiet. If you want them to know how much you are giving, give anonymously.

Resist the temptation to parade your righteousness. Instead, focus on the kindness, forgiveness, and power of God, and look at the many opportunities to serve God as expressions of love for the one who died for you. There's not much pride in that! But there's a lot of joy and fulfillment.

—Be still. Listen to what God is saying to you.

1. Give your own definition of "walking worshipers."

2. What do you think Jesus meant when he said to worship "in spirit and truth"? What are some ways we fail to do that?

3. How would it help you to use those four suggestions when you sing?

—Let the song be a spotlight on sin.

—Let the song be the cry of your heart.

—Let the song be a benchmark of integrity.

—Let the song be translated into action.

4. How are you doing these days in connecting the dots of praise songs and obedient actions? Explain:

5. Read Romans 12:1-2. Think about each verse, then use it as a guide as you pray.

Memorize Psalm 116:1-2.

DAY 21

JOURNAL

Lord, today you are calling me to die to selfish desires by:

You are calling me to obey in these areas:

You are calling me to intimacy with you by:

DAY 22

BE A DOER

"DO NOT MERELY LISTEN TO THE WORD, AND SO DECEIVE YOURSELVES. DO WHAT IT SAYS. BUT THE MAN WHO LOOKS INTENTLY INTO THE PERFECT LAW THAT GIVES FREEDOM, AND CONTINUES TO DO THIS, NOT FORGETTING WHAT HE HAS HEARD, BUT DOING IT—HE WILL BE BLESSED IN WHAT HE DOES."
– JAMES 1:22, 25

Our churches are full of armchair Christians. We watch people who are actively serving God and give a play-by-play analysis: "He should have done it this way." "She shouldn't have done it that way." Armchair Christians are faithful to go to groups and services. We enjoy singing praise songs. We know a good sermon when we hear it, and we appreciate a well-constructed message. We read our Bibles from time to time and pray occasionally. We may even go to a retreat and get excited about what God is doing.

But when it comes to taking action, we balk. When God asks us to apply the Scriptures and make genuine changes in our lives, we find excuses. We are hearers, not doers. James recognized our tendency to "sit, soak, and sour," to listen but not take action, so he admonished us in his letter to get in gear and get moving. Good Bible study contains three parts: observation (What does the passage say?), interpretation (What does it mean?), and application (What does it mean to me?). Of these, application is the hardest because it requires change. We may get excited about observation and interpretation, but we can leave them in our heads. Application moves our feet and hands.

James tells us to take action, but what is he talking about? Does he want you and me to jump on the next boat to South America and be a missionary to some natives nobody has ever heard of? Maybe, maybe not. We probably need to take some shorter trips first, maybe like walking across the street to greet the new neighbors and invite them to church, or to notice that somebody is down and give them a word of encouragement. The examples James uses are the most common things in the world: "to look after orphans and widows in their distress and to keep oneself from being polluted by the world." In James' day, disease and death ran rampant. Almost all families lost a father, a mother, a spouse, and several children. Widows and orphans were everywhere. James was saying, "Hey, open your eyes! The people you need to show God's love to are everywhere!" They are everywhere today: people whose parents are divorced, people who are depressed, people who have been emotionally or physically hurt in a painful relationship, people who have been abandoned, people who have moved to a new community and the fabric of their relationships have been torn apart. Being a doer of the word means we notice these people and reach out to help them. And, as James noted, being a doer means we also protect our commitment to avoid being stained by the greed and lust of the world.

Jesus calls us to be "doers of the word." He wants us to apply all of God's word in our lives by acting on it. This is in stark contrast to how the Pharisees "applied" the truth of God. They studied the law of God. They memorized it, and they even put it in little boxes on their foreheads. They were so committed to God's truth that they expanded the law by writing a new book, the Talmud, to make sure people understood what God wanted. They studied the Law to an incredible degree, even to the point of counting each letter to be sure every manuscript copy was exactly perfect.

But they failed to *do* God's law. Jesus called their bluff. He knew their hearts. In Matthew 23:23, Jesus declares, "Woe to you, teachers of the law and Pharisees, you hypocrites! You give a tenth of your spices—mint, dill and cummin. But you have neglected the more important matters of the law—justice, mercy and faithfulness." On the outside the scribes and Pharisees appeared to be righteous, but on the inside they were full of hypocrisy and wickedness. Strong medicine. The Pharisees were doing some of the right things but with the wrong intent—self-glory.

Some of us are just like them. Instead of applying all of God's truth, we apply only the parts that are convenient to us and make us look better publicly.

Paul was a man who knew truth. He was one of the leading Pharisees. He had been taught by Gamaliel, probably the leading Pharisee of that day. But something was different about this Pharisee—God got hold of him. When Paul met Jesus Christ, it turned his world upside down. He became the greatest activist the world has ever seen! Everywhere he went, he not only talked about Jesus, he acted out his faith. He went to the lost to tell them about Christ; he healed the sick; he argued with those who questioned Christ's deity. Paul was a man of action. In fact, all the disciples were men of action. That's why the Bible's history of the early church is called "Acts."

When we are committed to applying God's truth, he affects every aspect of our lives. His truth gives us direction about loving God and honoring him through forgiving those who have hurt us, reaching out to the lost, serving God, and how to handle our time and money. The word of God doesn't just tickle our minds. It challenges our hearts, our motives, our wallets, and our schedules. In fact, if the truth of God doesn't make a difference in these areas, we aren't really doers of the word at all. We're not even really good listeners.

Application of God's word brings three benefits:

Strength

In the Sermon on the Mount, Jesus told the parable of two builders. One built his house upon the sand; the other upon a rock. The one who hears and applies God's truth can withstand the storms of life because his life has a strong foundation. But Jesus warned, "But everyone who hears these words of mine and does not put them into practice is like a foolish man who built his house on sand" (Matthew 7:26). That house was washed away when the rains came. Strength comes not from only hearing God's word, but putting God's word into practice.

Joy

On the night before he was betrayed, Jesus was with his men, washing their feet as an example to them of serving each other. After he has given them insight about what he had done to them and for them, he said simply, "Now that you know these things, you will be blessed (or joyful) if you do them" (John 13:17). Real joy, Jesus explains, doesn't come by only listening to someone teach God's truth or reading it on our own. Real, lasting joy comes when we act on the word and witness God's work in us and through us.

More Truth

The law of sowing and reaping applies here, too. When we act on truth, God opens our minds and hearts to understand more truth. When we feast on God's word regularly, we are compelled to put it into action. This action leads to continual fulfillment in Christ. This continual fulfillment gained through communicating with God through his word and prayer leads to increased action and hunger for more of God. So the cycle continues.

Over the next few days, we will look at several specific steps we can take in applying God's word. Today, however, I only want us to do a heart scan to see if the flow of God's truth is flowing freely in your life. Be a doer, not just a hearer.

—Be still. Listen to what God is saying to you.

1. What are some characteristics of people who are hearers but don't apply much of God's word? (How do they relate to God? How do they relate to others? What is their attitude?)

2. What are some characteristics of people who are doers of the word?

3. Is it harder to apply God's truth than it is to observe and interpret it? Explain:

4. Are there areas in your life that you know what God wants you to do but you avoid obeying him? If so, what are the results?

5. How does applying truth bring:

   —strength?

   —happiness?

   —more truth?

6. Read James 1:19-27. Think about each paragraph, then use it as a guide as you pray.

   Memorize: Write Psalm 116:1-2 three times.

DAY 22

JOURNAL

Lord, today you are calling me to die to selfish desires by:

You are calling me to obey in these areas:

You are calling me to intimacy with you by:

DAILY GRACE

"THE TEACHERS OF THE LAW AND THE PHARISEES BROUGHT IN A WOMAN CAUGHT IN ADULTERY. THEY MADE HER STAND BEFORE THE GROUP AND SAID TO JESUS, "'TEACHER, THIS WOMAN WAS CAUGHT IN THE ACT OF ADULTERY. IN THE LAW MOSES COMMANDED US TO STONE SUCH WOMEN. NOW WHAT DO YOU SAY?'" – JOHN 8:3-5

One morning Jesus was teaching in the Temple. Suddenly, some lawyers and Pharisees burst into the room dragging a woman in front of Jesus. When they accused her, the people understood why her hair was messed up and she was barely clothed. She had been caught in the act of adultery, and these religious leaders wanted to have her stoned to death for her sin. Imagine how she felt at that moment! Caught in the act...dragged out and accused publicly... facing a horrible death. Jesus could have said, "Yes, that's what the Law says. Come on, everybody. Pick up a rock, and let's get it over with!" But he didn't.

She deserved death. Jesus gave her grace. After all the accusers had left the room, Jesus stood alone with the woman. Jesus asked her, "Woman, where are they? Has no one condemned you?"

"No one, sir," she said.

"Then neither do I condemn you," Jesus declared. "Go now and leave your life of sin" (John 8:10-11).

God's grace is not a new concept. It is as old as God himself. In fact, grace is God's very nature. He forgives sinners because it pleases him to be kind to us. His grace doesn't excuse sin and say, "Oh, she couldn't help it." Grace doesn't minimize it and say, "It wasn't that bad." The grace of God looks sin in the face in all its ugliness—and forgives. Our sins deserve condemnation. They deserve the righteous wrath of God to be poured out to punish us. That's why God's great grace is so wonderful: We deserve just the opposite! Speaker and author Jerry Bridges once said that grace is "God's goodness displayed toward our unworthiness."

Have you noticed all the rules and commands listed in the Scriptures? Do they seem to be demanding, difficult, and guilt-producing? These laws are God's perfect standard of holiness for us, and they show us how far we miss that standard. Paul wrote, "The law was added so that the trespass (and our awareness of sin) might increase. But where sin increased, grace increased all the more" (Romans 5:20). Do you see it? The more we are aware of our sinfulness, the more we will be aware of God's grace! Those who think they don't sin very much don't have much appreciation for the forgiveness and kindness of God, but those who are very aware of the dark parts of their hearts are very thankful for God's grace. Paul then asks a question: "What shall we say then? Shall we go on sinning so that grace may increase?" He answers that question: "By no means! We died to sin; how can we live in it any longer?" (Romans 6:1-2). Paul's conclusion is very similar to the statement Jesus made to the woman caught in adultery: When we are gripped with the grace of

God, we won't take forgiveness for granted. We will "go and leave our life of sin."

No matter what you've done, God's grace is greater. No matter how big or how bad your sin may be, God's grace provides forgiveness, hope, and restoration. His grace is unlimited. His cookie jar of grace is never empty.

Almost every relationship we experience, every class we take, and every job we hold is based on performance. We get what we deserve. That perspective is so pervasive that it is difficult for many of us to realize that God breaks this mold. He treats us very differently. We don't get to heaven based on what we've done. We get there *in spite of* what we've done—even the worst of us.

If I showed up in heaven, and I found that getting there was based on my performance, I'd know I sure didn't belong! God would have to grade on a curve—a *huge* curve—for me to make it on my own! But God doesn't grade on a curve. His standard is perfection. You and I can't possibly achieve that, so we have to turn to someone who did. We can walk boldly into the gates of heaven, and if the guy at the ticket booth says, "Hey, do you belong here?" we can tell him, "No, not on my own. Jesus paid my way."

Some of us think of grace only in terms of the point of our salvation experience. Certainly, the grace of God brings us to repentance so we are born again, but grace is an "all day, every day" thing. We don't dip our toe into it only when we become Christians and when we blow it really badly; we dive in head-first and soak our hearts in it. Over and over again in the New Testament, the writers use the term "in Christ" to describe believers. When God looks at you and me, he sees the righteousness of Christ because we are "in him." How much does the Father love you and me? As much as he loves Jesus. How much does he provide for you and me? As much as he provides for Jesus. How much does the Father accept you and me? As much as he accepts his own Son, Jesus, because we are "in Christ." All day, every day.

And some of us think God shakes his head and grimaces when he dispenses grace to us. We think he is reluctant to be kind to us, but that's not true at all. God delights in showing his goodness and forgiveness to us. When

Jesus talked to the woman caught in adultery, I think he was smiling when he told her, "Neither do I condemn you." I think she felt his love because his smile was genuine and obvious. The grace of God reveals his glory and his nature. When we understand more about grace, we understand more about God's heart. It changes us.

We tend to make two mistakes regarding the grace of God: When things are going well, we don't even think of God; but when things are going bad, we think it's so bad that even God can't fix things. In his tape series, "Disciplines of Grace," Jerry Bridges says, "Your best days are not so good that you are beyond the *need* of God's grace, however, on your worst days, you're not so bad that you are beyond the *reach* of God's grace."

The grace of God is at work in our lives from beginning to end. Even our desire to please God is a result of his grace working in our hearts. Our choices to obey are by the grace of God. The changes we experience and the ways God uses us to change others' lives are by the incredible grace of God. No, the grace of God is not an ointment we dab on when we feel bad. It is the air we breathe in our relationship with Christ.

As we soak up the grace of God, we gain three things:

- We have hope and assurance that God forgives, God cares, and God provides. No sin is bigger than God's grace, and no situation is too difficult for it.
- We are full of thankfulness. Like the woman in John 8, we realize that we deserve condemnation, but we received kindness and love.
- Our motives for obedience are clarified. Grace turns a teeth-gritting, "do or die" attitude into a thankful, "do because he died" gratitude. We obey out of love, not because we're afraid of him.

By now you've been working through this book for a few weeks. You may have really struggled with some things you feel that God has told you to do. You may have disobeyed God, and you feel conviction. If that is the case, remember the grace Jesus showed to the woman caught in adultery. She blew it, too—big time!—but Jesus spoke to her with kindness, gentleness, and forgiveness. He encouraged her to respond to his grace by doing better.

Or in the past few weeks, you may have been faithful to do every exercise in this book and you've learned a lot. You're so proud of yourself that you can't wait to tell people how great you're doing and the pearls of wisdom you're learning every day! You need to remember the grace of God, too. You aren't more acceptable to God because you've done your homework. You are acceptable only because Jesus Christ died to pay for your sins. Including the sin of pride.

How are you responding to the darkness in your life? If you are down, remember God's grace in his kindness and encouragement. Or maybe you are seeing wonderful changes God is making in your life. If you are doing great, remember that these changes are not your doing. They are the deep work of the goodness and power of God. Either way, his grace is truly amazing.

"Amazing grace! how sweet the sound
That saved a wretch like me!
I once was lost but now am found;
Was blind but now I see.

'Twas grace that taught my heart to fear,
And grace my fears relieved.
How precious did that grace appear,
The hour I first believed."[5]

—Be still. Listen to what God is saying to you.

5 "Amazing Grace," by John Newton, 1831.

DAY 23

1. Describe the situation of the woman brought to Jesus in John 8:1-11. (Who, what, when, where, how, why?)

2. What do you think she may have been thinking and feeling at the beginning?

   ...at the end?

3. When have you felt the grace of God most strongly and clearly? Describe that time.

4. What do you typically believe about God's grace on your worst days?

   ...on your best days?

5. How can a deeper grasp of the grace of God give you:
   —hope and assurance?

   —gratitude?

   —clearer motives?

6. Complete this prayer: Lord Jesus, I want to experience your grace much more because...

7. Read John 8:1-11. Think about each verse, then use it as a guide as you pray.

   Memorize: Say Psalm 116:1-2 aloud. How can you apply this passage of scripture today?

DAY 23

JOURNAL

Lord, today you are calling me to die to selfish desires by:

You are calling me to obey in these areas:

You are calling me to intimacy with you by:

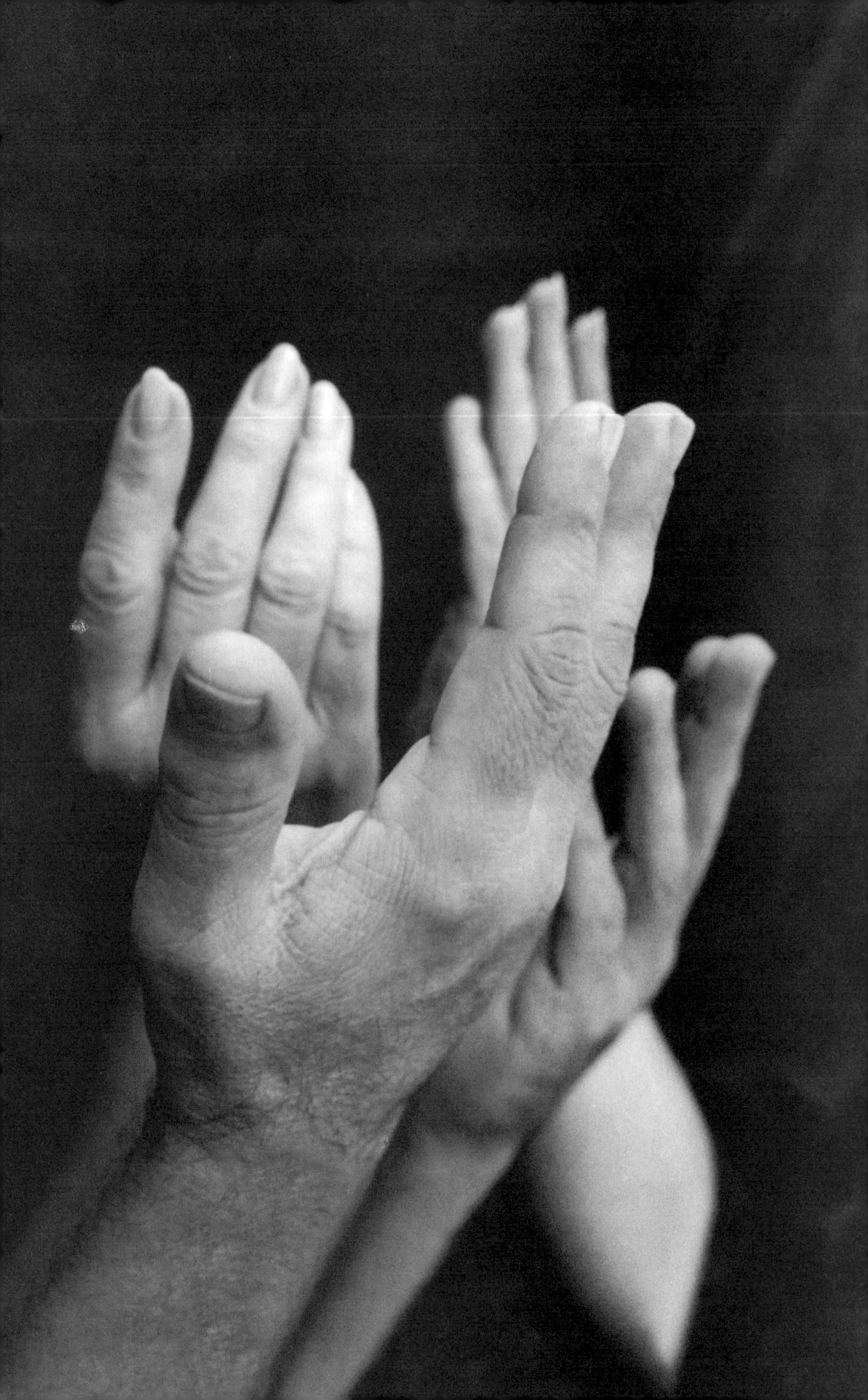

DAY 24

OUR #1 PRIORITY

"ONE OF THEM, AN EXPERT IN THE LAW, TESTED HIM WITH THIS QUESTION: 'TEACHER, WHICH IS THE GREATEST COMMANDMENT IN THE LAW?' JESUS REPLIED: '"LOVE THE LORD YOUR GOD WITH ALL YOUR HEART AND WITH ALL YOUR SOUL AND WITH ALL YOUR MIND." THIS IS THE FIRST AND GREATEST COMMANDMENT. AND THE SECOND IS LIKE IT: "LOVE YOUR NEIGHBOR AS YOURSELF."' ALL THE LAW AND THE PROPHETS HANG ON THESE TWO COMMANDMENTS." – MATTHEW 22:35-40

The Old Testament contains hundreds of laws given by God about every conceivable relationship, motivation, and behavior. At this point in Jesus' life, he was confronted by religious leaders who wanted to catch him in saying something unwise. They tried over and over again, and over and over again they were disappointed. This time, a lawyer asked him which was the greatest commandment. He was looking for an edge. He and his buddies hoped Jesus would say something they could use against him. Instead, Jesus challenged their hearts. He said, "Loving God above all else, thus bringing glory to him, is the most important thing God wants. If we love him, we'll love people. That's about it. Now, go do it."

Our first priority is to love God. Simple, isn't it? But if it's so simple, why do we get off track so far and so often? Some of us get off track because we are so caught up in pursuing riches, popularity, and pleasure. We let these things crowd God out of the center of our lives. Others of us are closer to the mark, but we get confused. We focus on the things of God (prayer, Bible study, etc.) instead of on God himself. The Bible says in 1 John 4:19, "We love because he first loved us." Our love for God is begun and built only and always in response to his love for us. We can't manufacture it. We can't read about it and take "four easy steps" to love God. We can't find a list of things we can do to create love in our hearts for God. No, our love for God is always in direct relation to our perception of his love for us. He isn't a list of principles or steps. He is the lover of our souls. He passionately pursues you and me to sweep us off our feet and convince us of his incredible love. How much does he love us? Enough to give his life for us.

He didn't have to do it. When Jesus was being arrested, Peter tried to stop the soldiers from grabbing Jesus. He cut off a guy's ear with a sword. (Bad aim, Pete!) Jesus stopped Peter and told him, "Do you think I cannot call on my Father, and he will at once put at my disposal more than twelve legions of angels?" (Matthew 26:53). Most people think of angels as happy, fat babies with bows and arrows, or after watching the television show, really nice celestial folks who want to help but sometimes are confused. Angels are some of the most powerful beings ever created. In 2 Kings 19:35 we read of a single angel who killed 185,000 Assyrians in one night. Jesus said he could have called twelve legions of these guys! A legion was usually 3000 to 6000 soldiers, so that would be 36,000 to 72,000 of these amazing beings!

Jesus could have stopped the process leading to the cross right then and there, but he didn't. Dr. Adrian Rogers, pastor of Bellevue Baptist Church in Memphis, Tennessee, paints this picture of Jesus and the cross:

> "In response to mankind brutally mocking and murdering their Lord, it was as if the mighty angels peered over the parapets of heaven with their swords drawn and their teeth clinched, shouting, 'Lord Jesus, say the word and we'll slay them all!'
>
> But instead, Jesus looked at those who were killing him and said, 'Father, forgive them, for they don't know what they are doing.'"

This image tell us of the incredible love of Jesus—for you and for me. He could have escaped the pain of the cross, and he could have annihilated the entire planet in an instant, but he endured the suffering to glorify God and demonstrate his love for us. No, the love of God is not just a principle or a theory. It is a powerful, life-changing commitment by God to bring us into his arms and restore us to a love relationship with him.

All we do is reach back. We would call that "loving God."

David was the king of Israel. He had all the perks of power and all the responsibilities of being king, but one desire passed all that. He wrote:

> "One thing I ask of the Lord,
> this is what I seek:
> that I may dwell in the house of the Lord
> all the days of my life,
> to gaze upon the beauty of the Lord
> and to seek him in his temple" (Psalm 27:4).

David had all kinds of priorities, but he made sure one was at the top. Most of us would say, "I've got so much king stuff to do today! I'll see if I can squeeze in a few minutes with God along the way." But David didn't want a little of God; he wanted to feast on him. David wanted to be intimately acquainted with him. He said he wanted "to gaze on the beauty of the Lord." When I read that, I had to ask myself, "Is the Lord beautiful to me? Is he my greatest delight?" If not, then I need to reassess my view of him.

Romans 5:8 says, "But God demonstrates his own love for us in this: While we were still sinners, Christ died for us." However, for many of us, our view of God is distorted and clouded. Some of us have had authority figures in our lives who have been harsh and condemning. We assume God grits his teeth at us, too, and snarls when we mess up. Some of us have been neglected by those who are supposed to love us, and we believe, "God may love Jim or Mary, but he sure doesn't care about me." We feel alone, abandoned, an outcast far from God. We may see God as a cop, a judge, a waiter, or a kind (but slightly senile) grandfather. None of those are accurate pictures of God. Only Jesus is.

If you don't delight in the beauty of the Lord, begin by being honest. Start right where you are. Tell him how you see him, and ask him to take you down the path of new insights about his character. Some of us can look at our parents and say, "I can see some of what God is like because I've known the love and strength my parents provided for me," but some of us need to say, like King David, "Even though my parents abandoned me, God is different. I know I can trust him" (see Psalm 27:10).

Remember, God is not just a principle or a theory. He's a person who loves you so much he's seeking you out—even when you don't understand. When you try to push him away, he is still nearby with his heart open and his hand out, waiting. Always waiting. In fact, Paul lets us know in Romans, Chapter 8, that absolutely *nothing* can separate us from the love of God.

The number one priority in our lives is to love God, but our love for him is only a response to his incredible love for us. Once we have truly experienced that love, we are overwhelmed by it. We want more of it, and we can't stand for anything to get in the way. Like someone hopelessly in love, we long to spend time with our lover. David wrote about this longing for God:

DAY 24

"O God, you are my God,
  earnestly I seek you;
my soul thirsts for you,
  my body longs for you,
in a dry and weary land
  where there is no water.
Because your love is better than life,
  my lips will glorify you" (Psalm 63:1, 3).

Look through the Psalms and experience the beauty of the Lord. Let your heart be filled with his kindness, compassion, and joy. He is thrilled when we respond to his love, and he is always ready to comfort us when we are honest that we don't feel his love. Both responses are open doors to letting God convince us of his love for us.

—Be still. Listen to what God is saying to you.

1. What are some characteristics of people who love God?

2. Why is the second commandment to love others "like" the first one?

3. Is the Lord beautiful to you? Why or why not?

4. Is your concept of God that of a cop, a judge, a waiter, a grandfather, or some other distortion? If so, what is that concept?

   How has that concept shaped your relationship with God?

   Why do you think you have that concept of God? (What important people have played that role in your life?)

5. Paraphrase Dr. Adrian Rogers' statement about Jesus on the cross:

6. Write your own prayer to God:
   Lord, I love you because...

7. Read Matthew 22:35-40. Think about each verse, then use it as a guide as you pray.

   Memorize: Go over the last three passages you have memorized (Psalm 56:3-4; Psalm 115:1, 17-18; and Psalm 116:1-2) until you can quote them without looking.

DAY 24

JOURNAL

Lord, today you are calling me to die to selfish desires by:

You are calling me to obey in these areas:

You are calling me to intimacy with you by:

DAY 25

BE RECONCILED

"THEREFORE, IF YOU ARE OFFERING YOUR GIFT AT THE ALTAR AND THERE REMEMBER THAT YOUR BROTHER HAS SOMETHING AGAINST YOU, LEAVE YOUR GIFT THERE IN FRONT OF THE ALTAR. FIRST GO AND BE RECONCILED TO YOUR BROTHER; THEN COME AND OFFER YOUR GIFT" - MATTHEW 5:23-24

One summer, when I was pastoring a youth camp on Lookout Mountain in Georgia, I witnessed one of the most painful things I've ever seen. A student was doing some rollerblading and showing off for the ladies, when he fell and broke his arm. He was in some serious pain. He was taken to the hospital where they set and cast his arm. Later on that week, the student had to be taken back to the hospital, where, brace yourself, they had to re-break his arm. They realized it had been set incorrectly and that unless it was re-set, it would grow back crooked and cause a lifetime of pain and problems.

You and I know we live in a broken world full of broken relationships. Just as broken bones need to be set correctly so they'll heal and grow properly, our broken relationships need to be set correctly in order to heal healthily. If we allow these relationships to try and heal without setting them correctly through God's word and Spirit, we can be in for a lifetime of pain and problems.

It takes courage to take these steps required to mend a broken relationship. But "doers of the word" can ask God to fill them with the courage to take that step as often as necessary.

In Matthew 5:23-24, Jesus acknowledges that the person in this scripture is serious about following God. The person is seen at the altar giving an offering. At that moment, he remembers that he has hurt somebody. Instantly, he gets up and goes to that person and makes it right. Only then does he come back and complete his gift. This story includes several important points for us as we consider righting our wrongs.

First, God uses the light of his presence and his word to show us when we've hurt others. Sometimes we know that instantly. Sometimes we find out when they tell us or when the Holy Spirit or scripture reveals it to us. More often, we know it but we rationalize it and try to forget it. We think, *He deserved it! Besides, what I did wasn't as bad as what he did to me!*

But we don't forget. It haunts us and colors every interaction we have with that person. If somebody talks about him, we may chime in with a sarcastic remark. If somebody praises him, we might say, "Well, you don't know the whole story," and our anger eats away at us.

When we are "at the altar" worshipping God in church, listening to a Christian CD, praying, tithing, or serving, we may be in tune with God. He may choose that moment to shine the light of the Holy Spirit on our sin against that person. We can offer our excuses and defiance, and quench the Holy Spirit's work in our hearts. Or we can respond and say, "Yes, Lord. I did that."

Jesus indicates that we need to act immediately. Leave the gift at the altar. Write a letter and put it in the mail. Make the phone call. Go see that person.

Now. If you wait, you'll think of a hundred reasons to delay. You might even rationalize that you really didn't do anything wrong after all. Everything in us wants to run the other way, but Jesus wants us to act.

Be reconciled to that person. What does that mean? Reconciliation involves three things: confession, repentance, and restitution. Confess your sins to God and ask him to forgive you. Then go to that person and confess what you did. Say, "I was wrong when I ________. Please forgive me." Be specific, but don't grind the point into the ground. You don't need to go into graphic details. The person probably is well aware of those details. Don't defend yourself by telling of any extenuating circumstances. Own your choice to sin, and confess it clearly. Don't make excuses or drag anyone else into it. Stand there alone and honest.

Express appropriate sorrow. You may not get emotional, but if you do, it's OK. Sin is serious business. It hurts people. Deeply. Pray before and as you are going. Reflect on how your sin has hurt that person. Think of how you have suffered when people have hurt you. That will help you understand what that person has lost and suffered by your actions. Express your sorrow by saying, "I know what I did hurt you very badly. I'm really sorry." Let the person respond. Some people feel the need to let you know just how much your actions hurt them. Keep your mouth shut and listen. Don't say much other than, "Please forgive me for ________." Then, keep listening.

Finally, make restitution. When our sins have taken something away from someone else, we need to restore what was taken. If you vandalized someone's car, you need to pay for the repairs. Yes, you. If you stole money, repay it. If you ruined someone's reputation by lying, you need to go to those who believed your lie and tell them the truth. This step is costly, but it is an absolutely necessary step in reconciliation.

When Jesus entered Jericho near the end of his earthly ministry, a short man climbed a tree to see him. It was Zacchaeus. Jesus spotted him and told the little guy that he'd like to have dinner with him. Some of those in the crowd were angry and confused. Zacchaeus was a hated tax-collector who took his fellow Jews' money for the Romans—and kept some of it for himself. Why would Jesus spend time with a thief like him? But a God-thing happened at Zacchaeus' house that night. Ol' Zach found forgiveness, and forgiveness worked itself deep into his heart. He told Jesus and the disciples, "Look, Lord! Here and now I give half of my possessions to the poor, and if I have cheated anybody out of anything, I will pay back four times the amount" (Luke 19:8). That's true repentance.

Does this mean that you and I need to repay people four times what we took from them. If their repair bill was $200, do we need to pay them $800? Maybe. That's what Zacchaeus did. His response is an illustration of how far we might be willing to go to make things right between us and other people. God is just as concerned with the attitude and spirit in which we pay someone back as he is with the actual restitution. True repentance leads to paying someone back—in the attitude of humility and love.

Often, when the Lord taps us on the shoulder and says, "Remember this? Make it right," we come up with a lot of "what ifs":

- What if he hurt me, too?
- What if he yells at me and refuses to accept my apology?
- What if it happens again?
- What if I get tongue-tied and can't say anything?
- What if I can't stand him?
- What if I don't have the means to make restitution?
- What if it's really embarrassing?

Those are just a few of the excuses we might use at that moment. Here are some practical ways to die to those excuses:

- If that person hurt you, then forgive him. Look at Ephesians 4:32 to get a right perspective on forgiveness. In strained relationships, both people usually are offended and offenders. Own up to your part, and confess your sin to that person. If he confesses his sin to you, that's great. If not, you must forgive him anyway.

- If that person yells, blames, and accuses, and at the end refuses to be reconciled, you've done all you can do. You can't make someone change. Pray for that person that God will change his heart. You must be responsible for your own behavior, pray, and offer a hand of forgiveness and friendship.
- The process of reconciliation is humiliating and painful. God can use the process itself to keep us from doing it again. However, we should confess, repent, and if needed, offer restitution as often as we sin against others.
- Many of us get tongue-tied when we have to say painful things to someone—especially when we have done something unwise. Pray that the Holy Spirit will give you the words he wants you to say, then write out exactly what you want to say, and memorize the first line. If your brain turns to jelly, take the paper out of your pocket and read it. Do whatever you have to do to make it happen!
- In many (if not most) cases, we feel distant from the person we've wronged. Maybe we've blamed that person for the trouble; maybe that person initiated the trouble in the first place. Going to someone you don't particularly like is a hard part of the process of reconciliation. But God is honored in our obedience to him, even through embarrassing times like this.
- If you have stolen or destroyed property and you don't have the means to repay, go to the person and be honest. Pray and ask God to provide a way for you to earn the money. Work out an arrangement to pay it back over time. Make plans to get a job and earn the money, and be faithful to pay it all off. Remember, Christ paid our debt in full.
- Don't worry if you feel embarrassed. That's a natural, normal part of going to someone and saying, "I blew it. Please forgive me."

All of us hurt people from time to time. The wisest among us are those who do something about it—confess our sin, express genuine sorrow, and make restitution as quickly as possible. How do we learn to do it quickly? By experiencing the pain and shame of having to go to someone that we've wronged and confessing, repenting, an offering restitution to them.

When we take these steps, God is honored through our obedience. Callousness in our spiritual lives is chipped away, and we have a new appreciation for God's great mercy and grace. In a new and fresh way, we appreciate what the cross bought for us: salvation, yes, and a clean heart today, too.

—Be still. Listen to what God is saying to you.

1. Describe the three parts of reconciliation:

   —confession:

   —repentance:

   —restitution:

2. What are some excuses people use for not being reconciled to people they've wronged?

3. What are some excuses you've used?

4. Why is it important to go quickly? (What might happen if you don't?)

5. Look over the "what ifs." Which of those are significant to you? Explain:

6. As you've read today's message, has the Holy Spirit tapped you on the shoulder and reminded you of something you've done which has hurt someone? If so, describe it here:

7. What is your plan to deal with it appropriately and immediately?

8. Read Matthew 5:21-26. Think about each verse, then use it as a guide as you pray.

Memorize Psalm 86:11-12.

DAY 25

JOURNAL

Lord, today you are calling me to die to selfish desires by:

You are calling me to obey in these areas:

You are calling me to intimacy with you by:

DAY 26

SEX

"BUT I TELL YOU THAT ANYONE WHO LOOKS AT A WOMAN LUSTFULLY HAS ALREADY COMMITTED ADULTERY WITH HER IN HIS HEART. IF YOUR RIGHT EYE CAUSES YOU TO SIN, GOUGE IT OUT AND THROW IT AWAY. IT IS BETTER FOR YOU TO LOSE ONE PART OF YOUR BODY THAN FOR YOUR WHOLE BODY TO BE THROWN INTO HELL." – MATTHEW 5:28-29

The guy was obsessed with sex. He lived to get in bed with his girlfriend, and they hopped in the sack at all hours of the day and night. He told a friend that his mind didn't drift toward thoughts of sex; it was riveted on those thoughts! No matter how much sex he had with her, he craved more. All day every day, all he could think about and dream about was sex.

But it was never enough.

Then, one day, this young man had his life turned upside down by Jesus

Christ. His powerful urges came under the Lordship of Christ, and the direction of his life changed dramatically. Does this story sound familiar? Does it sound like a guy you work with or someone in your chemistry class? The young man lived in the city of Hippo in the fourth century. His name was Augustine, and he became one of the greatest Christian leaders in the history of the church: Saint Augustine.

Sexual lust can be an addiction, for women as well as men. We usually think of addictions being connected with a substance or drug. In this case, the drug is adrenalin. The rush of sexual experience, and even of sexual fantasies, sends a surge of adrenalin through our bodies, and that feeling is addictive—and destructive.

Lust is the belief that sex with that person will meet your needs and give you fulfillment. That is a lie, and if it is not arrested, it quickly leads to sin. How serious is this sin? Jesus must have thought it was pretty serious because he told his followers to gouge out the lustful eye and cut off the lustful hand and throw them away. Was he serious? Was this a metaphor? He continues, "It is better to lose part of your body than for your whole body to go into hell."

When Jesus made dramatic statements like this, it means he wants us to go to the extreme in our devotion to him. In the area of sex, he wants us to be pure. Completely pure. Too often, I hear young men and women say they've signed a pledge not to have sex until they are married, but they watch sexually explicit movies, view porn sites on the web, and talk about sex with their friends. They think they can go to third base with their dates, and it's OK because they didn't go all the way. Purity means more than not going all the way until marriage. A lot more. It means we guard our hearts, we protect our minds, we put a lock on our tongues. It also means we think of others as people bought by Jesus Christ, not as objects to please our sinful desires.

Our culture is flooded by sexual messages. It's hard to avoid them. But we need to do just that. Too often, we make excuses like, "Oh, that doesn't affect me. I'm used to it." Paul didn't brush it off that easily. Corinth was a city that was much like yours and mine in its obsession with sex. Paul's encouragement to the believers in that city was: "Flee from sexual immorality" (1 Corinthians 6:18). That's pretty clear. Paul's reasoning was that our bodies are temples of the Holy Spirit, so we should use our bodies (including our brains) only in ways that honor God.

In that same passage of scripture, Paul reminds us that we "are not our own"; we have been "bought at a price." When we are tempted by lustful thoughts, we need to remember that we have been bought with a price. We can't just do whatever our hormones suggest. We have a much higher calling, a much more important role in the scheme of things, and a Lord who deserves more from us. When we look at someone and are stimulated by that person's appearance or touch, we need to remember: That is a person for whom Christ died. He wants the best for him (or her), and I do, too.

Some people will say, "Well, as long as I don't actually have sex with that person, it doesn't matter what I think about." Jesus doesn't leave that door open to us. He says that adulterous thoughts are just as sinful as the act itself. How can that be true? It is true because sin is primarily of the heart, and lust is the desire to have our own way in spite of what God wants for us. That selfishness and rebellion is certainly sin.

In our sex-saturated culture, we need some guidelines to help us follow Christ in this area. Here are a few suggestions for you:

1. Don't look twice.

There's nothing wrong with noticing somebody looks good. You'd have to be unconscious not to notice! But you don't have to stare. You may glance at someone and think, "Wow!", but you have the choice—and the responsibility—to avoid looking back and staring. Yes, it's hard, but it is a clear choice you and I can make.

2. Avoid stimulating movies and songs.

When Paul said to "flee," I think he would have easily applied that statement to sexually explicit and implicit movies and music. Change the station.

Pop in a Christian CD. Don't rent that video. Walk out of a movie if it has skin (or even the implication of skin) in it. Does that sound too narrow? I can hear people saying, "That doesn't leave anything but *Bambi* to watch!" Maybe so, but what is more important to you: walking hand in hand with Jesus, or doing what pleases you for the moment?

3. Develop friendships.

Many of us have the idea that sexual stimulation is a necessary ingredient in cross gender relationships. We simply don't have the concept of hanging out with a guy or girl without something sexual happening. Change the game plan. Develop a completely new perspective. Make it a point to develop friendships with no (that's NO) hint of sexual overtones at all. Learn to talk and laugh and do things that friends do. Far too many of us define our relationships on the basis of sexual advancement, and we fail to learn to communicate with each other in any other way. Change that. Learn to communicate very well verbally. Make lots of friends with people of the opposite sex, and eventually, when and if you get married, your relationship will have a strong foundation of quality communication skills—and a lot less guilt.

4. Stay on step 1.

Some people identify steps of sexual intimacy from talking, to holding hands, to arms around each other, and on and on to sexual intercourse. Once a couple begins taking those steps, they have a hard time stopping. If you begin dating someone, stay on step 1 for a long, long time. (And even longer!)

5. Go to war against your sin.

If you struggle with lust (and if you're normal, you do), don't make excuses. Do whatever it takes to focus your attention on Jesus and off sex. In this passage, Jesus says to pluck out your lustful eye and cut off your lustful hand. What does this mean for you and me? It means to take any porn sites off our browser. It means not going to a certain movie, even if all your friends are going. It means not participating in a conversation about sex. It means memorizing scripture and quoting verses when lustful thoughts fill our minds. It means finding someone to confide in and hold us accountable if we continue to struggle with lust. It means honoring Christ with our thoughts, words, and behavior.

If you have already gone far past step 1, this is the time to turn to Jesus and be honest about your sin. Confession means that you agree with him that your sin is wrong, disobedient, and destructive. It means that you will make changes to ensure that it doesn't happen again. You can be assured of God's great forgiveness, and you can also be sure of his power as you tell that person you must make drastic changes in your relationship. Get some help. Find a Christian counselor or pastor to give you encouragement and wisdom so you can stay strong in the face of confusion and criticism.

6. Wait for God to provide.

Many young men and women believe they need to experiment with as many people as possible in order to find "the right person." Even Christians fall into this trap. Instead, we need to look to God to provide someone for us when and if that is his plan for us. We are his, and he wants the best for us. We need to find our completeness in him. That means he will lead us in one of the most important decisions we will make in our lives.

Avoiding sexual lust is part of the answer. The other part is the pursuit of purity of heart and mind. The standard Jesus sets is very high in this area, just as it is in every other area of life. Fall in love with Jesus. Let him be the one who fills your heart and gives you joy. Then treat every person and every situation so that Jesus is pleased.

When we deny our selfish ambitions, take up our crosses of obedience, and follow Jesus in the area of sexual purity, we will be different—really different—from this culture. When we walk out of a movie or change a radio station, some will shake their heads, some will condemn, and some will laugh at us. But Jesus will smile.

DAY 26

—Be still. Listen to what God is saying to you.

1. Think back over the last 24 hours. What sexually suggestive or explicit messages have you been exposed to (including songs, commercials, ads, movies, magazines, conversations, web sites, etc.)?

2. Why do you think Jesus equated lust with the sin of adultery?

3. What does it mean to "pluck out" a lustful eye and "cut off" a lustful hand? (Hint: This is not a call to physically hurt yourself.)

4. What are some ways you can flee sexual immorality? (Think back on the messages you listed in Question 1. How can you avoid these?)

5. Describe what it means to be pure in your thoughts and actions regarding lust and sex.

6. Look over the suggestions. Which of these do you need to act on? What specific action do you need to take? What assistance do you need in order to take it?

7. Read Matthew 5:27-32. Think about each verse, then use it as a guide as you pray.

   Memorize: Write Psalm 86:11-12 three times.

DAY 26

JOURNAL

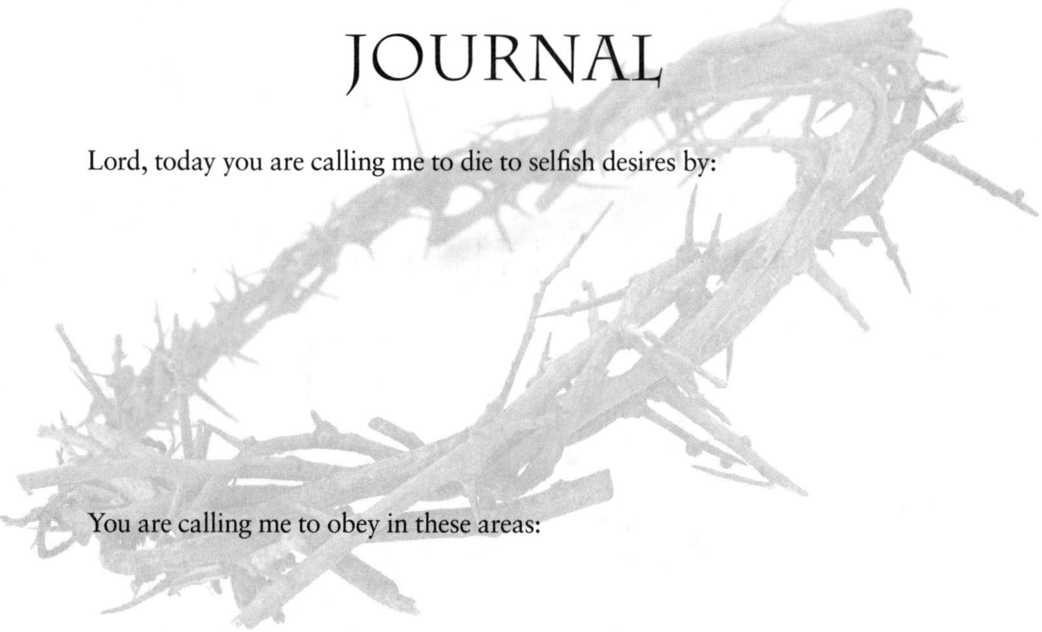

Lord, today you are calling me to die to selfish desires by:

You are calling me to obey in these areas:

You are calling me to intimacy with you by:

DAY 27

SPEAK THE TRUTH

"AND DO NOT SWEAR BY YOUR HEAD, FOR YOU CANNOT MAKE EVEN ONE HAIR WHITE OR BLACK. SIMPLY LET YOUR 'YES' BE 'YES,' AND YOUR 'NO' BE 'NO'; ANYTHING BEYOND THIS COMES FROM THE EVIL ONE" – MATTHEW 5:36-37

In Jesus' day, people used oaths to show how serious they were about telling the truth. One would swear by the temple, and the next would one-up him by swearing by the altar in the temple. Each person tried to outdo the other in promising truthfulness. We do the same thing today. A guy says something, and a girl says, "Do you promise?"

The guy replies, "I promise."

The girls isn't convinced and asks, "Do you really promise?"

If the guy doesn't come back with, "I *really* promise!", she thinks he's lying.

Jesus recognized our desire to force people to tell the truth by demanding oaths—and our desire to use oaths ourselves to prove our truthfulness—but he says there's a better way. A simple way. Just tell the truth. Period. Let your "Yes" mean "Yes" and your "No" mean "No." It's simply integrity. Don't spit hairs and try to trick people by using word games. Simply tell the truth plainly and clearly. Let the truth of Christ be your integrity. Let the chips fall where they may.

People lie to cover their sins. We weave elaborate stories to hide what we've done. In fact, most of the novels we read and movies we see focus on hiding truth. It is the uncovering of the truth that forms the plot and the drama of the stories. On a personal level, we often lie to each other because we are ashamed of our behavior and we want to avoid the consequences. Jesus spoke about this tendency in his conversation with Nicodemus. He said, "This is the verdict: Light has come into the world, but men loved darkness instead of light because their deeds were evil. Everyone who does evil hates the light, and will not come into the light for fear that his deeds will be exposed" (John 3:19-20). Exposure...that's what we try so desperately to avoid. We hope a lie will end the matter, but it rarely does. Instead, we have to lie again to cover the first one, and then another one and another. Soon, we are tangled in the web of deceit. Or, it would be too embarrassing to explain why we lied in the first place. So we leave it there.

Every lie drives a wedge in our relationship with others. We may get away with some of them in our earthly relationships, but to God we are completely transparent in our thoughts, motives, and actions. The writer to the Hebrews stated, "Nothing in all creation is hidden from God's sight. Everything is uncovered and laid bare before the eyes of him to whom we must give an account" (Hebrews 4:13). Who will give an account? All of us. Eventually, we all will stand before God in judgment. We will be asked about every word and every action...every lie and every truth we've said. We may think we are escaping the consequences of our sins by lying, but even if we aren't caught by our friends, our parents, our teachers, or our employers, God sees it. Or should I say, sees through it. Realize that God is not a "peeping Tom" ready to pounce on us for every sin. He loves us and no matter what lie we tell, his love for us doesn't vanish. However, in his holiness, God cannot be nonchalant about even the "smallest" sin.

We as people sometimes engage in a form of deception that we don't think of as lying, but it is. It's exaggeration. We make good things a little better, and we make bad things a little worse. Why? To impress people a little more. We laugh about this and call it "evangelastic," but when we make a statement that isn't true, it's sin. Often people ask me, "David, how many people were at that revival last weekend?" I might want to stretch the truth and say there were 400 when only 350 were there. Why? Because 400 sounds better than 350. It's that simple.

Why do we exaggerate? Maybe because we are insecure. We are afraid that person won't think as highly of us if we tell the truth. We want to be accepted. We want to impress. We want them to think we're hot stuff. So we stretch the truth—just a little—to get that smile and that pat on the back. When we have the urge to exaggerate, we need to look at our hearts and ask, "What's going on here? Am I secure in the love and strength of Jesus, or do I think I need to lie to get this guy's approval?" Act with integrity and honesty. Tell the truth.

As we walk in the light, we can be honest about our own sin, about our circumstances, and about God. We lose the opportunity to honor God as long as we try to rationalize or hide our sin. When his light shines on our misbehavior, we need to say, "Yes, Lord. I did that. Thank you for forgiving me." As we walk with God and observe our circumstances, we can be honest about the hurts and the joys. If we are truthful with God about them, he can soothe the hurts and magnify the joys, and we can be honest about the character of God.

I love the Psalms. In those pages, we see David, Asaph, and the other writers pouring out their hearts to God. Sometimes they are disappointed with God; sometimes they are angry. But in virtually every case, their honesty leads to fresh insights about the wisdom and love of God. It takes a lot of courage to be honest with God, but the results are wonderfully liberating.

Paul commanded the believers in Ephesus: "Therefore each of you must put off falsehood and speak truthfully to his neighbor, for we are all members of one body" (Ephesians 4:25). One of the reasons to be honest with each other is that we are connected to each other. Christians are the body of Christ. Imagine the problems we'd have if our body didn't communicate truth to other parts of the body! If your brain told your legs, "Hey, watch out! A train is coming!" when you're sitting in class or at work, people would surely misunderstand if you dove into the hall! But that's a picture of what happens is the body of Christ. We, often intentionally, tell each other lies, and then we make misinformed decisions based on what others tell us. When we find out someone has lied to us, we are devastated and often have somewhat of a mess to fix. Trust is violated, and we have a hard time trusting next time. Instead of speaking the truth—and sometimes the truth is hard—we lie, we hide, we exaggerate, and we erode the relationships with fellow believers that should be some of the strongest, most transparent and honest relationships in our lives. Telling lies can also severely damage our witness. Non-believers may distrust Christ if they have been lied to by Christians—the very ones who call themselves his ambassadors. If we claim to represent Christ, we must be careful to always speak the truth. Remember, if we call ourselves Christians, we are to be the very example of the one who is "the way, the truth, and the life" (John 14:6).

Speak the truth about yourself, about others, and about God as if you are in the presence of Christ—because you are. The truth may be hard at first, but walking in the light will result in forgiveness and strength instead of always looking over your shoulder to see if you are going to get caught.

Does this mean we should go out of our way to be disrespectful or impolite and excusing it as "just telling it like it is"? No, God gives us wisdom. Paul wrote, "Do not let any unwholesome talk come out of your mouths, but only what is helpful for building others up according to their needs, that it may benefit those who listen" (Ephesians 4:29). So...don't tell somebody, "You sure are annoying!" even if it's true! Be wise. Speak truth in love.

—Be still. Listen to what God is saying to you.

1. What are some consequences when people are caught lying?

2. What are some consequences they experience even when they seem to get away with lying?

3. Why do "men love darkness rather than light"?

4. Read the Hebrews 4:13 passage again. Does it comfort you or scare you? Explain:

5. Are there any recurring situations in which you tend to exaggerate? If so, identify them:

Look at your heart. What do you hope exaggerating will do for you? What does it actually do for you?

6. How does lying and exaggerating affect your Christian relationships? What can you do about the problem?

7. How does it shape your words to realize that every word you speak is spoken in the presence of Christ?

8. Read Matthew 5:33-37. Think about each verse, then use it as a guide as you pray.

Memorize: Say Psalm 86:11-12 aloud. How can you apply this passage today?

A CALL TO DIE

JOURNAL

Lord, today you are calling me to die to selfish desires by:

You are calling me to obey in these areas:

You are calling me to intimacy with you by:

DAY 28

DON'T TAKE REVENGE

"YOU HAVE HEARD THAT IT WAS SAID, 'EYE FOR EYE, AND TOOTH FOR TOOTH.' BUT I TELL YOU, DO NOT RESIST AN EVIL PERSON. IF SOMEONE STRIKES YOU ON THE RIGHT CHEEK, TURN TO HIM THE OTHER ALSO."
– MATTHEW 5:38-39

Nobody has to be taught to take revenge. It is a basic instinct of our sinful nature. You hurt me, so I'm going to hurt you. It's the law of the jungle... and the school...and the workplace...and the family. Jesus is saying, "Yes, I know you've learned to take revenge, but I have a better way for you. Return kindness for evil." Wow! That takes incredible character and courage! But that character and courage don't come from a vacuum. They are rooted in our experience of the grace of God.

In an article in the magazine *Christianity Today*, author Philip Yancey wrote that forgiving those who have hurt us is "an unnatural act." Everything in our flesh cries out for justice, and in reality, for revenge. We demand that the person pay for what he did to us. Forgiving that person cuts across the grain. It doesn't feel normal and natural, but it is the mark of a true disciple of Jesus Christ.

I believe it is important for us to absorb two important truths in order to forgive those who hurt us: Our ability to forgive others comes from our experience of being forgiven for our own sins, and we can leave justice in God's righteous hands. Let's look at these.

In his letter to the Ephesians, Paul wrote: "Be kind and compassionate to one another, forgiving each other, just as in Christ God forgave you" (Ephesians 4:32). Do you see it? We can forgive others only to the extent that we have allowed ourselves to experience God's forgiveness. If we have drunk deep of God's grace, we will be able to forgive even those who have hurt us deeply. If we have only sipped of that grace, we may harbor resentment against those who only mildly offend us. I have known people who experienced horrible, traumatic hurts at the hands of others: sexual abuse, beatings, and betrayal. A few of these people have been able to forgive the offender and reach out to those who hurt them so badly. They allowed themselves to experience the fullness of God's forgiving grace. However, I've caught myself many times being offended by someone making fun of me, ignoring me, or cutting in line in front of me. In reflection, I realize that the fact that I'm so easily unforgiving is paralleled by my own acceptance of the forgiveness Christ has for me.

The first and foremost step in learning to forgive is to focus our attention on the cross. As we spend time in God's word, the light of the Holy Spirit shines on our sins. As we experience and reflect on the cleansing grace of God, we will be much more likely to forgive those who offend us. Let me put it another way, if you and I are having a hard time forgiving someone, we need to dig into the Scriptures and spend time allowing the Holy Spirit to remind us of the forgiveness Christ offers us. This allows us to be overwhelmed by God's mercy and grace that we don't deserve.

The second important thing to remember is to leave justice in God's hands. Paul wrote to the Romans: "Do not take revenge, my friends, but leave room for God's wrath, for it is written: 'It is mine to avenge; I will repay,' says the Lord" (Romans 12:19). One of our primary reasons we don't want to forgive is that we don't want people to be off the hook. They aren't. We can be assured that there will come a day that they will give an account before God for what they did, and on that day, he will handle it. Paul tells us this to encourage us to let go, to let God in his sovereignty have the responsibility for justice. If we truly believe he is handling it, we can release the bitter venom in our hearts and forgive. God will then infuse us with his strength to pray for that person and situation.

When we refuse to forgive people who have hurt us, all kinds of bad things happen to us:

1. We become bitter.

The feeling of anger is not wrong, but harboring anger leads to sin and bitterness. Some of us are so bitter for so long that our hatred gives us our identity and energy. When we talk about ourselves, we talk about "how much we've been hurt" and "what he did to me." We get up in the morning thinking about how to get back at that person, and the adrenalin that keeps us going comes from our hatred.

2. Our hatred drives wedges in our relationships.

Not only do we hate the one who hurt us, our anger may make other believers feel uncomfortable around us, and they keep their distance. Imagine how non-believers perceive the forgiveness that Christ offers them through the cross when they see his followers unwilling to forgive someone who's wronged them. We can also experience a distance in our relationship with God. We may blame him for letting the hurt happen in the first place, and we may become angry at him for allowing us to struggle with the pain and raw emotions.

3. We could experience psychosomatic problems.

Some of us struggle with bitterness that is so strong that it affects us physically. We may have too much acid in our stomachs and our digestive system has problems. The tension could give us headaches, and we could develop high blood pressure. Depression could set in. To the bitter, depressed person, life can seem empty, hopeless, and meaningless. God doesn't want this kind of life for us. Jesus says, "The thief comes to steal and kill and destroy; I have come that they may have life, and have it to the full" (John 10:10).

All of us get hurt from time to time, and most of us are hurt very badly at some point in our lives. Christians have the incredible resource—and the responsibility—to forgive. Not out of our own strength, but out of the strength God provides through our experience of his forgiveness. When we choose through Christ to forgive, we can experience true joy and freedom. We will find the determination and the strength to pray that God will reveal himself to that person and draw him to God's heart. We can pray that God will help us love that person. Does this sound difficult? It's not difficult. It's impossible, unless you and I have feasted on the cross of Christ.

Our prayers for them don't guarantee that we will see repentance and a changed heart. However, God will change our hearts toward them and allow us not only to forgive them, but also to love them with the love of Christ. It will be a painful process, but there is joy and freedom in it.

Does this passage mean that there are no limits to what people can do to us? Should we "turn the other cheek" no matter what? No, I think there are limits. If we are being sexually, physically, or emotionally abused, we need to get help and put a stop to that trauma. Abuse victims need time and help to be able to forgive completely, but with God's love and power, it can be done.

When you are hurt and you want to take revenge by hitting, yelling, gossiping, withdrawing, or any other way you can hurt that person in return:

- Reflect on the cross and drink deeply of God's grace for your own sins,

- Get in the word and ask God to help you have the discipline to forgive that person, just as God in Christ forgave you, and
- Ask the Holy Spirit to help you pray for that person so he can experience the love and forgiveness of Christ.

What will be the earthly results? Jesus gave instructions on how to treat those who have hurt us. He didn't make any promises of how the person would respond. Paul tells us: "If your enemy is hungry, feed him; if he is thirsty, give him something to drink. In doing this, you will heap burning coals on his head" (Romans 12:20). I believe that the "burning coals on his head" may refer to the shame a person feels when he realizes he has been so ugly to you but you have returned his evil with kindness. It could also mean a form of discipline God will deliver. When will this happen? Maybe soon; maybe on Judgment Day. But you can be assured: It will happen.

If you and I return good when others are evil to us, believe me, people around us will notice. There may never be a clearer mark of Christ on your life and mine than this. Some people will misunderstand. They misunderstood Jesus, too. However, some will notice our response and say, "I don't understand. After what you've been through, how can you forgive this person?" That gives us the opportunity to talk about the incredible love of Jesus.

Jesus' instructions in this passage are not difficult. They are impossible in our strength. If we are true disciples who have experienced his love and grace on a very deep level, and if we "trust the Lord with all our heart and lean not on our own understanding," God can make genuine love and forgiveness be born in our hearts. Let the bitterness die.

—Be still. Listen to what God is saying to you.

1. What are some of the biggest hurts you have experienced in the past year or so?

2. How did you respond?

3. How would a deeper experience of forgiveness enable you to express forgiveness to that person?

4. Look at the results of not forgiving people. Have you seen any of those in your life? In your family's life? Explain:

5. Read Romans 12:17-21. Paraphrase this passage:

6. Think of those who have hurt you. Write out a plan for how you want to respond to each one in light of these passages of scripture:

7. Read Ephesians 4:30-32. Think about these verses, then use each one as a guide as you pray.

   Memorize: Go back over the last three passages you have memorized (Psalm 115:1, 17-18; Psalm 116:1-2; and Psalm 86:11-12) until you can say them without looking.

A CALL TO DIE

JOURNAL

Lord, today you are calling me to die to selfish desires by:

You are calling me to obey in these areas:

You are calling me to intimacy with you by:

DAY 29

LOVE ONE ANOTHER

"DEAR FRIENDS, SINCE GOD SO LOVED US, WE ALSO OUGHT TO LOVE ONE ANOTHER." – 1 JOHN 4:11

Jesus continues to go against our natural instincts when he tells us to love the people who hurt us and aren't like us. He commands us, just as he loved all kinds of people, to actively love people from all walks of life. In Matthew 5:38-42, Jesus overturned the Law of Retribution ("an eye for an eye..."), and now he overturns the Law of Exclusion. Instead of excluding the different, we are to love them.

This is another of those things Jesus asks us to do that we simply can't fake—at least, not for long. We may grit our teeth and say "Hello" to someone we usually don't associate with, but that is hardly what the Lord had in mind when he said "Love one another." Jesus set the standard in this passage when he said,

"If you love those who love you, what reward will you get? Are not even the tax collectors doing that? And if you greet only your brothers, what are you doing more than others? Do not even pagans do that?" (Matthew 5:46-47).

Basically, Jesus means non-Christians. Generally, they love only those who love them and greet only those who are their brothers. The mark of a person who is filled with the love and grace of Jesus Christ is that he is set apart. Radically set apart. That person looks beyond the surface and sees the heart. He goes beyond a person's callousness or anger or pride. Instead, he sees a needy person for whom Christ died. He reaches out, even to those who have a hard time accepting love and friendship.

Who are the unlovables? We all know people who are very different from us—and to be honest, we just don't want to be around those people. I believe there are four categories of unlovables:

1. Bullies

These are the people easiest to identify. They may be loners or they may be in gangs. They delight in tormenting weak people and showing how tough they are. They harass innocent people and get a kick out of putting fear in a person's heart. When bullies are challenged, many of them back down. Some of them, however, fight back.

2. Competitors

Almost all of us know people who compete with us overtly or covertly in sports, grades, looks, dates, and any other area. In most cases, these competitors are friends, but when one of you gets a little more attention than the other, jealousy rises and both of you want to win. Friendly competition can turn ugly, and friendships can be ruined by the need to be one up.

3. Loners

These people don't threaten us, but we don't accept them in our social circles. In that sense, they can be considered outcasts. These people may look or dress differently from us, have different interests, behave different socially, or be in certain classes at school. We avoid them because they don't seem to be like us.

4. Too Cool

On the other end of the spectrum are the people who seem to have it all together, and they know it! They drive nice cars, wear the sharpest clothes, say the funniest things, and hang out with other cool people. They seem to look down their noses at us—if they notice us at all—and we can't stand them!

These are the people Jesus wants us to love. Did Jesus love people like this? You bet he did! He went to a party at Matthew's house, and Matthew was a hated tax gatherer. Jesus talked to prostitutes and outcasts. He didn't start the conversation by showing them Bible verses. Jesus made sure he got to know them first, then he explained the love of God to them. He spent time loving bullies and the "too cool" set—the religious leaders. Jesus talked to Nicodemus, Simon the Pharisee, and any others who wanted to know him. Many of these leaders hated Jesus and plotted to kill him, but to the ones who responded to his love, he made sure he was there for them. No, loving these people didn't guarantee their lives would change, but a few did.

Do you see how different this is from gritting your teeth and trying with all your might to be nice to somebody who is different from you? This is a completely different way to live! God doesn't ask us to give out anything we haven't freely received (Matthew 10:8). But since we have received so much love and kindness—even when we were enemies (before we came to know him and follow him)—we can then share that wealth with those we rub shoulders with every day. If we have truly experienced the love of Christ, that will overflow to the point that we are compelled to share this love with the lonely, hurting, dirty, and empty.

Loving those who are different doesn't necessarily mean you feel mushy love toward them. Jesus certainly didn't feel that kind of love when he was in the Garden preparing to die. But he acted. He obeyed. We can, too. Here are some suggestions:

- ***Let God show you who to love.*** Did somebody come to mind when you read the four categories of people? Maybe you thought of a family member, someone in class, or a person at work. Scriptures show us who to love. Let the Holy Spirit direct you who to love and how to love them. You may have a gut reaction against loving that person. If so, that may be the one!
- ***Soak in the love of God.*** Remember that this passage teaches us that it is uncomfortable to think about loving this person. Go back to the passages about God's incredible grace, mercy, and love for you. Drink it in. Fill your tank. Then let God show you that person in a new light so you want the best for him—you want Christ for him.
- ***Go out of your way to speak to that person.*** Jesus said to "greet" that person. When we greet someone, we don't mumble as we run past. We look that person in the eye, extend a hand of friendship, and open a conversation. We may have developed a strong habit of avoiding that person (and he or she may have the same habit with us), so ask God to give you the courage to take this step of faith.
- ***Listen.*** Ask a good question, and listen. Really listen. Find out what that person is interested in (even if you aren't interested at all) and ask about it. Then, listen to what he has to say. You may want to ask follow up questions to find out more, but show you are interested by asking about what he likes.
- ***Invite that person to church or Bible study.*** After several conversations, casually invite that person to go with you to

your church or Bible study. He may say "No" at first, but don't be discouraged. Ask again sometime. You might be surprised to find he wants to go with you. When we first moved from Iran to America, I would have gone with anyone to anything they invited me to—because I was so lonely and empty. The problem was, no one asked.

- ***Pray.*** One of the best indicators of our love for our enemies is how and how much we pray for that person. Consider what God wants for that person: to know his love, forgiveness and peace. Let that person's needs shatter your prejudice, and ask God's blessing on him.
- ***Take the flack.*** When Jesus spent time with outcasts and tax gatherers, the religious leaders gave him a hard time. When he spent time with the religious leaders, I can imagine that some of the common people gave him flack. When we love the unlovely, people may misunderstand and attack our integrity. Remember, you are doing this to honor the one who died for you...and for the person to whom you're showing love. Let any flack you receive toughen your skin a little.

Loving our enemies, similar to the principle of not taking revenge when people hurt us, is a clear mark of someone seeking to please the heart of God. If you have a hard time loving those who don't love you, don't get down. All of us have that problem! But use that realization as an encouragement to grasp the bigger picture and to experience the goodness of God more deeply than ever before. Out of a full heart, love them.

—Be still. Listen to what God is saying to you.

1. Did the Lord remind you of people in any or all of the four categories of people? List them here:

   —Bullies:

   —Competitors:

   —Loners:

   —Too cool:

2. Look at I John 4:11 and Romans 15:7. Describe your ability to show love to those who are unlovely and accept those who are unacceptable:

   Do you need to drink more deeply of Christ's love and acceptance so you can love and accept others? Explain:

3. Pick out one or two people from your list and write out a plan for how you will act lovingly toward them. (Use the suggestions as a guide.)

4. Read Matthew 5:43-48. Think about these verses, then use each one as a guide as you pray.

Memorize Psalm 91:1-3.

JOURNAL

Lord, today you are calling me to die to selfish desires by:

You are calling me to obey in these areas:

You are calling me to intimacy with you by:

DAY 29

DAY 30

HOLD THINGS LOOSELY

"BUT WHEN YOU GIVE TO THE NEEDY, DO NOT LET YOUR LEFT HAND KNOW WHAT YOUR RIGHT HAND IS DOING, SO THAT YOUR GIVING MAY BE IN SECRET. THEN YOUR FATHER, WHO SEES WHAT IS DONE IN SECRET, WILL REWARD YOU" – MATTHEW 6:3-4

People can talk about what they value and what they believe all day long, but we know what a person really values by looking at his schedule and his checkbook: how he spends his time and his money. In this passage of scripture, Jesus addresses the issue of giving. Many of us feel we are exempt from this topic. We say, "I don't have any money. How can I give any to God?" Or for those who are early in their careers, some say, "I'm just getting started and I have all kinds of expenses. I'll give to the church later." God doesn't buy either of these arguments.

We live in the richest society the world has ever known. Even the most modest incomes provide lifestyles far above those of wealthy people only a few decades ago. Whether on an allowance or a tight budget, we can give if we want to.

It's the "want" that's the problem. In our consumer mindset, we expect to have more and better all day every day. That expectation creates a built-in dissatisfaction with whatever we've got because we *have to have* whatever's next. We are so focused on having a better car, a faster computer, and nicer clothes that we are only content for the day that we get the next big purchase. After that day, the thrill wears off, and we are dissatisfied again.

In most cases, we don't own our possessions. They own us. We live for them, we dream about them, we work to have more, and our lives revolve around getting them, fixing them, upgrading them, protecting them, and replacing them. We're in this rat race simply because we want to have as much as the next person (and maybe a little bit more).

Giving, not acquiring, is the lifestyle of the person who is sold out to Jesus Christ. Not to say that we're not consumers, but hopefully we're not consumed with consuming. If we get it, fine. If not, that's fine, too. We live to give, not to get.

And when we give, we're not to call attention to ourselves. Often we give primarily so others will notice. The Temple in Jerusalem had metal containers for people to put their offerings. Paper currency wouldn't be invented for over a thousand years. People used coins. When they put their coins in the metal containers, some of them let the coins drop as loudly as possible to broadcast their generosity. The sound was as loud as a trumpet! Jesus said, "If you are giving just so people will notice, then their praise will be all the reward you'll get. The Father isn't honored by that motive." Remember that he is more concerned with our motive for giving than our actual gift.

I can hear those people justifying clanging the container, "I'm doing this as an example to others. We all need examples, don't we?" Isn't it amazing how creative we become to justify sinful behavior? We want the praise of people for our generosity, and we call our pride in showing off "an example" to others. Jesus didn't buy it. Jesus cut right through that.

In stark contrast with this practice, Jesus told his followers to give in secret. Don't let anybody know what you're doing. But be sure, he promised, that the Father will know, and he'll reward you richly for your giving.

Because money reveals so much of our heart, that topic is addressed very often in the pages of Scripture. Paul gives several principles about giving in his second letter to the Corinthians. Here are some things for us to know:

- ***Give generously.*** Paul wrote: "Remember this: Whoever sows sparingly will also reap sparingly, and whoever sows generously will also reap generously" (2 Corinthians 9:6). I've heard people say, "You can't outgive God." He always blesses with his blessings when we are generous. We have to be careful, however, that we don't give with the idea of getting something in return. We should give out of a heart full of gratitude for what Christ gave for us.

  Giving starts with a minimum of 10% (the tithe) that Malachi 3:10 tells us to give back to the storehouse (the church). When God leads you to give above and beyond the tithe—great. (After all, all our physical resources are his anyway, right?) Distribute your offerings however the Spirit leads you. But make sure you practice the discipline of giving back one tenth of your earnings to your church. It's not an option.
- ***Give cheerfully.*** Paul continues, "Each man should give what he has decided in his heart to give, not reluctantly or under compulsion, for God loves a cheerful giver" (2 Corinthians 9:7). If you can't give cheerfully, by all means, don't. God doesn't need your money or time or energy. He is God. He can accomplish his purposes with or without us. However, he offers us the incredible privilege of being involved in bringing glory to him through a physical act of sacrifice.

What an act of worship! If we understand that offer, we will be thrilled to give.

- ***Don't compare.*** How often to you see people stealing a look at the folded bills and checks in the offering plate to see how their contribution matches up? Paul told us not to compare our gift to what someone else may give: "For if the willingness is there, the gift is acceptable according to what one has, not according to what he does not have" (2 Corinthians 8:12). Don't feel guilty if you can't give as much as someone else. Give whatever you can, and be glad you can give it.
- ***Give something you value.*** In most cases, we give money because it can be distributed to meet needs very easily. But we can also give other things we value: time, energy, and possessions. I know one lady who selects something she values from her home a couple of times of year and gives these things away. She gets great satisfaction in seeing the joy on someone's face who gets these treasures. She exercises her dependence on God, not on possessions, by giving away some possessions she really likes. My sister once went to feed the homeless in downtown Birmingham on a cold Sunday afternoon. When she got home, my mother asked, "Nastinka, where is the new coat I bought you?" Nastinka explained that she had given it to a lady who was cold and didn't have one. My Mom smiled and said, "I'm so proud of your generosity." That is a small picture of the Father's joy when you and I give cheerfully and generously to someone in need. The homeless lady may never see my sister again, but that doesn't matter. My sister had given out of a heart of gratitude and out of God's abundance.

Many times we think we're doing someone a favor when we donate our old, worn out clothes, some broken toy, or half-used item. The Bible tells us that we are to "give as unto the Lord." Just as God freely gave us the immaculate gift of his grace, we should follow his example and give out of our abundance, not from our cast-offs.

Whenever possible, we need to give anonymously. If we find out somebody doesn't have enough money to go to a retreat, we can go to the youth pastor privately and give him the money. Or we may even want to put the money and a note in an envelope and put it in the youth pastor's mailbox. Either way, we will be doing what Jesus told us to do: Give secretly.

If you're on a tight budget or an allowance, you can still follow the guidelines Jesus and Paul outlined. First, pray and ask God for wisdom in your giving, then reflect on all God has generously given you. Then, as Paul said, purpose in your heart what you want to do, and give it cheerfully. It may be only a few dollars a week. That's fine. The issue is not how much. It's why. Begin today, and enjoy seeing God work in people's lives—including yours—through your generosity.

And what are the rewards for giving? The rewards are the fact that you've glorified God. You have demonstrated that Christ is more important to you than any possession you have. God is honored when we help lift someone's burden and point them to God's saving grace through our gifts.

The way we use our possessions, including our money, is an indication of our commitment to Christ. Denying our selfishness means we identify and overcome our tendency to want more and more and more stuff, and then we follow Christ's example by generously giving in the name of the Lord. Generosity is both a heart attitude and a habit. Ask God to develop both in you.

> "Watch out! Be on your guard against all kinds of greed; a man's life does not consist in the abundance of his possessions" (Luke 12:15).

—Be still. Listen to what God is saying to you.

1. Think about what you have as compared to someone in another country (such as Russia, Brazil, or Ethiopia). Are you wealthy? Why or why not?

2. What are your resources to give (salary, allowance, savings, earnings of any kind)?

3. Give yourself a progress report on how you give . . .

   —generously:

   —cheerfully:

   —not comparing your giving to what others can give:

   —giving something you value highly:

4. Of the reasons to give we've listed, which ones motivate you to give? Explain:

5. In what ways is giving a heart attitude, and in what ways is it a habit?

6. Read 2 Corinthians 8 and 9. Write out your plan of how you are going to give.

7. Read Matthew 6:1-4. Think about these verses, then use each one as a guide as you pray.

Memorize: Write Psalm 91:1-3 three times.

JOURNAL

Lord, today you are calling me to die to selfish desires by:

You are calling me to obey in these areas:

You are calling me to intimacy with you by:

DAY 30

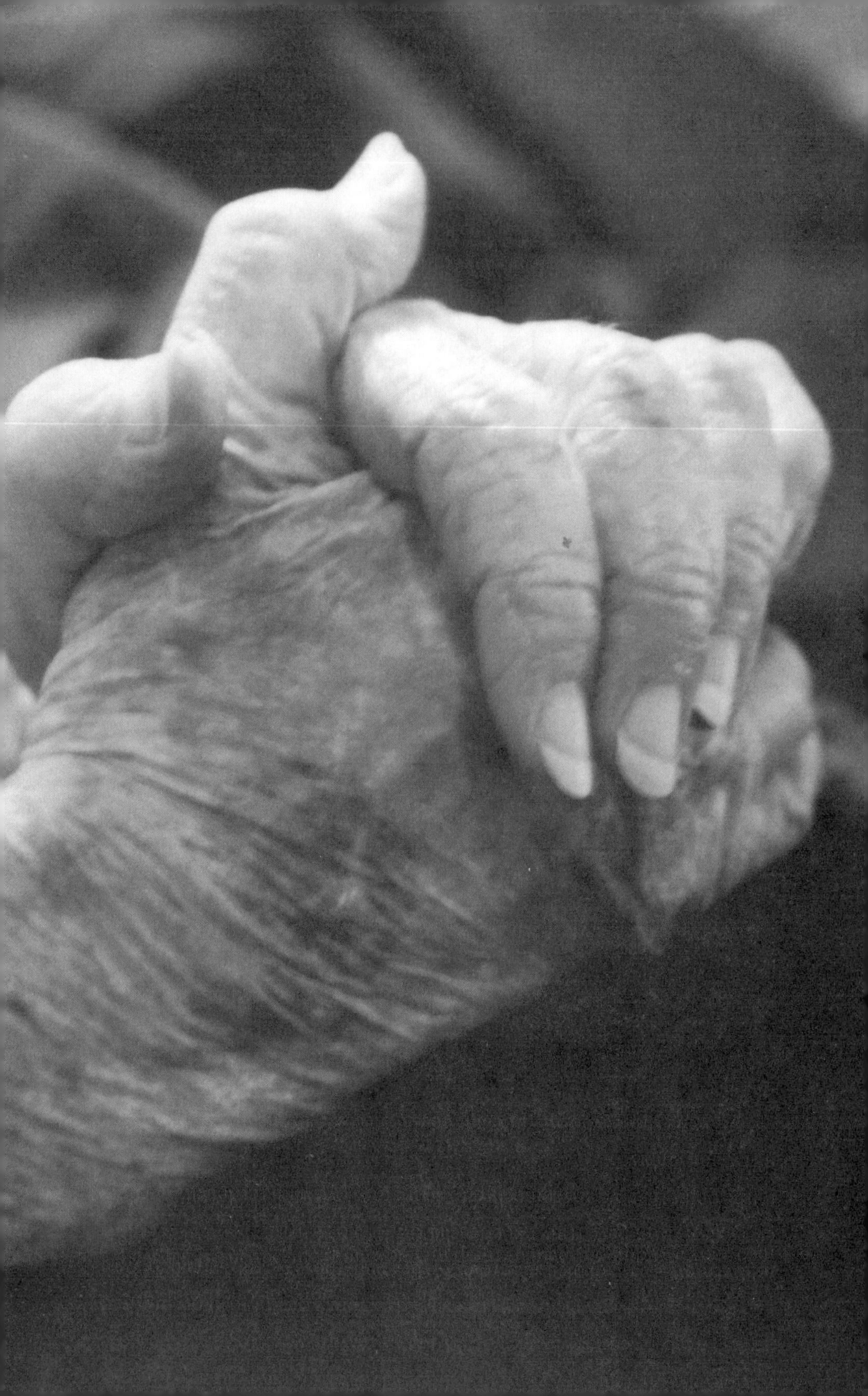

DAY 31

PRAYING

"AND WHEN YOU PRAY, DO NOT KEEP ON BABBLING LIKE PAGANS, FOR THEY THINK THEY WILL BE HEARD BECAUSE OF THEIR MANY WORDS. DO NOT BE LIKE THEM, FOR YOUR FATHER KNOWS WHAT YOU NEED BEFORE YOU ASK HIM" – MATTHEW 6:7-8

Prayer is simply talking to God. When we pray, we tend to make one of two common mistakes: We use too many words, or we use too few. Some of us think we can twist God's arm by praying long and hard. We believe more in the "power of prayer" than in the power of God. Others of us don't play that game. In fact, we don't play any game at all. We don't pray. We don't believe God needs our prayers, so what's the use?

The purpose of prayer is not to change God's mind. It is to get our hearts in line with his will and his Spirit. It helps us continually recognize our complete dependence on him. Far too often, especially with young Christians, prayer is tremendously self-focused. We bring our wants to God, and we give him the whole truck load! Certainly, asking God to provide is an important part of prayer, but it is only a part.

The primary purpose of prayer is to give us a vehicle to praise and worship him and help us know God and discover his will. Take a look at the prayers Paul records in his letter to churches. He asks God to fill the Colossian Christians "with the knowledge of his will in all spiritual wisdom and understanding, that they might walk in a manner worthy of the Lord and to please him in all respects." For the Philippians, Paul asks God to help them know "love (that) abounds more and more in knowledge and depth of insight, so that you may be able to discern what is best and may be pure and blameless until the day of Christ." For the Ephesians, Paul prays in Ephesians 3:16-19 "that you, being rooted and established in love, may have power together with all the saints, to grasp how wide and long and high and deep is the love of Christ, and to know this love that surpasses knowledge—that you may be filled to the measure of all the fullness of God." Paul asked God to work so deeply in people's hearts that they were overwhelmed with the love of God, they understood the will of God, and their lives reflected the character of God. That was his primary focus in prayer. It should be ours, too. As we praise and worship him through prayer, we understand more and more of the character of God. Our prayers will be filled with thanksgiving and praise, not just "gimme, gimme."

Another important part of prayer is listening. If, as Jesus said, we babble lots of words in prayer, we sure won't be good listeners. When we stop speaking and take time to listen to God as we pray, we probably won't hear audible voices. The Holy Spirit will, however, remind us of passages of scripture which apply to what we are praying about. Sometimes God speaks the loudest in the hush—the "still, small voice of God" breaking into our consciousness. Caution: not every idea that floats into our consciousness is necessarily from God. Make sure it lines up with scripture and is consistent with God's character.

How do we know we are understanding the will of God? That's a good question. The first and foremost way to know if you are in tune with the will of God is to see if your thoughts and direction line up with the Scriptures. What does the Bible clearly teach about the issue? God won't tell you something in prayer that conflicts with his word. Another way to discern God's will is to talk to several people who are mature in their Christian faith. Let them pray with you and ask questions to help you uncover what God's Spirit is saying to you. Over time, you will have a sense of "rightness" or "wrongness" about the direction. God will open and close the doors. Don't rush your decision. Let God confirm the direction he wants you to go. Far too often, young Christians think God tells them to do something, so they impulsively jump to do it—and they experience disaster. We need to learn the wisdom of waiting and discerning the will of God.

Jesus reminds us that our Father knows what we need, so we can ask in faith. Faith is the essential ingredient in prayer. If we don't believe God is good and he only wants what is best for us, then we think we have to wow him with a ton of words, or we give up entirely. As you pray, pour out your hurts and hopes to a Father who really cares about his children. As my friend, evangelist and author Dr. Jay Strack always says, "God loves you just the way that you are, but he loves you too much to leave you that way."

During the last night before he was betrayed, Jesus said many things to his disciples. He said one thing four times: "The Father will give you whatever you ask in my name." Man, what a promise! But what does it mean to pray "in Jesus' name"? It means to pray as his child, in his will, and for his glory. Are you his child? Do you have an intimate relationship with him? Do you pray more to a black void than to a Christ you know personally? If you don't know him, you can ask to receive him as your Savior and Lord. Are your prayers in his will? Hmmm. That's a little harder to answer. We have to check them out with scripture and see if our requests are in line with his will. Are they for his glory? That one can be really tough! Our selfish nature wants to honor ourselves, not Jesus, so we may need God to do some spiritual surgery to repair our hearts before he will answer. In my experience, many of us fail the second requirement because we don't know God's word well enough to discern his will. Many others of us, however, wrestle with the third one because we struggle with pride and self-love. Jesus gave us a fantastic promise.

Some of us pray at two specific times: on Sunday morning and when we're really in trouble! In his book, *Practicing the Presence of God*, Brother Lawrence talks about the possibility of constant prayer. He doesn't mean that we verbalize prayers twenty-four hours a day, but it is possible, he says, to have an attitude all the time of "What's next, Lord?" Whenever we get a phone call, before we answer we can pray, "Father, give me wisdom." When we meet with a friend, we can ask, "Lord, give me words of encouragement for her." Whenever we change from one activity to another, we can pray, "Lord, I need you here." Paul tells us in 1 Thessalonians 5:17 to "pray continually." This simply means to constantly try to be in a receptive, communicative position with God.

As we pray to know the character and the will of God, we will also ask God for things. At that point, pray specifically, and listen as you pray. When you bring a need to God and ask him to meet it, his plan may be to answer your prayer immediately. However, he may use that opportunity to get your attention and say, "OK, I hear you. Request registered. But before I answer, I want to talk to you about something." Requests and listening go hand in hand. He may want to redirect our request, or he may want to change it entirely. Rest assured, God always answers our prayers, but sometimes his answer may be, "No," or "Wait." He always wants us to be in a position of complete dependency on him.

Those who want to really know God and follow him will carve out time to spend in secret prayer. Jesus said, "But when you pray, go into your room, close the door and pray to your Father, who is unseen. Then your Father, who sees what is done in secret, will reward you" (Matthew 6:6). Praying in church or in a group is necessary, but there are also things God wants to tell you that must be told in private. Think of the best friend you've ever had. You enjoyed doing things with a crowd of friends, but the most treasured moments together were shared just between the two of you. That's how it is with God, too. This book has given you some time to spend alone with God every day. When you close this book for the last time, I hope the discipline of going to God every day in secret will be with you for the rest of your life.

Prayer is not magic. It is a holy conversation between the Creator of the Universe and his beloved child and friend.

—Be still. Listen to what God is saying to you.

1. What has been your purpose for prayer in the past? (Be honest.)

2. What difference would it make if your purpose in praying was to know God and uncover his will?

3. Write a short summary of what you learned about each of these aspects of prayer:
   —Listening:

   —Discernment:

   —Praying in faith:

—God's promise to answer if we pray "in Jesus' name":

—Constant prayer:

—Praying in secret:

4. What is one specific thing you will do to change and improve your communication with God?

5. Read Colossians 1:9-14. Think about these verses, then use each one as a guide as you pray.

   Memorize: Say Psalm 91:1-3 aloud. How can you apply this passage today?

DAY 31

JOURNAL

Lord, today you are calling me to die to selfish desires by:

You are calling me to obey in these areas:

You are calling me to intimacy with you by:

DAY 32

FASTING

"WHEN YOU FAST, DO NOT LOOK SOMBER AS THE HYPOCRITES DO, FOR THEY DISFIGURE THEIR FACES TO SHOW MEN THEY ARE FASTING. I TELL YOU THE TRUTH, THEY HAVE RECEIVED THEIR REWARD IN FULL. BUT WHEN YOU FAST, PUT OIL ON YOUR HEAD AND WASH YOUR FACE, SO THAT IT WILL NOT BE OBVIOUS TO MEN THAT YOU ARE FASTING, BUT ONLY TO YOUR FATHER, WHO IS UNSEEN; AND YOUR FATHER, WHO SEES WHAT IS DONE IN SECRET, WILL REWARD YOU" – MATTHEW 6:16-18

Each of us are experts on fasting. Maybe not physical fasting, but we definitely apply the concept of fasting in our daily lives. When you have a big exam in school or a major project at work, you do whatever it takes to concentrate on learning the material and getting the job done. You miss (or fast from) your favorite television program, you tell your friends you can't talk on the phone, you go to bed late and get up early, and you may even miss a meal to be sure you accomplish what you need to do. You concentrate on your academics and work. Fasting is spiritual concentration. In this case, you are concentrating your mind, soul, and body to know God and to know his will.

In much of the last couple of millennia, fasting was a common practice among Christians. Notice that Jesus didn't say "if you fast." He said "when you fast." Today, fasting is not a common spiritual discipline, especially among evangelical Christians. However, recently God is using certain Christian leaders such as Richard Foster, John Piper, and Bill Bright, to revive the significance of this spiritual discipline.

If you have read the Gospel of Matthew, you are familiar with Jesus' forty-day fast before he began his earthly ministry. He went into the wilderness to spend time with his Father and to prepare himself for his ministry of teaching and redeeming sinners—you and me. A more common practice today (and more common in Jesus' day) was to fast for twenty-four hours, from sundown to sundown. Some people fast for two or three days. In each case, if God calls you to a physical fast, you need to drink plenty of water and possibly even consult your family doctor to make sure that you're not bringing physical harm to your body.

When you began this book, I asked you to pray about fasting from a particular activity for forty days. This is not technically a fast, but the exercise is in the spirit of a fast. Some Christian traditions advocate abstaining from a common, pleasant activity during the forty days of Lent before Easter. Giving up this activity is a sacrifice which reminds us every day of the sacrifice Christ made for us on the cross. Giving up television or red meat, or drinking only water for those days can't approach the blood sacrifice and agony Jesus experienced, but at least it reminds us to think about him and what he did for us. That's the spirit of Lent, and it is the spirit of the exercise I asked you to do.

Fasting may be situational, or it may be a habit. Some people fast when they have a major decision to make, when they are confused about God's will, or when they are very discouraged. Their fast concentrates their attention on the Lord and drives them to the Scriptures to discern God's will. Others make fasting a habit in their spiritual walks. Many people begin fasting because they face a difficult circumstance, and when they see how it helps them concentrate on God, they make a habit of it.

Like any other exercise you do for the first time, the initial efforts can be awkward. When you learned to ride a bike, it took a few tries before you kept the bike under you. It's the same way with fasting. Some people complain that they have bad headaches and that keeps them from concentrating. In most cases, the headaches occur from the shock the body feels from the sudden absence of donuts and Cokes. The headaches usually go away in an hour or so. Other people report that the only thing they can concentrate on is the Big Mac and fries they plan to eat after sundown when their fast is over. Concentration is hard work. Focus your attention on the Lord, his will, his word, and his work in your life. That will help you overcome your mind's wanderings.

Jesus gave two simple instructions about fasting: don't tell anybody, and look good while you're fasting. The Pharisees fasted twice a week, but we get the idea that God wasn't too impressed because they made sure everybody knew they were fasting.

Bragging about your spirituality just doesn't cut it. Our natural (and sinful) tendency is to want people to know how incredibly committed we are to the Lord, and what shows our commitment more than fasting? Jesus said, "Don't tell a soul." In fact, make sure nobody can tell you are fasting. Guys, comb your hair (if you have any), and girls, put on make-up. Look good! Don't try to look like a ninth-century monk who just dragged himself in from the desert.

As lunch approaches, you may want to find a secluded, quiet place to read your Bible and pray. If somebody asks you, "Hey, aren't you going to eat lunch?" you can say, "I'm already full. Thanks." You don't have to tell him you are full of the love of God—unless he asks. Your parents may not understand if you say you are going to miss dinner and breakfast. You might want to tell them you are going to take that time to go to the park to spend time with the Lord. If they ask questions about what you plan to eat, it's fine to tell them you are fasting so you can concentrate on the Lord. "And no, mom and dad, I'm not becoming a weirdo fanatic. I just want to spend some good time with the Lord." If you tell them in a way that is natural and not defensive, they will probably let you go without saying anything else. If your parents don't agree, take time to tell them why you want to go without eating for a day. If they refuse to see your point, then graciously follow their wishes. There will be a lifetime of opportunities to fast after you leave home. For now, honor your parents by obeying them. God is pleased with the attitude of your heart and your desire to seek him, not just with the disciplines themselves.

What can you expect from fasting? It is not magic. We can't expect God to jump through our hoops just because we do something out of the ordinary. Our fasting doesn't twist his arm and get him to do what we want. Fasting doesn't put pressure on God; it clears our minds and hearts so we can be closer to him. In the freshness and intimacy of that experience, we can listen to his word, understand his will, and respond to his love for us.

—Be still. Listen to what God is saying to you.

1. Write a statement on the purpose of fasting:

   Is this purpose different than you thought before? Explain:

2. Do you know anyone who fasts regularly? If you do, what are the benefits to this person?

3. Have you fasted? What happened? What were the benefits? What obstacles did you encounter?

4. Are there situations you have experienced recently in which it would have been good to spend more concentrated time with God to discern his will? Explain:

5. Do you want to fast? Why or why not?

   If you do, how and when do you plan to do it?

   How will you make sure you do it in secret?

   What rewards do you hope God will give you?

6. Read Matthew 6:16-18. Think about these verses, then use each one as a guide as you pray.

   Memorize: Go over the last three passages you have memorized (Psalm 116:1-2; Psalm 86:11-12; and Psalm 91:1-3) until you can quote them without looking.

A CALL TO DIE

JOURNAL

Lord, today you are calling me to die to selfish desires by:

You are calling me to obey in these areas:

You are calling me to intimacy with you by:

DAY 33

SERVING YOUR MASTER

"NO ONE CAN SERVE TWO MASTERS. EITHER HE WILL HATE THE ONE AND LOVE THE OTHER, OR HE WILL BE DEVOTED TO THE ONE AND DESPISE THE OTHER. YOU CANNOT SERVE BOTH GOD AND MONEY"
– MATTHEW 6:24

A recurring theme in Jesus' teaching is that God requires complete, abject devotion. Anything less is idolatry, and it is destructive. Complete devotion, however, is difficult...very difficult. All people want a purpose bigger than ourselves; we want to live for something significant. But we also want to live for something that is tangible. Many times God seems invisible. His purpose is often hidden and mysterious. It is much easier to let our hearts drift back to the seen and tangible: possessions, power, others, and ourselves. Our heart's purpose and passion, whether tangible or intangible, is where our treasure lies.

Charles Spurgeon once wrote, "When the Romans erected the statue of Christ and put it up in their Pantheon, saying that he should be one among their gods, their homage was worthless. When they turned their heads first to Jupiter, then to Venus, then to Jesus, they did no honor to our Lord; they did but dishonor him. Their service was not acceptable. And so if you imagine in your heart that you can sometimes serve God and sometimes serve self and be your own master, you have made a mistake."[6]

Every moment, every word, every choice is a deposit either heavenly or earthly. Our deposits are our treasure: our affections and efforts to honor God or our efforts to live by the world's standards. Not both. One or the other. Jesus' statement about "treasures in heaven" refers to the rewards we will get at the Judgment when we stand before him. Remember? On that day, every word and deed we have done for selfish reasons will burn up, and everything we have said and done for Christ will be rewarded by God.

Some of us are almost as blind as unbelievers when it comes to what is important. We know enough not to go after riches with our whole hearts, but we pursue Jesus and riches, Jesus and fame, Jesus and fun. Christ's statement in this passage is that we can't have both as our treasure. While God may choose to bless us with some material possessions, good looks, or athletic ability, he never intends or designs these to take any sort of foothold in our lives. We can enjoy them *only* as long as we don't rely on them or set them up as "gods" in our lives. We can't have God and...anything as our treasure. We must allow God to fill us so fully and completely that we will be perfectly content if we gave those things away (or God took them away). Hold things loosely.

Jesus said in Matthew 6:21, "For where your treasure is, there your heart will be also." What we value the most, are most attached to, have the most passion and affection for—this is our treasure.

We can serve only one master: us or God. We are devoted to one, and our choices show that we don't value one as highly as the other. No matter how

6 Quoted from Spurpeon at his Best, (Baker Book House, 1988), p. 263.

much we say we value Christ, we can look at our attitudes, energy, schedules, and finances to find out what we really value. They tell the real story.

Does this mean we can't be involved in anything but ministry? Can a devoted disciple of Christ go into business or nursing or teaching or any other profession to which God leads us? Certainly, but with a different goal in mind. Our goal will be to seek to please God and not ourselves. Our goal in any profession should be to glorify God. Work "as unto the Lord," and daily live out obedience to him. This will show up in what we talk about, what we get excited about, and how we handle difficulties. If we honor Christ and above all else value him in all these things, we'll stand out like lighthouses to those around us. Ministers aren't exempt from this either. We must constantly check our motives and focus on *who* we serve—not on our ministries.

If we aren't consumed with money, possessions, and prestige, and if we daily seek the heart and will of God, our lives will be filled with peace, joy, and purpose. When we serve our master, Jesus Christ, he has promised to provide what we need. We don't need to worry. He said, "Therefore I tell you, do not worry about your life, what you will eat or drink; or about your body, what you will wear" (Matthew 6:25). Jesus then describes the Father's care for the birds and the way God provides beauty for even plants in the field, and he remarks, "If that is how God clothes the grass of the field, which is here today and tomorrow is thrown into the fire, will he not much more clothe you, O you of little faith?" (Matthew 6:30). God has promised to provide for us, and he has proven it by providing for his creation. So we can have confidence that he will provide what we need. We are the children that he loves.

Jesus sums up his teaching on serving one master by giving us one of the most widely quoted verses of scripture in the Bible. In light of what is real treasure and who is our master, in light of his promises to provide if we trust him and follow him, he said, "But seek first his kingdom and his righteousness, and all these things will be given to you as well" (Matthew 6:33). What are "these things"? Enough food, enough clothing, enough shelter, and an abundance of his peace and his presence. We could call that a treasure, too.

Like the song says,

> "Turn your eyes upon Jesus. Look full in his
> wonderful face;
> and the things of earth will grow strangely dim in
> the light of his glory and grace."

—Be still. Listen to what God is saying to you.

1. Do you agree or disagree with the statement: No one can serve two masters. Explain your answer:

   What happens when we try to serve two?

2. What or who helps you value the treasure that is intangible over the one that is tangible?

3. Describe the connection between treasures on earth and worry, and between treasures in heaven and peace:

4. Read Proverbs 30:7-9 again. Does this passage describe your heart? Explain:

5. Read Matthew 6:19-34. Think about these verses, then use each one as a guide as you pray.

   Memorize John 14:6.

A CALL TO DIE

JOURNAL

Lord, today you are calling me to die to selfish desires by:

You are calling me to obey in these areas:

You are calling me to intimacy with you by:

DAY 34

NOT PEACE, BUT A SWORD

"DO NOT SUPPOSE THAT I HAVE COME TO BRING PEACE TO THE EARTH. I DID NOT COME TO BRING PEACE, BUT A SWORD" – MATTHEW 10:34

Huh? Did Jesus really say that? I thought he promised freedom from anxiety for those who trusted him!

Yes, Jesus said those who follow him will sense his presence and his peace, but we will have peace in our hearts, not necessarily in our relationships. Families can be the source of our greatest joy and security and comfort, but families can also produce our greatest pain. When you and I choose to make Christ Lord of our lives and obey him above all else, it causes a ripple in some families. In others, it's an exploding bomb!

I've talked to young people who decided to make this kind of radical commitment to Jesus, and after praying about how and when to tell their parents, they mustered up enough courage to say, "Mom, Dad, I've made a decision. I'm going to follow Christ with my whole heart."

In many cases, the parents don't understand what that means, so the mom may reply, "That's wonderful! I've made a decision, too. We're having meat loaf for dinner."

And the dad might respond, "And I've made a decision. I'm going fishing Saturday."

Some parents realize this is going to cause some changes in the family, but they explain to their friends that "Jimmy is just going through a phase. He'll grow out of it in a few months."

But in other families, our decision to follow Jesus is met by outright opposition and even rage. In some cultures in the world, a decision to make Jesus Lord is not amusing to the family. It doesn't confuse them. It results in serious consequences. As an eighteen year-old, the night I gave my life to Christ, my parents were not happy. There was an amazing amount of tension at the house, to say the least. It all came to a head the night I wanted to get baptized. When I came home, I had to leave the house. I've heard my dad say, in reflection of my conversion, "Because of the Iranian revolution, I lost my home, my friends, my country, my family, my heritage, and now because of David's acceptance of salvation through Christ, I'd lost my religion as well."

Now that my entire family, including my father, are Christians (an eleven year journey), I can see God's hand in all of this. But looking back eleven years ago, at that moment, there was opposition. If you're reading this and saying to yourself, "I relate to the tension he went through with his family," I want to tell you there's hope. The situation might be bigger than you, but it's not bigger than God. "What is impossible with men is possible with God" (Luke 18:27). Be encouraged!

As Paul says in 2 Corinthians 4:17-18, "For our light and momentary troubles are achieving for us an eternal glory that far outweighs them all. So we fix our eyes not on what is seen, but on what is unseen. For what is seen is temporary, but what is unseen is eternal."

This is a decision point for all disciples. This is the point many of us say,

"Man, I knew there would be some tough times if I followed Christ, but I just can't stand it for my Dad to be so upset with me." We redefine our commitment to be radical up to—but not past—the point of upsetting our families.

Jesus didn't give us that option. He said clearly, "Anyone who loves his father or mother more than me is not worthy of me; anyone who loves his son or daughter more than me is not worthy of me; and anyone who does not take his cross and follow me (there it is again!) is not worthy of me" (Matthew 10:37-38). Luke records a similar statement in which Jesus said, "If anyone comes to me and does not hate his father and mother, his wife and children, his brothers and sisters—yes, even his own life—he cannot be my disciple" (Luke 14:26).

When we try to obey both God's principles and a family not serving him, we end up with a divided heart. We please no one, and we are miserable. What kind of choices are we talking about? That depends on the family. Like the song says, "I have decided to follow Jesus, no turning back, no turning back." It doesn't say, "I have decided to follow Jesus—only if my parents understand and support me." We also sing "I surrender all," not "I surrender 28%."

Some of you might come from a great, God-serving family. But I assure you, your godly dad is only human. He would probably be the first to tell you that he wants you to find your standard of holiness in the example of Christ.

You may not face those major decisions right now, but be ready for them. Tension is also created when values are different than our family's:

- if God is leading you to change your lifestyle and walk away from any ungodly movies and music your family usually watches, or
- if God is leading you to change an ungodly circle of friends.

Tomorrow we will examine what it means for a disciple to honor his parents, so be sure to understand what Jesus is saying in this passage: He doesn't want you and me to create tension in our families because we become defiant and obnoxious about our faith! But as we walk in his love and wisdom and make decisions to love him above all and obey him, some of us may experience the tension between pleasing our families and pleasing Christ.

Jesus shows the spiritual logic of following him: "Whoever finds his life will lose it, and whoever loses his life for my sake will find it" (Matthew 10:39). If you and I try to find life in the old affections, old lifestyle, old values, and old goals, we will lose it; we'll be empty and spiritually dead. But if we give up those old things for his sake (that is, deny our selfishness, put off our old clothes of sin, etc.), then we'll find real joy, vitality, energy, and insight in him.

The choice to let our families continue to be our lord or to let Jesus be our Lord is one of *the* biggest—perhaps the biggest—test of a disciple of Christ. It is one we will be faced with over and over again.

—Be still. Listen to what God is saying to you.

1. In what ways did Jesus come to bring peace? In what ways did he come to bring conflict?

2. Paraphrase Jesus' statements in Matthew 10:37-38.

3. Describe what Jesus meant to "hate" your family members.

4. Have you experienced tension in your family as you have made decisions to make Christ your Lord? If so, describe those. If not, why not?

5. Choosing Christ over family is one of the hardest things we do as disciples. What resources do you need to help you make these choices—but not be defiant when you make them?

6. Read Matthew 10:34-39. Think about these verses, then use each one as a guide as you pray.

   Memorize: Write John 14:6 three times.

JOURNAL

Lord, today you are calling me to die to selfish desires by:

You are calling me to obey in these areas:

You are calling me to intimacy with you by:

DAY 34

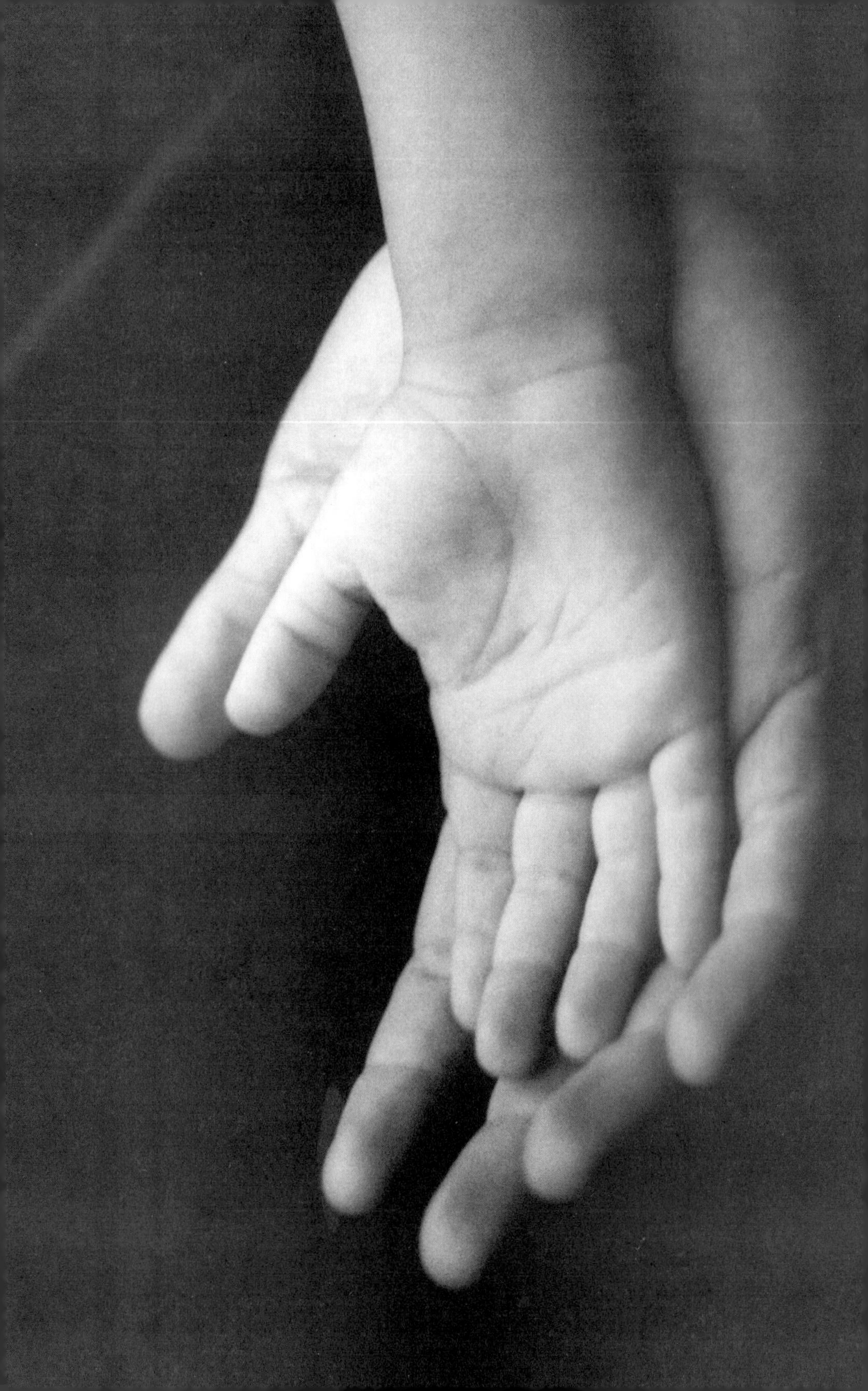

DAY 35

HONOR YOUR PARENTS

"FOR GOD SAID, 'HONOR YOUR FATHER AND MOTHER' AND 'ANYONE WHO CURSES HIS FATHER OR MOTHER MUST BE PUT TO DEATH.' BUT YOU SAY THAT IF A MAN SAYS TO HIS FATHER OR MOTHER, 'WHATEVER HELP YOU MIGHT OTHERWISE HAVE RECEIVED FROM ME IS A GIFT DEVOTED TO GOD,' HE IS NOT TO 'HONOR HIS FATHER' WITH IT. THUS YOU NULLIFY THE WORD OF GOD FOR THE SAKE OF YOUR TRADITION" – MATTHEW 15:4-6

The Pharisees knew the Law very well. They taught it, memorized it, and wrote it on little pieces of paper and put it in little boxes strapped to their heads (yes, they really did!). But they didn't always obey it the way God intended. Often, they obeyed only to the extent to which it was convenient for them. Jesus wasn't too happy about that. In fact, he was really angry at them. He goes on to say in Matthew 15:7-9:

> "You hypocrites! Isaiah was right when he prophesied about you:
> 'These people honor me with their lips,
> but their hearts are far from me.
> They worship me in vain;
> their teachings are but rules taught by men.'"

Ouch! Obviously Jesus thought the command to honor our parents was pretty important. It is one of the Ten Commandments. It is repeated in many ways and many times throughout the pages of scripture. God doesn't want us to miss the fact that he wants us to obey that command—even if it's inconvenient.

Those of us in our late teens and early twenties are in a stage when we are learning to be independent. That means we are exerting a little independence from our family. We take a bigger role in charting our own course for our lives, setting our own goals, choosing our own friends. In some cases, we and our parents both understand this stage and become partners in the process of change. In many cases, however, it causes strife. We demand freedom to make our own decisions, but our parents disagree. We want to "exercise our right" to be independent from them and make all our own decisions. Both want control, and anger flames at the tension points. If we are believers, a new ingredient is now added to the mix: the desire to please Christ above all, and the clear command of scripture to love Jesus more than our parents!

Jesus makes it perfectly clear that our Christianity is not about exercising our rights, but submitting to the authority of Christ. Dying to our rights. Paul urges us in Philippians 2:3-4 to "do nothing out of selfish ambition or vain conceit, but in humility consider others better than yourselves. Each of you should look not only to your own interests, but also to the interests of others." Especially those of your parents.

How do we put all this together? Here are some principles to make sense of this:

1. The role of parents or caregivers is very important to our development.

God instituted the family to give us stability and encouragement. Growing up may strain that bond sometimes or we may have stress in other ways, but we can be sure that God values the family relationship very highly. In fact, Paul reminds us that the command to honor our parents is "the first commandment with a promise— 'that it may go well with you and that you may enjoy long life on the earth' " (Ephesians 6:2-3). If we disobey this crucial command, God will oppose us. We sure don't want that! There are no excuses (like the Pharisees tried to use) to get out of fulfilling this command. God wants us to do it. We honor God when we honor our parents.

2. Put Christ first in your life.

Whether your parents serve Jesus or not, you can have Jesus as Lord of your life. Nobody and nothing on earth can prevent you from loving him. "But David, I can't honor my parents. You know what they're really like. They don't even serve God." Don't misunderstand. You dishonor your parents by being impolite, disobedient, disrespectful, or rebellious to your parents, whether inwardly or outwardly. Christ has a higher calling for us. Our submission to our parents' authority *does not* depend on our parents' submission to Christ's authority.

3. Prove yourself.

One of the most common conflicts between a young person and parents is when we want freedom but haven't paid the price. We may try to frame that freedom in Christian terms. ("I want to go to the retreat instead of doing my homework." "I was out until three in the morning because I was sharing the gospel with that person.") Our parents, however, may see it as an issue of our immaturity, not of our spirituality. We need to prove ourselves and earn the freedom we want to enjoy. That means we fulfill our obligations at school, at work, and at home—cheerfully. When you have shown your wisdom and maturity over months, your parents will be much more likely to give you more freedom. Even if your efforts don't "earn" your freedom in your household, we are still to sacrificially obey our parents or caregivers. It honors the one who sacrificially obeyed the Father for us. Our motive for obeying should always be to glorify and honor God, not obedience for the sake of getting what we want. As I've said before, God is just as (if not more) concerned with our motives and our attitudes as he is with our actions. This is truly dying to selfish desires. Paul tells us in Colossians 3:17 and 20, "Whatever you do, whether in word or deed, do it all in the name of the Lord Jesus, giving thanks to God the Father through him...children, obey your parents in everything, for this pleases the Lord." Paul also says in Philippians 2:14 to "do everything without complaining or arguing."

As a word of caution, if your parents or caregivers are requiring your obedience in areas that are abusive in nature (sexually, physically, emotionally, or otherwise) please seek Christian counsel immediately (pastor, teacher, principal, neighbor). God loves you and doesn't want you to suffer in that way.

4. Listen.

Yes, it seems sometimes our parents' don't have a grasp on what we go through every day. Your parents may not be cool, but they do have a lot of experience with life. When they offer advice, don't turn up your nose and shake your head in disgust before you've even heard them. Take time to listen. Ask them follow-up questions to find out more of what they have to say, then call 9-1-1 to have them resuscitated after they've passed out!

If you don't understand their decision, don't blow up and storm out of the room. You could politely ask them to clarify their reason. Just don't do it in a challenging or rebellious way. They may choose not to clarify their reasons, or you still may not understand. However, your listening and obedience is a response that not only honors them, but honors God.

Probably nothing shows them how much you value them than valuing their opinions. Godly authority figures in our lives often have perceptive insights into the character and will of God, and about life experiences in general. They can help us sort through the garbage of this world and lead us to the banqueting table of Christ.

5. Help out around the house.

Do *more* than is expected of you. If one of your chores is to clean your room, clean your parents' room or the den, too. If you wash dishes, dry them and put them up without complaining and without being asked. If your parents are stressed by having to take your little brother to soccer practice, take him yourself. We honor our parents by noticing what is going on in their lives and helping them. This is also a powerful way to show parents who are non-believers that we are serious about our commitment to Christ. It's a very visible sign of the change he is making in us. Cheerful obedience is one of the best ways we can witness to our parents of Christ's love.

One misconception is that these last two days are solely directed to the teenager. Wrong. Jesus' call to honor our parents goes beyond our adolescent years. It follows us to the grave. The adult reading this book who has loudly been "amen-ing" the last two days saying, "Yes, David, tell my teenagers a thing or two," should now reflect on his level of honor and obedience to his own parents and parents-in-law. No matter what the age. What are we teaching the students who watch our lives about humility and submission to authority when we disrespect, dishonor, disobey, ignore, or constantly question our own parents or parents-in-law? Do we chalk it up to, "They're just being difficult," or "I'm an adult now. I live my own life"? We should never "outgrow" this call from God.

—Be still. Listen to what God is saying to you.

1. Why do you think God gave a promise with this command to honor our parents?

2. Describe your relationship with your parents. (How do you communicate with each other on a daily basis? How do you communicate when there is conflict? What brings you together? What creates tension?)

3. Do you listen well to your parents? Explain:

4. What is your own personal motive for obeying your parents? Be very honest.

5. Do you agree or disagree with the statement: Honoring your parents doesn't necessarily mean you agree with them. Explain:

6. What one thing do you need to do to honor your parents more?

7. Describe how a sold-out disciple of Christ can put Matthew 10:34-39 together with Matthew 15:1-9.

8. Read Matthew 15:1-9. Think about these verses, then use each one as a guide as you pray.

   Memorize: Say John 14:6 aloud. How can you apply this passage today?

A CALL TO DIE

JOURNAL

Lord, today you are calling me to die to selfish desires by:

You are calling me to obey in these areas:

You are calling me to intimacy with you by:

DAY 36

WATCH YOUR WORDS!

"BUT THE THINGS THAT COME OUT OF THE MOUTH COME FROM THE HEART, AND THESE MAKE A MAN 'UNCLEAN.'" – MATTHEW 15:18

The Pharisees made sure they did all the right things. They went to the Temple on time; they attended every service; they gave ten percent of everything they got, including the garden herbs; and they prayed several times a day. Their culture was based on strict rules and ceremony. They could only eat certain things, and only when they had washed their hands in certain ways. They wanted people to look at them and say, "Wow! These people are really committed to God!"

But they weren't. They were committed to getting praise for looking like they were committed to God. In Matthew 23:27, Jesus called them "whitewashed tombs" who were neat and clean on the outside but dead and rotten on the inside. (How was that for some "hard words?") Their actions were made meaningless because of the sinfulness of their hearts.

Squeeze a sponge and what comes out is what's inside. When circumstances squeeze our hearts and lives, what's inside comes out of our mouths. In an earlier conversation, Jesus told the Pharisees: "You brood of vipers, how can you who are evil say anything good? For out of the overflow of the heart the mouth speaks. The good man brings good things out of the good stored up in him, and the evil man brings evil things out of the evil stored up in him" (Matthew 12:34-35).

"Out of the overflow of the heart the mouth speaks." What is flowing out of your heart and my heart through our mouths? Do we express thankfulness for what God is doing in our lives and how our parents, teachers, employers, and friends take care of us and enrich our lives? Do we find ourselves praising God for his goodness and strength? Do we speak words of encouragement to those who are down? Do we keep our mouths shut when we could say something that hurts another? Do we choose not to enter into a conversation that is tearing down someone's character? Do our words reflect a passion for God to move and work in everyday and in crisis situations? These reflect good words coming from a heart full of Christ.

On the other hand, do we laugh at other people's expense? When someone hurts us, do we make sure we tell everybody who will listen? When we fail, do we find someone to blame—even if it is ourselves? What level of pain, failure, or discouragement does it take for us to curse? These are evidences of a heart full of self. The problem is that often these evil words have become so common in our lives that we don't recognize them as wrong. We watch television shows and movies that make us laugh at sarcasm and be entertained by hatred. We have become numb to the evil, and we've allowed it to seep into our hearts without calling it what it is and rooting it out. Jesus told the people—in front of the self-righteous, evil-hearted Pharisees—that just doing the right things isn't enough. We have to pay attention to our hearts. He said, "But the things that come out of the mouth come from the heart, and these make a man 'unclean.' For out of the heart come evil thoughts, murder, adultery, sexual immorality, theft, false testimony, slander. These are what make a man 'unclean'" (Matthew 15:18-20). He was saying, "Don't be so impressed with these Pharisees. Don't be like them! Focus on letting God purify your heart, and your actions will follow."

James compares the tongue to a bit in a horse's mouth. It is a small piece of metal that controls the powerful animal. He also compares the tongue to a ship's rudder, "Although they are so large and are driven by strong winds, they are steered by a very small rudder wherever the pilot wants to go. Likewise the tongue is a small part of the body, but it makes great boasts" (James 3:4-5). James notes that many Christians praise God one minute and then blast people the next. He writes, "With the tongue we praise our Lord and Father, and with it we curse men, who have been made in God's likeness. Out of the same mouth come praise and cursing. My brothers, this should not be" (James 3:9-10).

I want you to test yourself in two ways. First, think back over the past twenty-four hours. Think of every conversation and everything you said, even if it was only to yourself. Make a detailed list, then next to each entry, record what those words reveal about your heart. I hope you'll find plenty of thankfulness and praise, but you may also find that some of your words reveal hurt, anger, and the desire to hurt others.

The second test is this: Over the next twenty-four hours, take a piece of paper with you. Make a note of every word that comes out of your mouth. You don't have to write down every word, but at least note the content and intention of every statement and conversation. As you do this, something incredible will happen: You will become aware of your words before you even speak them! You can make choices to change what you say. This is the essence of repentance, to change, to turn and go a different direction.

To be honest, it's pretty discouraging to look at my words as a thermometer of my heart. Far too much of what comes out of my mouth is designed to impress people, to make a subtle (or not so subtle) jab at somebody for offending me—or just to be different. That doesn't honor God.

As we look through the window of our words into our souls, we may conclude that, "Hey, that guy deserved it. He was mean to me first." We have failed to see the root of our problem—bitterness in our heart. Often, however, the too-sensitive among us react in the opposite direction. We believe, "My heart is so wicked that God can't possibly love me. I'll be like this forever!" Neither of these responses leads to growth. I'm encouraged by the example of David. He sinned terribly by committing adultery and then murder to cover up his sin with Bathsheba. When he came face to face with his sin, he threw himself on the grace of God in repentance. He experienced forgiveness. He was washed clean. His prayer in Psalm 51 is one of the most beautiful passages in the Bible. He didn't want to just be forgiven for his sin. He wanted God to change his heart, so he prayed:

> "Create in me a pure heart, O God, and renew a steadfast spirit within me" (Psalm 51:10).

We can't make our hearts pure. Only God can do that. The Holy Spirit identifies the evil there to us, and we confess our sins to God. Jesus blood has already washed them away, and our confession makes that payment real in our experience. But a pure heart is the work of God. He is the one who gives us love instead of bitterness, thankfulness instead of cursing, kindness instead of sarcasm, and silence instead of saying something stupid. Too often, we run hot and cold. We realize the wretchedness of our hearts and are very aware of cleaning up our act for a few days, but then we go back to the old patterns of talking. David also asks God to give him stability and persistence in purity of heart. Our stability and persistence comes through a daily walk with God. Daily recognizing our dependence on him and allowing him to purge and purify us. He prayed, "Renew a steadfast spirit within me." David asked God to change his heart.

You and I could use a heart change, too. Our words are an indication of our hearts, but if we only try to change our words, the change won't last. Ask God to change your heart as you learn to listen to the Holy Spirit who guides us to make better choices of what will come out of your mouth. Both need attention.

There will come a day, Jesus said, when we "will have to give account on the day of judgment for every careless word" we have spoken. "For by your words you will be acquitted, and by your words you will be condemned" (Matthew 12:36-37). A lot of our words are careless, aren't they? If we thought about them, we wouldn't say them. Jesus is telling us clearly, "Consider your words!"

—Be still. Listen to what God is saying to you.

1. Jot down a summary of every conversation and every statement over the last twenty-four hours.

   What does each one reveal about your heart?

2. What are the patterns in your words in the last twenty-four hours? (How much thankfulness, how much cursing, how much sarcasm, etc.?)

3. Are you at all like the Pharisees who did the right things but with selfish intentions? Explain:

4. How do you feel when you think of Jesus holding you accountable for "every careless word"? Explain:

5. Get a piece of paper to take with you over the next twenty-four hours. Note every statement and conversation, and note how your words reveal your heart.

6. Read Psalm 51, especially verse 10. Let God speak to your heart, and use this psalm to guide you as you pray.

7. Read Matthew 12:33-37. Think about these verses, then use each one as a guide as you pray.

Memorize: Go over the last three passages you have memorized (Psalm 86:11-12; Psalm 91:1-3; and John 14:6) until you can quote them without looking.

DAY 36

JOURNAL

Lord, today you are calling me to die to selfish desires by:

You are calling me to obey in these areas:

You are calling me to intimacy with you by:

DAY 37

A FORK IN THE ROAD

"AND WHOEVER WELCOMES A LITTLE CHILD LIKE THIS IN MY NAME WELCOMES ME. BUT IF ANYONE CAUSES ONE OF THESE LITTLE ONES WHO BELIEVE IN ME TO SIN, IT WOULD BE BETTER FOR HIM TO HAVE A LARGE MILLSTONE HUNG AROUND HIS NECK AND TO BE DROWNED IN THE DEPTHS OF THE SEA."
– MATTHEW 18:5-6

Jim Elliot experienced the grace of God, and that grace worked deep into his soul. He wanted more than anything in the world for his life to count for God. Every waking moment was given to that goal. His passion was for God to work through him in a powerful way, and that God would get the glory for it all. Elliot realized that ministry consists of a series of moments of crossroads in people's lives. In these moments, they make choices. Sometimes these are monumental, life-changing choices. He longed for every encounter he had with people to create opportunities for them to make a definitive choice about Jesus Christ—either for him or against him. Elliot prayed:

> "Father, make of me a crisis man. Bring those I contact to decision. Let me not be a milepost on a single road; make me a fork, that men must turn one way or another on facing Christ in me."[7]

Is that prayer boastful? It is if we think we, instead of God, can change lives. Is it harsh? It is if we try to force people to respond instead of presenting the bold message of Jesus love and truth. Jim Elliot was a radical, and some of us don't feel all that comfortable with radicals.

But Jesus was a radical, too. So was Paul.

Radical commitment to a cause doesn't mean that much. Look in history, and look around the world today. We find plenty of examples of people who are willing to die for their political cause in the Middle East, in the Sudan, and in a dozen other places. But a radical commitment to Jesus Christ is different: It combines zeal with compassion, conviction about the cause with kindness. Jesus said some really hard things to those who opposed him, but he reached out a hand of love to everyone, even those who despised him. Who could be more radical in his commitment to Christ than the apostle Paul? Paul waded in to the most difficult situations time after time to tell friends and enemies alike about Jesus. He never backed down. His toughness was awesome, but so was his gentleness. He compared his relationship to believers "like a mother caring for her little children" (1 Thessalonians 2:7). That combination of zeal and compassion is what makes us different from political zealots around the world.

The disciples were having a hard time understanding how Jesus wanted them to relate to people. They assumed Jesus would become king and they would be his cabinet. That would give them power to do what they thought needed to be done. In fact, they looked around the room and started jockeying for position among themselves. They asked him, "Who is the greatest in

7 Elliot, *Shadow of the Almightly*, p. 59.

the kingdom of heaven?" No, Jesus explained, they didn't understand. That isn't the way it works. Being great is actually a hindrance to his plan, not the fulfillment of it.

To illustrate his point, Jesus brought a little child in front of him. He told his guys, "I tell you the truth, unless you change and become like little children, you will never enter the kingdom of heaven." Whoa! Wait a minute! This was a shocker to the disciples. They were expecting to be powerful, and now Jesus was telling them that the ball game was completely different. They had to become powerless, like a child. "Therefore," Jesus continued, "whoever humbles himself like this child is the greatest in the kingdom of heaven" (Matthew 18:4).

Instead of having to position ourselves to get on top at work, at school, or in our church group, Jesus has a different (and opposite) agenda for us: to become like a child. What does that mean? I think Jesus means that real spiritual strength comes from enjoying being loved by our Heavenly Father, having a simple heart of trust in the Father, and not being concerned with power and authority. That's what it means to be a child, and that's what it means to be a kingdom person. If we have that kind of simple faith, God will use us in incredible ways, but if we are plotting to get power and recognition, God will oppose us (see 1 Peter 5:5).

Jesus gives us a word of encouragement and a warning as we are examples to others. He says, "And whoever welcomes a little child like this in my name welcomes me." That's cool! "But if anyone causes one of these little ones who believe in me to sin, it would be better for him to have a large millstone hung around his neck and to be drowned in the depths of the sea" (Matthew 18:5-6). Hurting other Christians by our lust for power and fame is sinful. The disciples were listening, and I can imagine their eyes being wide open when they realized that was exactly what they'd been doing. The desire for power is a natural, normal part of the world's way of doing things, but the family of God should be different. Very different.

The paradox is that we have the greatest impact for God when we don't care about fame, power, and approval. This is really good news for you and me. You see, this means we don't have to have a certain profile of ability for God to use us. I don't have to speak like Billy Graham. I just have to be faithful to speak the words God gives me to say. You don't have to be somebody you aren't, either. You don't have to have this ability or that spiritual gift. You don't have to have a certain position or status in the group or club. You just have to be faithful to let God communicate his love and grace in you and through you.

He will.

Christianity is littered with stories of men and women who had great talents but lusted for more power and more prestige until God pulled the plug on them. He is patient. He gives us plenty of warning and plenty of opportunity to repent of our desire for fame, but if we refuse, we lose. Power is intoxicating. We get hooked on it, and we need more and more. No matter how much we get, it only satisfies for a short while. Even if we are incredibly successful, if power is our aim, we live in fear that we will lose our position.

Christianity also has many stories of people—especially young people—who come like little children to Jesus. They say, "Lord, I'm not much, but I'm all yours. I'd sure like it if you'd use me to change people's lives." I believe God moves heaven and earth to use people who have that attitude! He brings people into their lives, and he gives them opportunities to tell these people about the life-changing grace of God.

You and I can be a fork in the road for people. As we live the grace and truth of Christ, it will ooze from every pore. When people met Jesus, they faced the truth about God and the truth about themselves. At that moment, they had a choice. Jesus never forced them to decide one way or the other. He simply loved them and pointed the way. In the same way, you and I have the unspeakable privilege to tell people about Christ in a way that communicates the truth about Jesus and the truth about them. We don't have to push. We just need to be clear. We don't have to force a decision. They will make one on their own. God is in control.

Some looked at Jesus' love and hated him for it; some embraced him; and some tried to ignore him. They will do the same with us. What a privilege! —Be still. Listen to what God is saying to you.

1. Why do you think the disciples assumed Jesus would give them positions of power and authority so they would be great?

2. What did Jesus mean to "become like children"?

3. When Christians try to gain power over others, what kind of impact do they have?

4. Have you wanted "to be great in the kingdom of God"? If you have, how has God opposed you?

5. Express your desire to be like a child in your walk with God:

6. What kind of influence do you want to have on others?

7. What are some opportunities you've had in the past few days to be a fork in the road for people? How did you respond to those opportunities? How did these people respond to Christ?

8. Read Matthew 18:1-6. Think about these verses, then use each one as a guide as you pray.

   Memorize Psalm 46:10-11.

A CALL TO DIE

JOURNAL

Lord, today you are calling me to die to selfish desires by:

You are calling me to obey in these areas:

You are calling me to intimacy with you by:

DAY 37

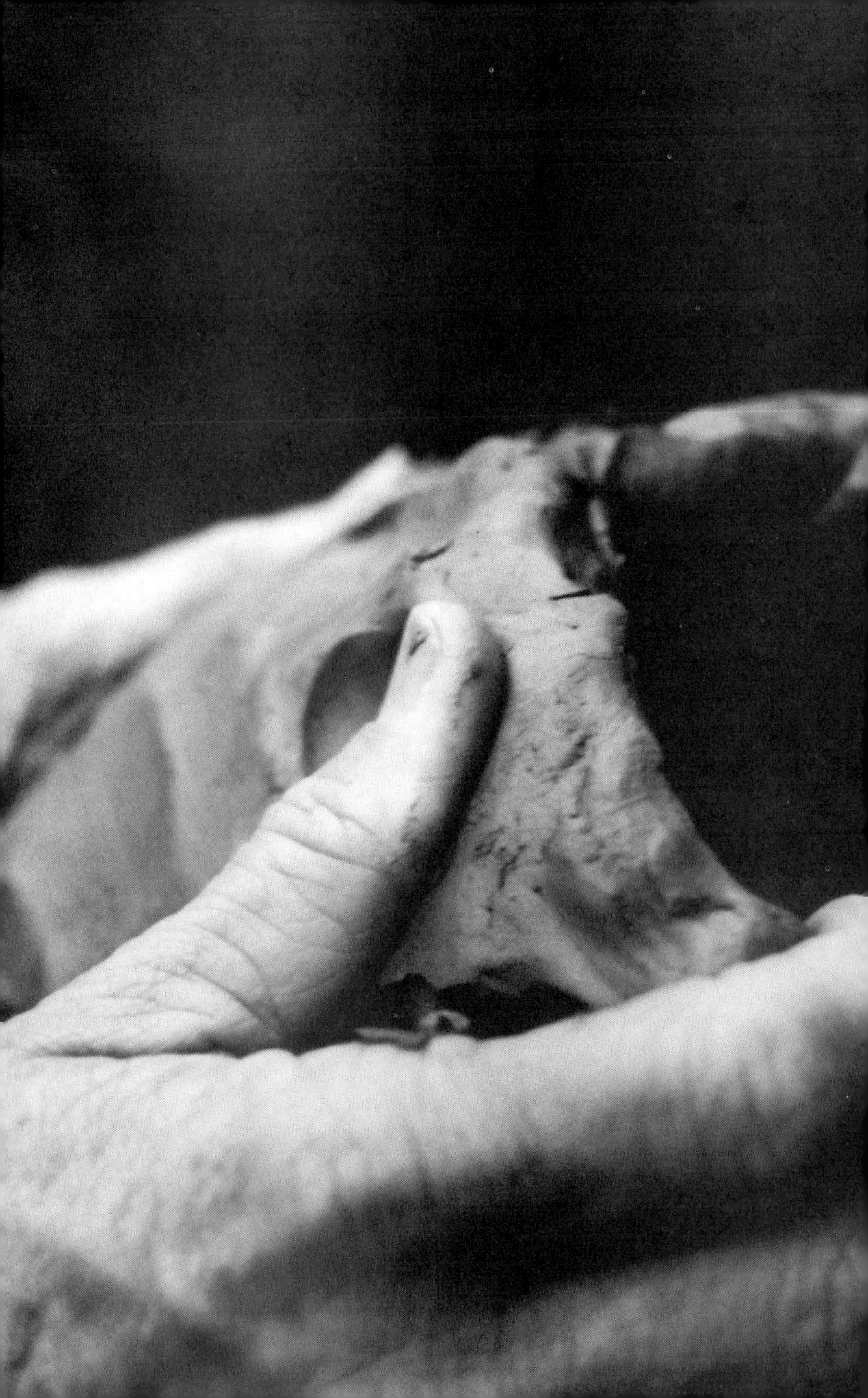

DAY 38

GOD CAN USE YOU

"JESUS SAID TO THE SERVANTS, 'FILL THE JARS WITH WATER;' SO THEY FILLED THEM TO THE BRIM. THEN HE TOLD THEM, 'NOW DRAW SOME OUT AND TAKE IT TO THE MASTER OF THE BANQUET.' THEY DID SO, AND THE MASTER OF THE BANQUET TASTED THE WATER THAT HAD BEEN TURNED INTO WINE."

– JOHN 2:7-9

Speaker/Bible study teacher Beth Moore tells a story in her Bible study series, "A Heart Like His," that has really affected my life. It powerfully illustrates how God can use us if we are simply available and obedient. We never know the scope of his grace until after we have trusted him and surrendered to his voice.

Beth tells of being in a busy airport waiting for her flight to board. As she was sitting, she noticed a man in a wheelchair sitting alone, close to the boarding gate. The gentleman was very old and was wearing wrinkled, unmatched clothing. Beth said, however, that the thing that stood out most was this man's hair. Everyone was noticing and whispering about it. It was very long, and very tangled and matted. It looked like it hadn't been brushed in ages. As she was sitting and waiting, Beth felt God saying to her spirit, "Go and brush that man's hair." Had she heard correctly? Was God telling her to go and ask a stranger if she could brush his hair? She had to be mistaken. It was crazy! Sure, she had little girls and was used to taking a brush and gently working the tangles out of their hair, but this was different. However, the longer she sat, the stronger God spoke. Finally, she very nervously got up and walked over to where the man was sitting. She went up to him and asked quietly, "Sir, may I please have the honor of brushing your hair?"

"Speak up, please," he said.

She asked the question again louder. He still couldn't hear. God didn't tell her he was hard of hearing! So, she had to practically shout, "Sir, may I please have the honor of brushing your hair?" So much for doing this inconspicuously. At this point, everyone sitting in the boarding area was staring and whispering. The old gentleman looked at Beth with wide eyes and said, "Yes, there's a brush in my bag."

Beth says she sat beside him, took the brush, and began to gently try to work the tangles out of his dirty, matted hair. As she brushed, tears began to run down the man's face. He began to explain that he had been very sick and had been away from his wife for a long time. He was flying to see her for the first time in several years. He had wanted to brush his hair, but he had no one to help him because he couldn't do it by himself. He had prayed earlier that God would somehow let him not look so ugly and unkempt when he got off the plane and saw his beloved bride for the first time. Because Beth had been available and obedient to God, he had used her to be the hand of Christ to this man. Meanwhile, unknown to Beth, a flight attendant was getting ready to board the plane. She watched Beth serving this stranger, despite the fact that all the people in the area were whispering and pointing. Later, during the flight, the attendant approached Beth and asked her why she did it. God used this to allow Beth the opportunity to share with this attendant the love of God.

We are not always promised that God will show us the "big picture." It's not obedience if we only obey when we know the great things that will come out of it or when it is convenient for us. God wants our availability and obedience to him simply because he asks. If anyone has the right to ask for this kind obedience, it would be the sovereign, Holy God, right?

Our availability allows us to do the things that we can do to set a backdrop for God to do the mighty things only he can do.

We are called to let him use us to accomplish the things he asks us to do. What a privilege to be asked by God to be a part of his amazing, life-changing work!

In John, chapter 2, Jesus is at a wedding. The host runs out of wine. Coming from a culture where generous hospitality is of utmost importance, I imagine that he was in a panic. What was he going to serve all of these guests? Mary brings this to Jesus' attention. Jesus then asks the servants to go and get the six stone water jars, fill them with water, and bring them to him. He then performs his first miracle. Jesus turns water into wine.

Could Jesus have performed the miracle by creating from nothing the jars, the water, and the wine? Absolutely! However, he allowed ordinary people to participate in the miracle. In fact, if you look at most of Jesus' miracles, he usually involved regular, everyday people by asking them to do regular, everyday things. That's how he works with us. He allows us to participate in his miracles. God calls ordinary people to do ordinary things so he can do the extraordinary work only God can do. Our obedience in even the little things allows God to set a backdrop to show his power in saving people, healing broken hearts, restoring wounded marriages, and performing the miracle of molding us into the image of his Son. In the earlier story, Beth was not the miracle worker—God was. He is simply looking for us to listen and respond to his voice. No matter how strange we think the task is. He is the only one who can perform miracles.

When we listen to the voice of God by bringing a friend to church, telling someone about Jesus, visiting someone in the nursing home, babysitting for a single mom, or even going to Africa to be a missionary, we are exercising obedience in doing our part. Then we can relax to know that God will do the rest. He will perform the miracle of healing, saving, restoring, changing. Now, don't misunderstand. Just because we allow God to use us, that doesn't mean that we will automatically see the results we think should happen. We let God handle the results—that's his department.

I have teenagers and adults alike come to me all the time and say, "I feel like God is calling me into full-time ministry. What are the first steps I need to take?" I usually tell them that God is looking for their obedience in the "small," everyday things he is asking them to do. When God sees that we can be trusted to obey in those things, he may entrust us with bigger responsibilities. Often we want God to use us in mighty ways. We may feel like he has blessed us with special or extraordinary talents and gifts. However, in the parable of the talents in Matthew 25:21, Jesus explains that the master in the story says to the servant, "Well done, good and faithful servant! You have been faithful with a few things; I will put you in charge of many things." Let God freely use you in the small things and when you're ready, he will use you in bigger ways as well.

Be encouraged! God will use you. He just needs your availability and obedience.

—Be still. Listen to what God is saying to you.

DAY 38

1. Have you ever heard God's voice speaking to your heart and telling you something specific to do? What was it?

2. How do you feel when God specifically tells you something to do? Are you nervous, scared, embarrassed, etc.?

3. In Jesus' first miracle, what was the job of the servants? Did they fill up the jars half way with water, or did they fill them to the brim? How can we apply this when God asks us to do something?

4. Are we responsible for the results when God calls us to do something specific? Why not?

5. Explain why you think God will give us greater responsibilities only after we've proved to be faithful in the smaller things.

6. Read John 2:7. Think about how and to what extent the servants responded to Jesus.

Memorize: Write Psalm 46:10-11 three times.

DAY 38

JOURNAL

Lord, today you are calling me to die to selfish desires by:

You are telling me to obey in these areas:

You are calling me to intimacy with you by:

AS YOU GO...

"THEN JESUS CAME TO THEM AND SAID, 'ALL AUTHORITY IN HEAVEN AND ON EARTH HAS BEEN GIVEN TO ME. THEREFORE GO AND MAKE DISCIPLES OF ALL NATIONS, BAPTIZING THEM IN THE NAME OF THE FATHER AND OF THE SON AND OF THE HOLY SPIRIT, AND TEACHING THEM TO OBEY EVERYTHING I HAVE COMMANDED YOU. AND SURELY I AM WITH YOU ALWAYS, TO THE VERY END OF THE AGE.'"
– MATTHEW 28:18-20

Jesus was standing on a hill outside Jerusalem. He was getting ready to go up into heaven, and he had some last words for his disciples. Think about it. These eleven men had consistently misunderstood Jesus all the time he was with them. He had talked about being as humble as a child; they argued about who would be the greatest. He told them he was going to be killed; they wanted him to be king. He asked them to pray for him; they went to sleep. At his moment of greatest need, they ran away. But here he was with the eleven who were left, and he was entrusting to these guys his heart and his mission to save the lost of the world. Amazing!

It's the same with you and me. We have failed to understand him over and over again. He has wanted us to be as humble as children, but we have wanted fame, power, and freedom. When he has given us things to do for the kingdom, we have been too preoccupied with our selfishness to even notice, and even when we noticed, we found excuses to avoid responding to him. Yet Jesus looks at you and me and he says, "I'm entrusting my entire venture to reach the world to you. I have confidence in you. Go for it!" Lord, shouldn't you use angels? They are more loyal than us humans. Lord, maybe you could align the stars to spell out John 3:16 so everyone will see. That would be cool.

He has, however, chosen you and me to help take his kingdom message to the entire planet.

Jesus begins his last word to his guys by reminding them that he's the boss. All authority in heaven and on earth is his. That's a lot! So what he says goes, and what he says is "Go." Actually, Jesus makes the assumption that we are already on our way. The original text reads: "As you are going..." Jesus assumes that we are responding to his marching orders to follow his commands—and if you are this far into this book, I pray that you are responding to his marching orders!

As you and I are on the road of obedience, Jesus gives us instructions about how to be as effective as we can be in our kingdom work. First, he tells us to "make disciples." Not pew sitters, disciples. Not retreat goers, disciples. Not people who just buy Christian CDs and books, but people who obey Jesus Christ. The law of nature is that like produces like. A tomato plant doesn't produce pineapples. Horses don't produce cows. You and I can't produce disciples if we aren't disciples ourselves, and the level of commitment of those we influence is seldom higher than our own. Dr. Howard Hendricks, professor at Dallas Theological Seminary, says, "If you want people to bleed, you have to hemorrhage!" He's right. If you and I want people to follow Christ, we have to live and breathe the grace and truth of Jesus. If we want people to be radical about Christ, we have to show them.

And what do we do with those disciples we are making? We baptize and teach them. We looked at baptism earlier in the book. It is a symbol of a dramatic change in our lives. We go into the water and come out, just like we are buried and are raised again in Christ. Our identity is changed. We are new people because we are Christians. Things that used to matter don't matter anymore. We are consumed with a new passion and we follow a new Master. You and I are to have the disciples we are making baptized so that the world knows they are now different, too. This is a dividing point for each of them. Baptism is a public statement that they are going in a new direction and have a new Lord. Life has changed.

Jesus called us to teach the world his truth. Teaching is not just from a book. Jesus taught his disciples with a combination of words and actions. If we think we can teach everything Jesus commanded from a book or in a class, we are mistaken. Which do you think the disciples remembered more clearly, a talk about the power of God or the times Jesus touched people and healed them? Both are important, but we need to be sure to take people with us and let them see the power of God in action as we minister to others. There comes a time that we send the disciples out on their own, just as Jesus sent out the twelve on one occasion and seventy on another. Two by two, without Jesus walking with them. Just them, Jesus' clear instructions, and their faith. God used them incredibly! Do you think that was an important lesson in the school of discipleship? Sure it was!

This kind of teaching takes time and energy. We live in an instant society of drive-thru windows, ATMs, and high speed modems. The kingdom of God doesn't operate at that pace. Spiritual depth is achieved slowly by reflection, long walks and long talks with our Heavenly Father; by being still and listening to the Spirit. We may learn a great truth at a retreat or a church service, but it takes time to learn to apply it deeply and specifically in our experience. Disciples learn to be patient. Radically committed, but patient in absorbing and applying the truth of God's word in situations and relationships.

Jesus was well aware what kind of command he was giving the eleven men who where with him, and to us, too. He knows that our closest friends might neglect us and our families might reject us. Satan and his demons throw up every kind of temptation to get us off track and obstacles to block our path. We will experience discouragement. When we read the accounts of the disciples in Acts and in Paul's letters, we find God at work in incredible ways, but we also read about hardships and difficulties of every stripe. Jesus knew this was coming, so his final words to his disciples and to us were: "And surely I am with you always, to the very end of the age." When things go well and we see God's hand at work, we don't need to wonder if he's around. It is, however, when we encounter difficulties, and our prayers seem to bounce off the ceiling that we need to be reminded Jesus is with us. He cares. He gives us hope, and we can go on.

I speak to students and young adults all the time, and I hear of how God is using them in incredible ways. Frankly, I'm amazed that the God of the Universe would choose to use people like you and me.

I love this passage of scripture because I remember to whom Jesus is talking. Those guys were just as clueless as you and me, and yet Jesus chose to use them anyway to take his love and his truth to the entire planet. They did. Within a few years, the gospel of Christ was known throughout the entire world. If God could use those guys like that, he can use you and me.

Amazing grace.

—Be still. Listen to what God is saying to you.

1. Peter denied Christ three times on the night he was betrayed. Jesus had talked to him a few days after his resurrection and forgiven him. How do you think Peter felt as Jesus was saying these final words in Matthew 28?

2. What does Dr. Hendricks' statement: "If you want people to bleed, you have to hemorrhage" mean to you?

   Are you hemorrhaging for Christ? Why or why not?

3. How is someone teaching you to follow Christ these days? Are you learning from the Bible, from watching someone, and from being involved in serving God yourself? Explain:

   What are some holes in your own discipleship experience you need to fill?

4. Are you discipling someone? If you are, how are you doing according to this passage?

   If not, do you want to? Explain:

5. Why is it important to remember that Jesus is with us? What happens when we forget that fact?

6. Read Matthew 28:18-20. Think about these verses, then use each one as a guide as you pray.

   Memorize: Say Psalm 46:10-11 aloud. How can you apply this passage today?

JOURNAL

Lord, today you are calling me to die to selfish desires by:

You are calling me to obey in these areas:

You are calling me to intimacy with you by:

DAY 39

DAY 40

THE NEXT STEP

"THEN JESUS SAID TO HIS DISCIPLES, 'IF ANYONE WOULD COME AFTER ME, HE MUST DENY HIMSELF AND TAKE UP HIS CROSS AND FOLLOW ME. FOR WHOEVER WANTS TO SAVE HIS LIFE WILL LOSE IT, BUT WHOEVER LOSES HIS LIFE FOR ME WILL FIND IT. WHAT GOOD WILL IT BE FOR A MAN IF HE GAINS THE WHOLE WORLD, YET FORFEITS HIS SOUL? OR WHAT CAN A MAN GIVE IN EXCHANGE FOR HIS SOUL? FOR THE SON OF MAN IS GOING TO COME IN HIS FATHER'S GLORY WITH HIS ANGELS, AND THEN HE WILL REWARD EACH PERSON ACCORDING TO WHAT HE HAS DONE.'"

– MATTHEW 16:24-27

We are at the end of this book, but I hope you are at the beginning of a fresh, dynamic relationship with Jesus Christ. We have looked at some hard things in these pages, and we have been encouraged by some of the most positive, uplifting words ever spoken by Jesus. Some are designed to blast; some are to build. All are to change our lives so that we walk more closely with Jesus.

The message of Jesus calls us to make choices about him, about ourselves, and about how we live. If it doesn't shake us up from time to time, we must already be dead! But too many of us read a book or go to a retreat and make changes, only to slip back into the same old patterns in a few days or a few weeks. With this in mind, hopefully this forty-day journey has allowed God to change your identity—not just your behavior. Change your behavior, and you'll probably go back to your old behavior. Let God change your identity, and you'll never be the same. We need consistency in our walk with God.

The message of Jesus is really very simple: If you try to selfishly grab for all you can get, you'll lose everything, but if you are willing to lose what you have for Christ's sake, you will be rewarded with meaning, purpose, rich relationships, and eternal rewards. The message is clear, but the heart is evil. The lure of the world causes Christians to look away and think real life is found apart from Christ. Even strong Christians can get off base. One of the saddest stories in the Bible is of a little-known man named Demas. His spiritual decline is noted in three passages written by Paul. In Colossians, Demas is walking with God and is effective in his ministry alongside the great apostle. Paul mentions Demas in the same verse with Luke: "Our dear friend Luke, the doctor, and Demas send greetings" (Colossians 4:14). But Demas began to slip. In his letter to Philemon, Paul only mentions Demas is there with him. In his last letter to Timothy, Paul tells the sad story: "For Demas, because he loved this world, has deserted me and has gone to Thessalonica" (2 Timothy 4:10).

Did Demas intend to slide downhill in his spiritual life and his ministry? Of course not. But his affections changed. He went from loving Jesus to loving this world. It probably didn't happen in an instant. It may have happened when he saw some other Christian who had more than he did. Demas may have sulked, "Man, I'm doing all this for God, and this bum has a lot more than I do. It's not fair!" The devil got a foothold in his heart.

Be on guard. Be aware of your own heart's wandering, and rein it back to Christ when it starts getting away. Be aware of Satan's schemes to get you to sin, and then to get you to feel so rotten that you don't experience God's forgiveness. Peter said that Satan "prowls around like a roaring lion looking for someone to devour" (1 Peter 5:8). What kind of animals do lions devour? I've watched enough nature shows to know the answer to that one: They eat the ones that aren't careful, those that aren't wary, those who are sick and wounded, and those that are slow to respond to danger. Don't let Satan eat you, too.

I am a fan of "last words." I like to read what people wanted to say right before they died because those words were tremendously important to them. Jesus' last words to his men were incredibly encouraging and challenging. He gave them the privilege of representing him to every person who ever lived! He reminded them: "I am with you always," so they would never be alone. In Paul's last letter before he was executed in Rome, he wrote to his disciple Timothy. He wrote:

> "For I am already being poured out like a drink offering, and the time has come for my departure. I have fought the good fight, I have finished the race, I have kept the faith. Now there is in store for me the crown of righteousness, which the Lord, the righteous Judge, will award to me on that day—and not only to me, but also to all who have longed for his appearing" (2 Timothy 4:6-8).

To Paul, his struggle to walk with God all day every day was a fight, and the strain of obeying day after day in all kinds of situations was like running a marathon. He may have stumbled sometimes, but he kept fighting and kept running. He finished. That's an incredible thing to be able to say at the end of your life, and because of that, Paul looked forward to the "crown of righteousness" God would give him—and which he will give to you and me as we hang in there to fight and finish the race.

Will I be like Demas or like Paul? Which one will you be like?

One of my biggest hopes is that you have developed new disciplines as you have gone through this book. In the early days of this material, we talked about how Richard Foster compares the Christian walk to farming. A good farmer has to do certain things in his field, but he can't make the crop grow. You and I can be faithful to pray, study the Scriptures, spend time with strong believers, and be involved in ministry. Those are habits that can last for a lifetime, and as we do those, the soil of our spiritual lives will be ready to grow the seed of God's word. In these weeks, I hope God has opened your eyes as you have read the Bible; I hope he has given you insight as you have prayed; I hope he has used the passages you have memorized at times when you needed encouragement or correction.

And I hope you will continue these disciplines for the rest of your life.

What is the next step for you as you close this book? It would be easy for you to say, "Wow! That was good! (or That was hard! or whatever) I need a break for a while." Don't take a break. Find something challenging and encouraging to keep sharpening your spiritual sword. Here are some suggestions:

- ***Find another Bible study to go through.*** Talk to your pastor or a godly friend to find something to challenge and inspire you.
- ***Focus on one book of the Bible for the next month.*** I recommend John, Romans, or Ephesians. Study it, memorize large portions of it, and let it marinate into your heart. (In your study, use 2 Timothy 3:16-17 as a guide. First, read the book several times so you become familiar with it. Get a notebook, and each day study a paragraph. Ask yourself these questions: What does this passage teach me? How do I fall short? What am I going to do to change? How can I get that change into my daily schedule so it becomes a habit?

Don't try to rush this process. Good Bible study takes time. Feast on the word slowly.)

- ***Go back through* A Call to Die *again*.** Each time you go through material, you will gain more insights and apply the truths more deeply or in new ways. You might want to go through this material again right away, or you might want to pick it up again in a month or so. Either way, I encourage you to go through it again.

A Call to Die is designed to challenge you, but it is also designed to encourage you. The great grace of God shows us where we are sinning, but it always picks us up and points us in the right direction. My greatest hope through all this material is that you sense the overwhelming love of Jesus Christ. That's his goal for you and me, and if we experience his love, we will be radicals in following him. Ultimately, the greatest challenge in the world is to be open to all that God has for us.

In years to come, I pray that what has revolutionized your life would not necessarily be the statements and illustrations you read in this book. I hope that the marination process that has occurred in your life, through hiding God's word in your heart over the last forty days, will forever affect who you are. I pray God has given you clearer direction and stronger insight. However, even if all you've gotten out of this journey is a forty-day break from the world, know that God has been honored through your efforts.

I spoke in the beginning of this book about how *A Call to Die* was not a call to physical death; but one day, for all of us, that physical death will come. I hope that before this time comes for you, you'll be able to look back on your life and say to yourself, "It was on that forty-day journey in my life that God and I collided. He called me to die to myself, and I was never the same." That is my prayer for you.

"I pray that out of his glorious riches he may strengthen you with power through his Spirit in your inner being, so that Christ may dwell in your hearts through faith. And I pray that you, being rooted and established in love, may have power, together with all the saints, to grasp how wide and long and high and deep is the love of Christ, and to know this love that surpasses knowledge—that you may be filled to the measure of all the fullness of God.

Now to him who is able to do immeasurably more than all we ask or imagine, according to his power that is at work within us, to him be glory in the church and in Christ Jesus throughout all generations, for ever and ever! Amen" (Ephesians 3:16-21).

—Be still. Listen to what God is saying to you.

DAY 40

JOURNAL

Write a prayer to God telling him what you think he has been saying to you over the last forty days. Thank him for how he has strengthened you and guided you. Ask him to give you clear direction as you continue to seek to know him more.

MEET THE PHOTOGRAPHER

Jennifer Nasser chose to photograph hands for the majority of this project because hands are among the most expressive parts of our bodies. They can vividly represent desire, emotion, action, ownership, devotion, and sacrifice. She did not randomly choose hand models for this project. Behind each hand seen in this book is a life truly lived for the glory of God. Jennifer would like to thank each model for generously giving of his or her time, prayers, and patience to make *A Call to Die* happen.

In addition to taking the photographs for this book, Jennifer also happens to be married to the author.

MEET THE AUTHOR

In 1979 Iran was embroiled in a bitter revolution. Untold numbers of people were slaughtered everyday. Gas prices skyrocketed. Fear and panic gripped the Mid East. Fortunately, in the midst of this horrible turmoil, God was moving.

Leaving everything behind, nine-year-old David and his family were forced to escape their native homeland of Iran hoping to begin a new life in the vastly different culture of the United States. The following years, found a young and isolated David Nasser seeking and trying everything imaginable to be accepted, but was always left the outsider. Eventually, David found true acceptance at the age of eighteen, when through the persistent witness of a body of believers, David received salvation and purpose through a deep and personal relationship with Jesus Christ.

As one of the nation's forefront speakers and visionaries, God has blessed David with the talent to reach the high tech, attention-lacking culture of Generation Next. Involved in revivals, citywide rallies, camps, and school assemblies, David speaks to over 700,000 people each year. The heart's cry of D. Nasser Outreach is to effectively present the same relevant message, the Gospel of Christ, using fresh, innovative methods and resources. Alongside his own full time ministry, DNO is also growing rapidly as a mentoring and consulting ministry. DNO has worked extensively with ministries such as BGA, Youth Specialties, Student Life, Acquire the Fire, and many others. David, his wife Jennifer and their children live in Alabama.

Psalm 119, is the companion CD for *A Call to Die*. Scriptures are set to praise and worship arrangements that focus on the daily scriptures throughout *A Call to Die*.

Featuring Recordings by:
Joel Engle, David Parker, Jami Smith, Michael John Clement, Chris Davis, and Jeffrey B. Scott.

Glory Revealed, the Word of God in Worship is a ten song, Scripture-driven worship project. The songs on this CD are the passages inspired from *Glory Revealed*, the book.

Featuring Recordings by:
Trevor Morgan, Third Day's Mac Powell, Steven Curtis Chapman, Brian Littrell, Hyper Static Union's Shawn Lewis, David Crowder, Shane & Shane, Candi Pearson-Shelton, Josh Bates, Michael W. Smith, Starfield's Tim Neufeld, and Casting Crown's Mark Hall.

Formerly *A Call to Grace*, *Grace Anatomy* is a 39 day look at how the grace-filled life is not about doing but about being. New look, same scripture based message.

A 20 chapter exposition discovering how the invisible God makes himself known. See his Glory Revealed.

Contact D. Nasser Outreach at 205-982-9996 for more information or visit www.davidnasser.com.